New Plays
from the
ABBEY
THEATRE

1993–1995

Michael Harding
Tom Mac Intyre
Donal O'Kelly
Neil Donnelly
Niall Williams

Edited and with an Introduction by
Christopher Fitz-Simon *and*
Sanford Sternlicht

Syracuse University Press

First Edition
97 98 99 00 01 00   6 5 4 3 2

The paper used in this publication meets the minimum requirements of American National Standard for Information Sciences—Permanence of Paper for Printed Library Materials, ANSI Z39.48-1984. ∞

Library of Congress Cataloging-in-Publication Data
New plays from the Abbey Theatre, 1993–1995 / Michael Harding . . . [et. al] ; edited and with an introduction by Christopher Fitz-Simon and Sanford Sternlicht. — 1st ed.
p.   cm. — (Irish studies)
Contents: Hubert Murray's widow / Michael Harding — Sheep's milk on the boil / Tom Mac Intyre — Asylum! Asylum! / Donal O'Kelly — The duty master / Neil Donnelly — A little like paradise / Niall Williams.
ISBN 0-8156-2699-1 (alk. paper). — ISBN 0-8156-0345-2 (pbk. : alk. paper)
1. English drama—Irish authors.   2. English drama—20th century.   3. Ireland—Drama.   I. Harding, Michael P., 1953–   . II. Fitz-Simon, Christopher.   III. Sternlicht, Sanford V.   IV. Series: Irish studies (Syracuse, N.Y.)
PR8869.N48   1996
822'.914080415—dc20   95-53289

Contents

Christopher Fitz-Simon is the literary manager of the Abbey Theatre of the National Theatre Society of Ireland and the author of *The Irish Theatre.*

Sanford Sternlicht is a part-time professor of English at Syracuse University. He is the author of a number of books, most recently *All Things Herriot: James Herriot and His Peaceable Kingdom,* and the editor of three books by Padraic Colum, all of which were published by Syracuse University Press.

Illustrations

Introduction

The Abbey Theatre and Its History

The term 'The Abbey Theatre' is popularly applied throughout the world to all aspects of The National Theatre Society of Ireland, its building, situated on Lower Abbey Street in Dublin, its ethos, its players, its repertoire, and the playwrights associated with this repertoire. The present building, opened in 1966 on the site of an older theatre which the society leased in 1904, contains two performing spaces, the Abbey and the Peacock. These two spaces enjoy equal status: thus, the conventional arrangement of 'main stage' and 'studio,' prevalent in most theatres where there is more than one auditorium, does not apply here. The only difference is that of size: the Abbey is the larger, the Peacock the smaller.

The Company—referred to for convenience as 'the Abbey'—operates for fifty-two weeks of the year on both its stages, even when productions are on tour within the island of Ireland or fulfilling engagements overseas.

Before the formation of the Irish Literary Theatre, progenitor of the present National Theatre Society in 1898, the work of Irish-born and Irish-educated dramatists reached the stage mainly via the principal London playhouses. For two hundred years, from Congreve and Farquhar to Wilde and Shaw, the work of this school of (largely) pungent social satirists was seen by the lively audiences of Dublin, Belfast, and Cork at second hand.

The cultural nationalism which fuelled the political movement towards self-determination during the latter part of the nineteenth century did little to alter this state of affairs. This movement, manifested through archaeological research, through the rediscovery and translation of the literature of antiquity, through the collection of folklore and folk music, and, most importantly, through the revival of the Irish language, did not express itself to any significant extent on the stage, except perhaps in the patriotic melodramas of Boucicault and Whitbread, and in little plays and sketches put on by amateur dramatic societies. The 'Irish Literary Renaissance', a component of the so-called Celtic Revival, resulted in a host of publications in poetry and prose fiction; it was not until three energetic and determined friends met in a house on Galway Bay on a damp evening in the summer of 1898, that the absence of the theatre's place in this scheme came under serious scrutiny. As dusk fell, the arrival of a truly national theatre was auspiciously signalled.

The meeting of Augusta Gregory, Edward Martyn, and W. B. Yeats resulted in a manifesto which formulated a theatre that would 'bring on the stage the deeper thoughts and emotions of Ireland'. Theirs was an ambitious and imaginative project, but many such projects, announced in high-flown language by ambitious and imaginative people, have a way of evaporating when the progenitors move on to other enterprises, or because they have merely indulged in experiment for experiment's sake.

It is certainly within the bounds of reasonable speculation that the plans which ultimately resulted in what we now call the Abbey Theatre might have come to naught had it not been for the emergence of the playwright J. M. Synge, just at the right moment. Yeats's eclectic verse plays, Gregory's jaunty folk comedies and myth-inspired fantasies, and the dozens of dramas of contemporary social (and generally rural) life which they encouraged from other writers, were hardly going to keep a company with a carefully articulated artistic policy in business in a city-centre playhouse. Providence, however, does have a way of throwing the right people together at the right time, and Yeats's celebrated meeting with Synge in the Paris of *la vie de boheme* resulted in a collaboration which in turn created what the novelist and critic George Moore approvingly described as 'great literature in a barbarous idiom.' (A contemporary parallel may easily be discerned in regard to the relationship between the Moscow Art Theatre and the dramatist Anton Chekhov.)

While the subject matter chosen by writers for this eminently avant-garde theatre came from the legends and folk myths of the past on the one hand, and the everyday life of peasant, bourgeois, and landowner on the other, the stylistic inspiration came very much from Europe, and especially through Andre Antoine's *Theatre Libre* in Paris. The work of this quintessential 'little theatre' was much admired by William and Frank Fay, who proceeded to place an intimate and precise stamp on the Abbey's playing and production style, with long reaching effects. The first production of Synge's *Playboy of the Western World* in 1908, with the Fay brothers taking central roles in all senses of that term, crystalised everything which the company had been striving towards in playwrighting, direction, and performance since the official opening of its theatre four years previously. Tours with plays by Padraic Colum, Fred Ryan, Yeats, Gregory, and Synge to Britain and the United States demonstrated that this was a theatre of unique power and sensibility, but it was *The Playboy* which marked the Abbey indelibly on the international theatrical map.

.   .   .

However much the early Abbey drew sustenance from European sources—early French literature, for example, as much as from *Symboliste* poetry and art, the plays of Maeterlinck, the repertoire of the Théâtre Libre, the Meninger company, and J. T. Grein's Independent Theatre—the single European playwright who exercised the most lasting effect on Irish drama was Ibsen.

It is fair to say that Yeats's vision of a 'poetic' theatre in the narrower sense evaporated under the strong urges of writers younger than himself to deal—often in a 'poetic' manner in the wider meaning—overtly or covertly with contemporary social and political issues. The overwhelming number of new plays produced by this most generously new-play-producing management throughout the first half of the twentieth century owes more to Ibsen than to any other playwright, and Irish theatregoers eagerly embraced plays which presented to them a recognisable critique of this or that aspect of the Ireland in which they lived. The typical 'Irish problem play,' also categorised as the 'Irish Ibsenite play,' would more often than not have left that Scandinavian dramatist bemused in regard to the appropriation of his own name, for Irish playwrights in general are at their most serious when articulating their thoughts through veils of laughter. Even when the canvas is much broader, as in the satiric tragedies of Sean O'Casey which were the Abbey's chief contribution to the world theatre in the 1920s, the most appalling aberrations of human nature are more often than not devastatingly projected by comic means.

It must be emphasised that not all the major Irish plays of the past hundred years were 'Abbey plays.' There tends to be a confusion abroad between 'Abbey plays' and 'Irish plays'—not that it matters, so long as the plays reach the public. It is also irritating for writers to be labelled as 'Abbey writers,' as if their work was never produced elsewhere. Most of O'Casey's later work including, *The Silver Tassie* and *Red Roses for Me,* was first presented by other companies; the same is true for Brendan Behan's *The Quare Fellow* and *The Hostage* and for several of Brian Friel's greatest plays, including *Philadelphia Here I Come!* and *Faith Healer.* It is often forgotten that Bernard Shaw's *John Bull's Other Island,* written expressly at Yeats's request, was first produced in London by Granville Barker and had to wait twelve years until the Abbey was in a position to mount it satisfactorily—when, of course, it became one of the most popular plays of the repertoire. As it happens, these few examples have all been performed by the Abbey Players on many subsequent occasions—the point being that the Abbey possesses what may be described as a finely tuned sense of guardianship of the national theatrical deposit, constantly and responsibly reassessing and re-evaluating works which have been laid aside by their original promoters, or where, for one reason or another, the original promoters no longer exist. In Ireland, as everywhere else, managements come and go; but the Abbey continues through thick and thin; and sometimes, it has to be said, the thin has been of its own making.

· · ·

There was a period at mid-century when the National Theatre Society did not actively search for innovative work in the way that had earlier been the case, and which again became the case at about the time of the opening of the new building in 1966. A number of plays, which turned out to be important and exciting when performed elsewhere, written by authors who subsequently attained the forefront of Irish dramatology, were rejected by the society's managing director Ernest Blythe. Among these were John B. Keane's *Sive,* Tom Murphy's *a Whistle in the Dark,* and Hugh Leonard's *Poker Session.* True, there were many fine plays produced at the Abbey at this time—among them outstanding work by Seamus Byrne, Walter Macken, and Denis Johnston—and the Abbey remained a popular resort for theatregoers, but the willingness to experiment, and the willingness to risk failure in the process, was temporarily abandoned.

Perhaps in declining to stage certain new plays which, as we can now clearly see, spoke for their era more lucidly and astringently than anything staged at the Abbey from 1941 for almost a quarter century, Ernest Blythe may charitably be said to have merely displayed that paralysing trait which sometimes inhibits the elderly from responding positively to social change and to the legitimate demands of a younger generation. Whatever the reasons—and they were certainly more complex than that—neither board, nor professional staff, nor playwrights, rebelled against this *status quo* in any effective way. The best playwrights simply took their wares to other houses. The works of some established playwrights also seems to have been studiously ignored. It seems extraordinary, too, that no play by Samuel Beckett appeared on the Abbey stage until 1969, even though his work had been acclaimed elsewhere in Ireland and his presence was already felt among younger writers.

Beckett, who like Joyce and other expatriate Irish writers merges into the literary heritage of Europe without losing his Irishness, was, in his student and teaching days, a regular attender at the Abbey, and was later to acknowledge Yeats, Synge, and O'Casey as important to his own appreciation of the theatre. It is significant that towards the century's end, as at its beginning, the Irish theatre receives its signals from Europe rather than from Britain. Dr. Anthony Roche, in his recent and already indispensable book *Contemporary Irish drama,* succinctly identifies 'a rejection of naturalism and the linear plot of the well-made play as inappropriate to a post-colonial society like Ireland; a favouring dramatically on a imposed situation in which the characters find themselves and which they either disguise or subvert thorough rituals of gesture and play,' as preoccupations which Beckett "shares in common with more "rooted" Irish playwrights.' He proceeds to show that the Irish drama of today relies more on an explored central situation than on plot, and that this is 'as true for Behan's prisoners in Mountjoy [jail] and Frank McGuinness's sons of Ulster at the Somme as it is for Beckett's Vladimir and Estragon.'

．　．　．

It is, of course, barely a step back from the world of Beckett's articulate vagrants and lonely voices, passing the time of day (as we say in Ireland) in remote or vaguely identified landscapes, and uttering a flow of restless and arresting talk to Synge's world of grotesques and solitaries—distressed perhaps, yet eloquent and inventive; and also barely a step from Beckett to the 'dreaming back' ghost-ridden world of Yeats's later plays. Synge, writing in English, developed a language which many Englishmen find difficult to understand: a heightened version of the English spoken by farmers and fisherfolk who were only a generation away from being native Irish speakers and whose natural expression should have been the Irish language: English words but Irish idiom and constructions. It is no great distance from here either to the rich and quirky vernacular of Tom Kilroy's *Talbot's Box* (1977)—Matt Talbot himself is a grotesque if there ever was one—or to the desperately word-abounding world of The Irish Man and J. P. W. King in Tom Murphy's *Gigli Concert* (1983), or to the seemingly casual and incidental, yet vividly allusive, talk of those who await the illusory ferryman in Friel's *Wonderful Tennessee* (1993). However much Irish dramatists have departed, in the final third of the century, from the form of the 'traditional' Ibsenite three-act play, and however much they may from time to time have dallied with mime and dance and other physicalities of the stage, their theatre remains predominantly verbal. 'You've a fine bit of talk stranger,' says Nora Burke to the tramp in Synge's *In the Shadow of the Glen* (1904), 'and it's with yourself I'll go.' Talk is, and remains the key.

．　．　．

The Abbey Theatre has been in continuous management longer than any other repertory company in the English-speaking world.

While there is a constitutional commitment to present the work of
eminent foreign authors from time to time—for instance, in 1995
these included Miller and Kushner—the prime objective is to provide a performance space for Irish dramatic writing. The variety of
topics treated in the five plays in this volume, and the individu-
ality of styles which their authors have naturally adopted immediately answers that deadly question posed by many an academic as
to 'What is the Abbey's playwrighting policy?' The answer, as the
audience or reader immediately becomes aware, must be that the
policy is created by the playwrights as they come and go. Neil
Donnelly's suavely satiric home thoughts from abroad, Donal O'
Kelly's compassionate and angry exposure of society's treatment of
the underprivileged, Michael Harding's savage vision of an Ireland
brutally at war within itself, Niall Williams's gently comic *alleluia!* to the survival of the soul of a depleted rural community,
and Tom MacIntyre's folk play for the nineties which wings its
way in fantastic fashion between this world and the beyond (and
described by one critic as 'Synge on speed')—this assemblage is as
characteristic in its diversity as any the Abbey Theatre has produced in its ninety-two years of existence.

From the double bill which opened the theatre in 1904—Lady
Gregory's bucolic comedy *Spreading the News* paired with W. B.
Yeats's heroic verse drama *On Baile's Strand*—to Philip Davison's
Invisible Mending Company and Marina Carr's *Portia Coughlan* which
will open the latest season of plays as this collection reaches the
bookstores, the Abbey Theatre has given the first production of
over 700 plays by Irish dramatists.

Christopher Fitz-Simon
Dublin

The Plays and the Playwrights

Hubert Murray's Widow is Michael Harding's fourth play with the
Abbey. *Strawboys* was produced in 1988, *Una Pooka* in 1990, and
The Misogynist in 1992. The latter also received critical acclaim at
the 1992 Edinburgh Festival. His plays have also been seen in
London.

Harding's fiction has caused him in 1989 to be short-listed for

the Irish Times Aer Lingus Literature Prize and the Hughes Irish
Fiction Award. In 1990 Harding was awarded the Stewart Parker
Bursary. Harding lives in Carrick on Shannon, County Leitrim.

Hubert Murray's Widow opened in the Peacock on 21 April
1993. The play, a startling mystery of politics and passion, is set
in the present in a kitchen in a rural farmhouse just within County
Fermanagh, Northern Ireland. Two ghosts, Gene, who was a
young Protestant, and Hugh Murray, who was a crude man in his
fifties and a senior IRA operative, continue their rivalry for the
body if not the love of Murray's widow, Rhoda. In the front room
the wake of Hubert Murray is in progress under the guard of two
IRA youths with guns and masks. Murray apparently has been
blown to pieces by a bomb he had mishandled or by counter-
terrorists.

In a series of flashbacks in which Gene and Hugh are
sometimes speaking as the ghosts they are, awaiting transport to
purgatory, and sometimes as their living characters in their recol-
lections, as they relive the events leading up to the funeral and the
aftermath for Rhoda, Gene is besotted with Rhoda and, although
a Protestant, chooses, after learning of Hugh's death, to help the
IRA in gun smuggling across the border to County Cavan, expecting to be paid enough to take his one-time mistress to America.
This brilliantly plotted play contains a series of macabre surprises
and reversals that, excellent thriller that it is, must leave the audience gasping.

The scene-setting and scene-participating ghosts remind one of
the narrating ghosts in Yeats's and Padraic Colum's Noh plays.

Ostensibly a play about political loyalty and betrayal, *Hubert
Murray's Widow* is really about sexual passions and patriarchal jealousies of a loutish young man, a mean older man, a sanctimonious
Dublin Republican brother-in-law of Rhoda, and a fornicating
priest dutifully promoted to Monsignor, directed towards the attractive, sensual wife of an older, often absent sexually disinterested husband. The play is a powerful new version of the
Theseus-Phaedra-Hippolytus deadly triangle fashioned here within
the Irish tradition of mixing sex with guilt and siting the cause of
male conflict in a woman's natural sexuality.

As to the politics of the North-South conflict, Gene sums it
up: "You can't plan everything in life. And there's so much quar-
reling, arguing. Relentless. Obsessive. and every so often it all

comes together, coheres, in one beautiful creative act of violence. I understood that a long time ago about Ulster. The problem has no solution. Violence is just a way of imposing order on the chaos. . . . It's almost beautiful. It's almost like sex." Belatedly, Gene comes to understand that for "heroes" eroticism is "to take the chaos and fashion a little violence out of it. It's called history."

Because of its thriller plot, black humor, fine characterization, near Pinteresque dialogue, and O'Casey-like profound cynicism towards causes and activism, *Hubert Murray's Widow* is a play to be remembered.

·   ·   ·

Tom Mac Intyre is one of Ireland's most distinguished men of letters. He is widely published as a poet and writer of fiction. His plays produced by the Abbey include *The Great Hunger,* 1983; *The Bearded Lady,* 1984; *Rise Up Lovely Sweeney,* 1985; *The Great Hunger,* revised 1986; *Dance for Your Daddy,* 1987; *Snow White,* 1988; and *Kitty O'Shea,* 1992. *Chickadee* was produced in 1993 by the Red Kettle Company. Mac Intyre was born and lives in County Cavan.

Sheep's Milk on the Boil opened in the Peacock on 17 February 1994. The play is set on an island off the West Coast of Ireland. The time is now and yesterday and timelessness. *Sheep's Milk on the Boil* is a remarkable postmodern fable, a contemporary folk play, and a fantasy of great poetic vitality in which an earthy island couple, Biddy and Matt, celebrate life as they are observed and interfered with by the Inspector of Wrack, a character named Maggie Friday, a blacksmith, two ever-watchful bookkeepers, and other palpable and symbolic characters. But Matt and Biddy show us that the meaning of life is living and that one partnership, imperfect though it may be, is the only antidote to existential despair.

In *Sheep's Milk on the Boil* Mac Intyre reminds us of the Synge of *The Well of the Saints* and the Beckett of *Endgame* but with a *joie de vivre* beyond Synge's, a lyricism that contrasts sharply with Beckett's grim *Weltanschaung,* although the fragmented speeches, shots that miss and speed past the responses, bring Nag and Nell to mind.

Synge insisted that in a good play "every speech should be as fully flavoured as a nut or apple." Mac Intyre knows this well. In the best tradition of Irish dialogue, Mac Intrye's characters frolic and carouse in language as they sing, joke, curse, lie, joust, challenge, and tell tales in an idiom that is simultaneously West Country and universal. What a grand jest life is as long as the company is fine!

.   .   .

For the past ten years, Dublin-based Donal O'Kelly has combined writing and acting careers. *Asylum! Asylum!*, which opened in the Peacock on 27 July 1994, was O'Kelly's second Abbey-Peacock production; *Mamie Sighs,* the first, played in the 1990 Dublin Theatre Festival. Other plays by this prolific dramatist include *Rabbit,* the much traveled *Bat the Father, Rabbit the Son,* which played all over Ireland, New York, London, Edinburgh, Glasgow, Australia, and New Zealand, and *The Wake,* an adaptation of *Finnegans Wake* with Paul O'Hanrahan that received a Fringe First award at the Edinburgh Festival. O'Kelly coauthored and coperformed *Mulletman and Gullier* at the City Arts Centre. *The Dogs* was seen at the 1992 Dublin Theatre Festival and in Glasgow. *Hughie on the Wires* was produced in Dublin and Glasgow and on RTE radio. *Trickledown Town* was seen at the 1994 Dublin Theatre Festival.

O'Kelly has acted in films and many plays besides his own. He received a 1989 Arts Council Writers Bursary and a 1994 Scottish Arts Council Script Develop Grant, which resulted in the 1995 brilliant production of his latest one-person play, the "live movie" *Catalpa: the Movie,* in which O'Kelly plays all twenty-six parts!

Donal O'Kelly is a political activist, a cofounder of Calypso, a Glasgow-Dublin production company specializing in dramas dealing with human rights issues. Previously, he cofounded Parade, arts workers who mounted spectacular street events in Dublin campaigning for the release of victims of miscarriages of justice in Great Britain. *Asylum! Asylum!* is a product of O'Kelly's humanitarian concerns and commitments. It is his artistic response to past repressive and inhumane Irish Asylum regulations and the coming European Union (EU) cooperative controls of borders that will deny the human rights of asylum seekers throughout the Continent.

Two historical events helped precipitate the writing of *Asylum!*
Asylum!: in 1991 five prisoners in Bucoro, Bulu District, Northern Uganda, were put into a pit which then was covered by logs
and a fire was set on the logs. This horror was reported by Amnesty International. In 1992 Vietnamese immigrants were burned
to death in a hostel in Rostock, Germany, by a German mob as
the local police looked on. This event made the international
news.

Asylum! Asylum!, a realistic three-act drama, takes place in
present-day Dublin in various locations: a pub, a cell in a Garda
station, a visiting room in Mountjoy Prison, and the backyard of
Bill Gaughran, a widower and a recently retired sascristan, father
of Leo Gaughran, an Irish immigration officer, and of Mary
Gaughran, a newly qualified solicitor.

Joseph Omara is a Ugandan seeking asylum in Ireland, having
survived a massacre and torture in Bucoro. The ambitious and
cynical Leo is trying to further his career by deporting Joseph,
while the idealistic and sympathetic Mary attempts to save Joseph
from deportation and sure execution as a witness to military mur-
ders. The Gaughran family has been mutually estranged; and the
conflict between the siblings over the denial of sanctuary proceedings fires up old sibling jealousies, memories of Bill's coldness to
Mary, and the family's general disfunctionality. The war of conscience over Joseph Omara, with Mary and Leo on the front lines,
and Bill, the moral and ethical church servant, and the monolithic
Irish bureaucracy, in the strategic rear, both wracks the little family and reunites it.

Asylum! Asylum! is a powerful polemic of great dramatic inten-
sity in the tradition of the Theatre of Conscience that began with
Ibsen's *Enemy of the People* and whose many landmarks include
Galsworthy's *Strife* and Miller's *Crucible* and *After the Fall,* Vac'lav
Havel's *Garden Party,* and the dramatic works of the contemporary
playwright that *Asylum! Asylum!* is most akin to: Athol Fugard.

. . .

Neil Donnelly's *Duty Master* first opened in the Abbey's Peacock
Theatre on 8 February 1995 directed by Ben Barnes. Neil Donnelly was born in Tullamore, County Offaly. In the 1970s, along

with Martin Houghton, Donnelly cofounded Wheels, an early Theatre-in-Education touring company in Great Britain. In 1981 and 1982 Donnelly received the Harvey's Award for Best Play. He won the 1983 Best Script Award for the *Lifestyles* series written for the Health Education Bureau. Other educational series followed, including the 1987 *Just a Little Virus*. Donnelly was appointed Writer-in-Residence with the Mayo County Council in 1993–1994, where he edited *Mayo Anthology 5*.

Donnelly is a prolific dramatist whose plays have been well received in Ireland, Scotland, England, and the United States. *Dust* was seen in New York in 1972. The Edinburgh Festival featured *The Station Master* in 1974. *Upstarts* began eight years of performances at the Peacock in 1980. It moved to the Irish Arts Centre in New York in 1982. More performances followed at the Eblana and the Olympia in Dublin, and on a nationwide tour of Ireland with the Playwrights and Actors Company in 1984–1985. In 1990 *Upstarts* was performed at the Riverside, Coleraine, and in Perth, Australia, in 1990.

The Silver Dollar Boys opened in the Peacock's 1981–1982 season. An Abbey mainstage production followed in 1986, followed by an Irish national tour with the Playwrights and Actors Company in 1987. *Flying Home* appeared in the Peacock in 1983, followed by *Chalk Farm Blues* in 1984. *The Boys of Summer* was presented at the Gaiety Lunchtime and Project '85. The TEAM Theatre Company produced *Blindfold* in 1986, and the Peacock was the venue for *Good-bye Carraroe* and *The Reel McCoy* in 1989.

Currently, Neil Donnelly is a tutor with the Theatre Studies Course at the VEC, Inchicore, and Ansbacher Writer-in-Association with the Abbey Theatre.

Much of Donnelly's work is about Irish people in self-imposed or economically imposed exile in England. His characters journey through landscapes of housing cooperatives, Irish ghettos in English cities, and English institutions, often looking back for a fading identity and not knowing if their place in the cosmos is past or future.

The Duty Master is set in the present in a boys' public school in Leicestershire, England. Irish-born Patrick O'Rourke is an English master in the school, and his English wife Sarah is a successful professional artist about to have an exhibition that will move her toward the mainstream of the British art world. They are an unhappy couple, each involved with another person: Patrick with Estelle Hilton, the school secretary to whom he has promised that he will divorce his wife and move to another school with her; and Sarah with an Israeli sculptor, who is sensitive, understanding, and supportive of her work.

Patrick is ashamed of his Irish farming background. He has tried to become more English than the English. In the thirty-two hours of the play, during which time he is "duty master" for the school and responsible for the institution, Patrick is faced with the impending doom of his marriage and the specter of self-exposure as just another "paddy" when, unexpectedly, his brother Michael, the son who stayed with the old parents on the farm, appears without notice (how un-English) and has an attractive University College Dublin student named Brenda in tow. She is twenty years younger than the bachelor Michael.

The brothers have never gotten along. The first-born Patrick, Michael claims, was favored by their parents, who have asked Michael to try to get Patrick to return for a visit to Ireland while they are still alive. They want to see their grandchild, Pippa, Patrick and Sarah's only child once more. Sarah hates Ireland, and Patrick is so embarrassed by his background that he asks Brenda to request that Michael stop calling him Pat in public, which naturally Michael continues to do.

The tensions within this well-made, engrossing play revolve around the domestic drama of a marriage on the rocks, and more significantly, the perennial Irish theme of conflict between the son who emigrated and the one who remains behind to tend the farm and old folk. The two dialects employed by Donnelly, an effected U-language in Patrick's mouth, and a County Meath brogue laid on by Michael in part to tweak his brother, delightfully represent and symbolize the conflict between the two men and, as it develops, within Patrick, who in the crisis moment of the play must for once and for all either accept or reject his Irish heritage.

As precisely crafted as the best of Terrance Rattigan, and as insightful into the pains of a long unhappy marriage as an Ingmar Bergman drama, *The Duty Master* exhibits a profound understanding of the modern dilemmas faced by those who leave their native lands to live and mate with strangers, thinking they have left their otherness behind only to find that, shadow-like, it always follows them. Like Brian Friel, Donnelly believes that "concepts of Irishness" such as loyalty, marriage, generational respect, and religion are best addressed in the family context.

.   .   .

Niall Williams's *Little Like Paradise* opened at the Peacock on 29 March 1995. Williams was born in Dublin in 1958 and educated at University College Dublin. He lived in the capital until he moved to West Clare in 1985, where he and his wife, the artist Christine Breen, have written four nonfiction books about their life on the West Coast. In August 1991 Williams's first play, *The Murphy Initiative,* was produced on the Abbey stage, and then appeared at the Lyric Theater, Minneapolis. Williams's has also written a novel, *Four Letters of Love.*

A Little Like Paradise is set in the year 1992 in a village on the Atlantic coast of County Clare. On stage one sees Jay Feeney's bar and grocery. The beach and the sea are adjacent. The play tells the story of the dreams, disappointments, illusions, and follies of the inhabitants of this diminishing habitation on the extreme edge of Europe, seemingly forgotten by the powers in Dublin, let alone Brussels. The area needs rebuilding of its infrastructure and, most of all, it needs a hospital. The cynical natives say that the quickest way they can get to a hospital is to row out on the ocean and call for the Shannon rescue helicopter.

The local political leader, Senator Marty McInerney, is facile with the Blarney but ineffective in Dublin. He and the inhabitants of the village are more concerned with their shibboleths of memory, their individual lives, their health, and their personal problems than they are with the national and international issues of their time. Marty, a widower, wants to marry the widow Kay Breen, once a hospital matron, and sister of Jay Feeney, Marty's agent, informer, fixer upper, and local publican, undertaker, and grocer. Kay and Marty were fond of each other a long time ago and she is reluctant to marry him because she is now middle aged and bitter about her loveless first marriage, and furthermore, she thinks the optimistic and romantic Marty is really in love with the young girl she once was and no longer is.

Marty's son has gone to America abandoning his young wife Mary, leaving his father to look after her. She misses her husband terribly, and because she has read too much about "out of body" experiences, thinks that she can rekindle her husband's affection and bring him back to her through meditation, mental concentration, and deep breathing.

Mick Maguire, an elderly, alcoholic farmer, "dies" at the bar, and "returns" to life, becoming a religious celebrity as he recounts his brief experiences in the next world. He proudly exclaims: "I'm really living since I died."

The heroic, even tragic figure in the community is Father Francis McInerney, Marty's brother, who although dying of cancer, tries to keep the community together, fight superstition, build relationships, offer hope to those who have lost faith in the future, and deal through his great pain with his growing disillusionment with God.

Mary learns she is pregnant, and the fact that a child will be born once more in this seemingly doomed community, this microcosm of all of rural Ireland at the end of the twentieth century, raises some hope for the future.

To an American the portrayal of the atrophying community of Caherconn, sketched with humor, gentle satire, and pathos, is reminiscence of depictions of western American communities left behind after the exhaustion of mines, the end of the cattle drives, and the closing of the frontier; and peopled by the survivors: the broken, the eccentrics, the aged, and the ever-hopeful of revitalization. Caherconn is nearly a ghost town. In fact it seems more peopled with the ghosts of those who have died and those who have left than with the living wounded. Caherconn perches precariously on the edge of the eternal, mournful sea just as the western town waits for the prairie to overwhelm it.

Of course, *A Little like Paradise* is not at all like paradise, except that within those who love or remember with love a community, a little bit of paradise goes a long way.

Williams's play exhibits two particular strengths: fine characterization, especially of humorous figures, and a credible slice-of-life portrayal of a community. For an Irish audience *A Little Like*

Paradise offers the pleasure and satisfaction of seeing perhaps not a completely untypical community vividly reproduced.

.   .   .

The plays presented in this anthology of new Abbey Theatre work represent current directions in the Irish drama and are outstanding examples of the continuing creativity and vitality of that venerable institution. They foretell a sensitive, committed, linguistically vibrant, socially aware, and politically active Irish theater of the future.

Sanford Sternlicht
Syracuse

The Plays

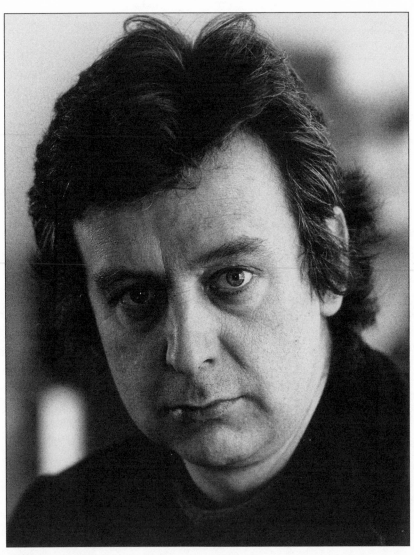

Michael Harding.
Courtesy Cowns & Associates.

Hubert Murray's Widow

MICHAEL HARDING

1993

Original Cast

Clive Geraghty	Phelim Drew
Gabrielle Reidy	Birdy Sweeney
Miche Doherty	Pauline McLynn
Sean Campion	Patrick Dawson

Director: Patrick Mason

Characters

RHODA, a vibrant woman, not yet forty
BOYLE, suave cleric of about the same age
GENE, mid-thirties, a cool dude, impulsive and comic
JENNY, just a little younger than Rhoda, meticulous
JOE, a very high opinion of his own importance
PHEILIM, small farmer, in his sixties
ENDA, cunning
HUGH, a big, heavy man in his fifties, self-assured in tone of voice
    and in his movements

The atmosphere of set and lighting should be claustrophobic, with tight spaces, lots of shadow, so that people fade in and out of conversations, while still remaining present.

In natural terms the action takes place in a kitchen as outlined at the beginning of Act I, but the entire set ought not be restricted to a vocabulary of naturalism.

ACT I

Scene

The play opens in a modern kitchen, in a rural farmhouse, just inside Fermanagh. All modern conveniences. A door to pantry upstage right, to hall upstage left, and to backyard, downstage right. The playing area ought to feel congested, claustrophobic, and the details of kitchen should not be presented as realism, but more akin to a dreamlike landscape. Gene stands centre stage as if in a dream. Upstage corner, Rhoda is seen, eyes closed, humming 'The West's Awake'.

GENE. She used to close her eyes and sing sad songs. In Gaelic. Songs she learned in secondary school, when she was growing up in the south of Ireland.

RHODA. (*Opens eyes.*) Eugene.

GENE. I loved her. But I didn't know what she was singing about. The rest of the pub was all Republicans. (*She closes eyes and continues her tune.*) I was the Protestant. Haunted by a woman from the other side of the house. I used to tell her she sang like a nightingale. All that Gaelic gobbledegook. But she used to sing so many of them sad songs, all keens and laments, I used ta say to her, 'Rhoda. How can ye be singing all them sad songs? It's unlucky'. It wasn't lucky. That was my opinion. But I was only joking her. (*Hubert Murray enters, and begins pacing up and down the kitchen. He is a stout man in his fifties. His movements are always slow and assured. There is a macabre aspect to his appearance. A chair somewhere upstage left is his main base, and he rarely moves much from it. At the moment he is waiting for someone.*)

GENE. He's waiting for me. And let's get one thing straight. This guy was a nasty bit of goods. She married him at the beginning of the troubles because he was some class of local hero and she was up on holidays from the south, a starry-eyed supporter of civil rights. She found out all about civil rights when she married him. (*Rhoda goes over to him. Almost touches. Withdraws and approaches Gene from behind.*) Then she started singing to me, and I would say, 'Feic it, Rhoda, the springs in this bed would wake the dead' . . . . (*They both look at each other, clasp hands, and swing each other in a single circle. Hugh stares over at them.*) Under the roof of a Republican gunman. His Catholic wife.

RHODA. And his Protestant labourer.

GENE. The two of us; laughing. (*The circle movement stops. They part.*) Then he started smelling a rat. I had to get out. Sort of suddenly. Went to New York. When I was in America, I used to phone her.

GENE. Rhoda. Rhoda.

RHODA. Gene. Gene is that you?

GENE. (*To audience.*) Jesus, America is incredible. The effect it has on ye. I started reading books. From a distance I had begun to see the real meaning of Ulster. And let's get one thing straight; Ulster is the politics of a thousand clichés. (*Mimics JFK.*) We may not achieve peace in our lifetime. But let us, at least, use that first cliché. Example: 'When the great deluge that had changed the face of Europe subsided', etc., etc., etc. Smart words. (*To Rhoda on phone.*) Rhoda, I never knew where I stood growing up. You know that.

RHODA. You're a prod.

GENE. I know that.

RHODA. You were born again in so many preachers' missions around Fermanagh and Tyrone, you never knew for sure which Jesus you belonged to.

GENE. There was so many of them.

RHODA. And then you turn around and start working for Sinn Fein. For Hubert. Gene, no one else ever knew where you stood either.

GENE. I was confused. (*To audience.*) Let's face it, and don't be shocked, please, but I worked for Hubert Murray. Oh, yes. I did occasional little jobs, for . . . our heroes; the boys. Simple things. Nothing medical. Delivering the odd message now and then, that sort of thing. Well, I mean, just because you've been born again doesn't mean you can afford to bite the hand that feeds you. (*To Rhoda.*) I swear to God, Rhoda, the way you could sing, with your chin in the palm of your hand, it was so good, Jesus, it frightened the shit out of me.

RHODA. You're only saying that now, Gene. You didn't mean it.

GENE. Rhoda, I swear to God.

RHODA. You left me high and dry, Gene. I was just one of your many little fantasies.

GENE. (*To audience.*) Then, after some time in New York . . . gradually, I realized for the first time, exactly which Jesus I belonged to. I did. I did. Truly. And I told her. (*To Rhoda.*) You see, Rhoda. I am my own Christ. That's the answer. Let the integrity of their quarrel continue. But far outside it there is enough air and enough space for every man to be true to himself. There's enough space for both of us, Rhoda, to be true to each other.

RHODA. You left me high and dry, Gene.

GENE. (*To audience.*) To thine own self be true. It was like a revelation to me. A new truth. But I suppose if I had really believe it, I might have stayed in New York. Fool that I was, I went back.

RHODA. You're coming back! Here?

GENE. (*To audience.*) The night Hubert Murray was killed, I was on the way back. For her. Jesus, when I think of it. I mean, why? To redeem her maybe? To give testimony to my most recently discovered truth? That there is no Jesus like your own Jesus. Be thou thine own Christ, and by thy bootstraps, liberate thyself from all the quarrelling of the world. Or maybe I was just lonely. And liked the sound of her voice.

RHODA. It was just a fantasy, Gene. Just a fantasy. (*She looks worried.*)

GENE. (*To audience.*) I went back. That was my mistake. That was my fatal mistake. (*Rhoda dashes off. Hugh notices Gene for the first time. He is not surprised.*)

GENE. Hello. (*Gene, a man in his early thirties, wearing a heavy-metal tee shirt, sleeveless leather waistcoat, jewelery, and jeans, shoes etc., in the American style. Gene moves about looking amazed.*)

HUGH. Correct. Your fatal mistake. Welcome to the house of the dead. Bang. And your head came off. One more dismembered carcass. One more ghost in the trees. Your little life has run out boy. Spilled itself into the ditch. May God have mercy on your soul. (*He laughs.*)

GENE. Well, holy shit. If it's not the notorious Mr Hubert Murray.

HUGH. Indeed.

GENE. Well, I always had a suspicion that the first person I'd meet beyond the grave wouldn't be Saint Peter.

HUGH. Sit down. And stop gawking round you.

GENE. But I didn't plan on joining you so soon.

HUGH. I'm well aware of that.

GENE. Mr Hubert Murray. Holy shit. So what in Christ's name am I doing back here? And what are you doing?

HUGH. It's a tradition, Mr Brady.

GENE. Yeah?

HUGH. When someone dies. They tend to hover round a place for some time. A few hours. We've got some time.

GENE. And then?

HUGH. We'll come to that later.

GENE. What about you?

HUGH. Me?

GENE. Yes, Mr Murray, sir. You. What about you?

GENE. I'm in hell, Mr Brady.

GENE. Jesus.

HUGH. Indeed.

GENE. You never liked me did you?

HUGH. That's an understatement. But I would prefer if you would stop gawking around, as if you had never seen the place before.

GENE. This is your place, of course.

HUGH. Correct.

GENE. So what the hell am I doing here? Talking to you. If I wasn't dead, I'd be terrified.

HUGH. (*Taking out dollar.*) Do you want a dollar, Mr Brady?

GENE. He's asking me do I want a dollar. The man wouldn't give you the steam of his piss. Now we're both walking ghosts, and he asks me do I want a dollar. Do I get a chance to spend it?

HUGH. No.

GENE. So what use is it to me?

HUGH. It's a game, Eugene. I know something that you don't know.

GENE. Like what?

HUGH. That's for me to know and you to find out.

GENE. Just gimme the dollar. (*Makes a grasp.*)

HUGH. Why?

GENE. I want it.

HUGH. It's not that simple.

GENE. You know, Mr Murray, since you died, you're really great crack.

HUGH. And you're confused.

GENE. Correct.

HUGH. And you know, Mr Brady, even before you died, you were really a waste of space.

GENE. Thanks a lot. Gimme the dollar.

HUGH. Why do you want the dollar?

GENE. I don't know.

HUGH. You know nothing. But work at it, my boy. Work at

it. And when you figure it out, you'll get your prize. One lovely American dollar. Can you remember anything of value in the way you lived?

GENE. I can't even remember how I died. Can you?

HUGH. I might.

GENE. Something went wrong. Didn't it?

HUGH. Precisely.

GENE. Story of my life. I always get something wrong. Here. You're to blame for a lot of this.

HUGH. I have nothing to answer in relation to your life, Brady.

GENE. I wouldn't be here only for your funeral.

HUGH. Was it a good turn out?

GENE. What?

HUGH. My funeral.

GENE. Are ye joking? It was like a feicing Patrick's Day Parade in New York.

HUGH. I'm glad to hear that.

GENE. Mrs Murray was very upset. Which surprised me. Oh, and Father Boyle spoke very eloquently, you'll be glad to hear.

BOYLE. (*Enters, and delivers in manner of sweet sentimental sermon.*) Hubert, we will this morning, lay to rest, my dear people, in the family plot, where, as you know, only too well, we buried his daddy, Stephen, just this time seven years ago. Stephen was then just eighty-nine years of age. This morning his son, Hubert, his wee child, will once again be placed in his daddy's arms, as we lay Hubert to his final resting place; and both of them, together, in the arms of their one great daddy in heaven. As all of us, someday, finally rest. In the arms of Jesus. The arms of Mary. The arms of holy Saint Joseph.

GENE. Final resting place my arse. And you were on the radio as well; (*He mimics voice of radio newscaster.*) Mr Murray's body was found this morning by his neighbours; he had been within a few feet of the bomb when it went off, and died instantly. Security forces say they are baffled by the killing, though local sources claim that the murder was the work of SAS units known to be active in the border area over the past few years, and that Mr Murray was singled out because he was a known Republican. (*Rhoda bursts into playing area, not yet forty, she is lively and attractive.*

As she enters, in a crazed fashion, she begins scrubbing the very odd-looking range. It is an old Stanley black. However, small bogey wheels have been attached to the bottom legs so that it can shift around the very large kitchen. An attractive piece of furniture.

HUGH. And my wife, Mr Brady. Don't pretend you have forgotten my wife already.

GENE. Okay, okay, cool it. Your wife was . . . very nice.

HUGH. Very nice. You found her very nice. You make her sound like ice cream.

GENE. (*To audience.*) You see what I mean? Mr Murray was never a pleasant man. But ice cream is not how I remember his wife. No. On the contrary, Rhoda was . . . all . . . blood. Blood . . . and . . . bones. She . . . was . . . clench fisted. Unbreakable. Her voice was blood and bones. She could stand up to anyone. Even if living with him for so long made her sound a bit shrill at times.

RHODA. (*Singing to the air of 'The West's Awake'.*)

Of all the men I've ever known, I've never known a one
    so sad, as he who sucks his chicken bones, or chains
    his dogs till they go mad.
He isn't happy with his wife, till her days are filled with
    pain and strife,
Come, oh my hero, set me free, from wedding bliss,
    please set me free.

(She continues humming.)

HUGH. Your dollar Mr Brady. Go on. Talk to her.

GENE. You mean it? Okay, then. (*To audience.*) So what do I care. They can't harm me now. The mystery of how I got to be so dead, has yet to be unraveled, but let there be no doubt about it; I . . . am . . . dead. Christ, can you not hear that sweetness of tone, that beautiful melody, wafting through the window down the valley and across the ocean, wafting in through the little gullies of my memory in New York? It brought me almost instantly to her side. (*He is instantly at her side.*)

RHODA. Gene, you're back.

GENE. Oh, my back, my legs, my belly, my balls; all yours.

RHODA. America didn't agree with you then?

GENE. How could I stay away from a funeral like this?

RHODA. But, damn it, you louse, you left. 'Oh, I'm only a

boy,' you said, 'and you are a woman. 'So let's make passionate love,' you said, 'in the grass. Right now. No one is looking. Make me a man', you said.

GENE. And you did. We did.

RHODA. And then you feiced off.

GENE. It was the noise, Rhoda. I mean it. I left because of the noise. There was just too much; I could never hear you sing clear enough.

RHODA. What are ye talking about?

GENE. Too much emotional disturbance. (*Stares at Hugh.*) I needed to clear my head in the quiet tranquility of downtown Manhattan.

RHODA. Really?

GENE. That's a fact.

RHODA. Well, pity you didn't stay there; not be coming back to me with more of your schemes.

GENE. (*To audience.*) True, I had a scheme. That night before the funeral of Hubert Murray, I came back with a brilliant plan. It involved me in a certain, what will I say, connivance with former acquaintances in the IRA, yes, and it involved Rhoda. But it also involved money. Lots of money. Enough money to make me and Rhoda happy. Now wasn't that a silly idea? (*To Rhoda.*) Rhoda, I have a confession to make. New York is empty without you. It was as if the Lord himself had abandoned me.

RHODA. Oh, piss off.

GENE. Without you, the light went out. All was darkness.

RHODA. Well, maybe you should just go back to one of your gospel halls and find it again, without me. Now get out of me way.

GENE. But you don't understand. I did. I did.

RHODA. You did what?

GENE. I found it again. Isn't that a strange thing? Just off the plane yesterday, and then, I'm passing through Irvingstown last night, big tent, preacher man, and there you are, I was born again.

RHODA. You're lying.

GENE. (*To audience.*) Of course, I'm lying. She knows I'm lying. It's just that I'm a Protestant, and this is a Catholic house, and the notion of Bibles and preachers and salvation was always close to the surface. That's all they every knew about me. That's the blueprint. So what if you're like me and have a sense of humour? Well, you just make up things. Tell lies. It's called codding. (*To Rhoda*.) True as God, Rhoda, this time, I have been saved, I have seen the light, I have discovered the truth.

RHODA. Yeah.

GENE. Yeah.

RHODA. Again. Born again. And again and again. And how many times is that?

GENE. Seven.

RHODA. Gene, I wish you would leave Jesus out of this, just for once.

GENE. (*To audience*.) She wishes I would leave Jesus out of this. I never brought him into it. After all, I had my plans to discuss with her. (*To Rhoda*.) We have other business. You and me.

RHODA. Mind. Out of me way.

GENE. What are you doing?

RHODA. I'm trying to clean this cooker, before the mourners arrive. It smells.

GENE. An odd way to be mourning your husband.

RHODA. Don't mock my husband.

GENE. He was a smart man.

RHODA. Aye. That's one thing he had over you.

GENE. Mrs Murray. Please. You know what an extraordinary intelligent man I am, of course.

RHODA. Of course.

GENE. I could be your very own personal saviour . . . if you were at all interested.

RHODA. What do you want?

GENE. Me? Nothing.

RHODA. Nothing?

GENE. Well. Actually, I do have a proposition. For both of us. (*To audience*.) And so I put it to her. As bold-faced and brazenly as I could. I laid before her the entire plan, and how we could make ourselves a tidy sum of money and a good life. And she listened. Oh, yes indeed, she listened. You could see a thaw begin inside her. An excitement in her eyes. Money. Escape. I felt like the hero in an opera, singing the big aria just before he whisks the lady away to safety. (*Sings. Affects an exaggerated theatricality*.)

Of all the women I've ever known
who scrub the floor to make a home
I've never known a wound so deep
as those inflicted by the creep
who turned the silence round your neck
and held the purse till you were wrecked
whose dignity was cruelty, when he demanded
    conjugality.

(*Laughs. Turns to Hugh.*) Ugh. You again.

HUGH. I wasn't even in the grave, when you were back stirring things between the two of yis again.

GENE. Hubert, come on.

RHODA. Gene, I've missed you.

GENE. Hey, so what's the problem? Here I am.

RHODA. It's too late. You let me down. You left me with him. You woke something up inside me, and then abandoned me.

GENE. (*To audience.*) She could put it more precisely if she wanted to.

RHODA. You gave me an appetite.

GENE. And then I feiced off.

RHODA. Before we could really sit down to dinner.

GENE. I was your dinner?

RHODA. You were my everything. My tootsie wootsie. But it's too late now.

GENE. Rhoda, it's never too late. He's gone now. You've won. You can sing a sweet little lament at his funeral if you like, but you can sing happy, too, because you are alive.

RHODA. I love you, Eugene. I always have. I'll do anything with you.

GENE. (*To audience.*) And that was her answer. I laid my master plan out, and she agreed. Just like that. What did I feel like? An opera singer? No, no. It was more like the sound of music. We were skipping over mountains of eidelweiss, singing a love duet . . .

RHODA. I'll do it. I'll do it with you, Gene. I will. Okay. Together. You and me. Later. (*She exits.*)

HUGH. You never had much integrity, did you?

GENE. You talk about integrity?.

HUGH. I asked you to do a few jobs for me, that was all. When you worked here, I trusted you. And what do you do? You compromise my wife, and then run off the America.

GENE. Oh, yeah? Simple jobs alright. Messenger boy to the national army of liberation. No thank you.

HUGH. They were young boys with courage; with more faith, hope, and love in their hearts for this country than you could ever dream about.

GENE. Courage? They were clowns. Eegids. They couldn't tell the difference between military manoeuvres and a pantomine. (*There is a rattle and fuss as Pheilim and Enda enter from yard, dragging with them three crates of guns. They titter to themselves as they proceed.*)

ENDA. Quick. Quick. Over here, Jesus Christ. Over here, in the pantry. Come on, Daddy.

PHEILIM. Oh, be jeepers, me back is killing me. (*Enda goes to range, tests it, and sets about fixing it. Pheilim remains in pantry or at door.*)

GENE. And by the way. Did you say something about boys? Boys. You call him one of the boys?

PHEILIM. Be jeepers, Enda, Enda, hi, a say, Enda, son, will ye look a here? Hi, Enda.

ENDA. Yeah, yeah, I know.

PHEILIM. Ah, no, but hi, come here, this is monstrous.

ENDA. Daddy, you'll not be thanked for sticking your nose where it's not wanted.

PHEILIM. Cripes, it's going to be some funeral, if she gets through that amount of booze. Too much booze isn't dignified at a wake. Do you think there's enough guns there for the firing party?

ENDA. Ouch. (*He is working on range.*) Nothing wrong with this, Daddy; just needs a new element.

PHEILIM. Guinness, lager, whiskey, vodka, gin, Bacardi, ... Bacardi, if ye don't mind.

GENE. You see what I mean? Bacardi. Not indigenous to the culture; a ladies' drink.

PHEILIM. Malibu. Malibu. What's that?

GENE. It's a hair conditioner.

PHEILIM. Is that what it is? And paraquet. Cripes. She has a bottle of paraquet sitting on the same shelf as her drinks.

GENE. Ah, ha. Poison, sir. And what about that, Mr Murray?

HUGH. For the rats. Out in the sheds.

PHEILIM. Sure a young lassie might not know that was poison, until she was dead.

ENDA. Daddy, we're fixing the frigging cooker.

PHEILIM. It's a range.

GENE. It's one of Hubert Murray's perverse attempts at creativity, actually.

ENDA. It's a cooker.

GENE. You know, when you've been away from Ireland for a considerable period, and then you return, you can find that rural society has the ability to simply ignore you exist.

PHEILIM. Didn't ould Murray make a grand job of it though? A mobile range. (*He moves the range, there being small wheels on it.*)

ENDA. Ah, stop it, Daddy, wait outside can't ye.

GENE. You got the guts of an old cooker, stuck it all inside the shell of a range, and put wheels on it. Feic it, you weren't right in the head.

PHEILIM. It's a wonder he didn't shove a juke box in there as well.

GENE. It was his wife liked the music. Not Hubert. Hubert hadn't a note in his head.

ENDA. Will ye for God's sake lave that drink alone?

PHEILIM. I'm only throwing this poison out. In case one of the mourners' tears their guts out.

ENDA. That's not what I meant. What is that in your hand?

PHEILIM. Whiskey.

ENDA. No one offered us whiskey, Daddy.

PHEILIM. Aren't we obliging the woman?

ENDA. I'm not so sure. More like she's obliging us. (*Exit Enda to collect element.*)

PHEILIM. Not that she deserves much obliging.

GENE. Ah, ha. Now that I remember it, there was precious little integrity about the way your heroes spoke behind Rhoda's back.

PHEILIM. (*Mimicing.*) Oh, anything to oblige Mrs Murray.

HUGH. He's a commedian. You don't appreciate the rustic sense of humour.

GENE. I don't understand the Catholic sense of humour. He's a two-faced, lecherous maggot.

PHEILIM. Anything to oblige, isn't that right? Like, Monsignor Boyle, to take one example, he's the man could oblige her.

GENE. (*To audience.*) You see, Rhoda was, let's face it, having something of an affair with the local prince of the church. Well, I mean, that was natural enough. The man was looking for all he could get, and her husband had practically forgotten what she looked like naked.

HUGH. That's a lie.

GENE. He probably couldn't have cared less. Nor could I for that matter. Seems as reasonable an act of liberation on a woman's part as blowing someone's head off. 'Cept I would have preferred it was me, rather than the bloody Catholic priest. That stung a little, I must admit. Christ I could have devoured her.

HUGH. You almost did. (*Rhoda rushes in to downstage position, looking around, excited and whispering.*)

RHODA. Gene. Gene. Eugene.

GENE. (*Rushing to her.*) Rhoda.

RHODA. Where are you?

GENE. I'm here in the kitchen. With the head engineer from the local brigade. I think he's converting the mobile cooker into a nuclear bomb.

RHODA. No one else?

GENE. Yeah, he's got Aristotle Maguire with him, leavening the conversation with the odd philosophical remark.

RHODA. They're bringing the body here. Then to the church. It'll be quiet later. (*Charming.*) We can make plans. About what you were saying. I'm pretending to be all heartbroken about Hubert you know.

GENE. Oh, yeah. Sure. So am I. Devastated. Just devastated.

RHODA. Terrible. See you later. (*Kisses. She skips off.*)

GENE. Well, you must admit, I did have a certain affect on her. You're not annoyed?

HUGH. Both of us are beyond being annoyed by anything, Mr Brady. As I told you before, I am also . . . suffering.

GENE. Yeah, I know. You told me.

HUGH. There is no time left, for things as trivial as annoyance.

GENE. You know something? You gave me the willies. I mean, not just now. But you always did. I never told you that, did I?

HUGH. That you were afraid of me?

GENE. Yeah.

HUGH. I'll be back. Maybe then you'll have figured out your arse from your elbow. Well go on, or are you afraid?

GENE. Mr Murray, would you not stay?

HUGH. You were always a coward. (*Hugh exits.*)

GENE. Yeah. You could be right there. (*He stares as Hugh exits into the shadows.*) (*To audience.*) The official story remained that he was blown to bits in his own meadow; presumably handling explosives. But then in Ulster, nothing is as it appears. Whatever was left of him was taken to the Erne Hospital in Enniskillen. The identification was made by these two gents. They said they recognized the shoes. (*Then he turns to Pheilim and Enda, still engrossed at cooker.*) Some animal, that Hubert. A say. Hubert. He was some animal. (*Neither of the other two notice him.*) My problem was I could never see anything; even when it was under me nose.

PHEILIM. See what?

GENE. Nothing. How are yis?

ENDA. Yes, Eugene.

PHEILIM. Be gawd, I hardly noticed ye Eugene. The last playboy of the western world himself.

GENE. Don't mock me now. Just because I'm a simple-minded eegid that threw up a wonderful destiny in the fight for freedom, all for to spend a couple of years broadening me mind in New York. Foolish of me, no doubt. But there's things about freedom that you've never even dreamed of.

ENDA. Is that a fact?

PHEILIM. Now, boy.

GENE. Aye. True freedom. And you know what that's about?

PHEILIM. What?

GENE. It's about love. Real freedom. Liberation . . . love. In a nutshell. Love.

PHEILIM. Well, to look at ye, you might make a better corpse than a lover.

GENE. (*To audience.*) You see, they were going to give me the money. If I helped out. Just one more time. Then me and Rhoda could fly away somewhere. The problem was, I thought I was codding them, when in fact, all the time, they were codding me. (*To Pheilim.*) Now now. Be not mocking poor foolish me.

ENDA. Lave him be, Daddy.

PHEILIM. Do ye be on drugs a lot, Eugene, over there?

GENE. Actually, I am waiting for Father Boyle. I'm anxious to explain to him the secret of the universe. Love.

ENDA. I think he knows that already.

PHEILIM. Maybe you're thinking of changing your religion. (*To Enda.*) He'd try anything.

GENE. I would. I'd try anything . . . for love.

PHEILIM. Of course, you could always turn the priest over to your side. (*Laughs. To Enda.*) It shouldn't be that difficult to make a pervert out of Monsignor Boyle.

GENE. Did you know, Mr Maguire, that it is a proven fact in anthropology, that even the tiniest of peasant brains can sometimes stumble on little gems of insight.

PHEILIM. Is that a fact?

GENE. It is.

PHEILIM. D'ye know I can't make head nor tail of most of what you talk about; but listen; I heard you chatting with Mrs Murray a while back there.

GENE. You did?

PHEILIM. Aye. So tell us.

GENE. Tell you what?

PHEILIM. Is it true?

GENE. Is what true?

PHEILIM. That you were born again on the way home.

GENE. In a tent outside Irvingstown.

PHEILIM. Let me get this straight. You seen the light again? For the seventh time?

GENE. Correct.

PHEILIM. So what was all that between you and Mrs Murray about . . . love or something? Maybe I didn't hear you right.

GENE. But isn't this what I keep saying; in a blinding flash I discovered that the mystery of the universe . . . is love.

PHEILIM. Oh, I see. And would this have anything to do with Jesus be any chance?

GENE. No. Nothing. It was a different sort of light.

PHEILIM. Is that a fact? A different sort of light. Now, Enda, d'ye hear that?

GENE. In fact, that's why I thought I would drop in and give these gentlemen . . . some assistance. (*To audience.*) Well, I was only fooling them really. Or so I thought. But there was a wisdom in there somewhere. The light was having the usual effect it tends to have in this part of the world. I was walking around blind. (*They smile at him. Gene, looking for Hugh.*) Hey, come here, come here.

HUGH. (*Entering.*) What?

GENE. Were you never suspicious?

HUGH. About the priest?

GENE. Yeah. Yeah.

HUGH. No.

GENE. No idea?

HUGH. Boyle was a man I respected. He attended my mother when she was dying. I trusted him. He was a man I thought we could do business with.

GENE. Yeah. Well, you were wrong there. Weren't you? Boy he sure lost the run of himself since they made him a monstrosity.

HUGH. A monsignor.

GENE. Yeah. A monsignor. Chief ecumenical bottle washer, yeah. You were wrong there. Boy, but you were wrong there.

HUGH. I made some mistakes. (*Rhoda and Boyle enter.*)

RHODA. No, I'm sorry. No.

BOYLE. Rhoda. Rhoda. Rhoda. For God's sake.

RHODA. No, sorry, I've heard enough.

BOYLE. Rhoda, will you, for Chirst's sake, listen to me?

RHODA. Listen to you? After that?

BOYLE. Rhoda, I love you.

RHODA. You made a fucking disgrace of me in there.

BOYLE. I tried to put my arms around you. That's all.

RHODA. That's all? You're so stupid Danny.

BOYLE. I tripped over the coffee table.

RHODA. I could see half the room sniggering at ye. I mean, who do you think you are when you go throwing your arms around people like that? The pope in Africa? Jesus, I know you got promotion, but there's no need to get totally carried away with yourself.

BOYLE. That's enough, Rhoda.

RHODA. I mean what is it with you? Up in the middle of my husband's funeral. You want the whole bloody perish to know that I'm your 'bit on the side?'

BOYLE. I . . . told . . . you . . . that's . . . enough . . . Rhoda. You . . . are . . . a selfish . . . awkward . . . female. I told you before. Any promotion I get, doesn't affect . . . our relationship. (*Bang and clatter from range.*)

PHEILIM. (*Cough.*) We left the bits for your washing machine in the pantry, Mrs Murray. In the crates. Gene, here, knows what to do with them.

BOYLE. What washing machine?

ENDA. Oh, and the cooker. Just needed a new element.

PHEILIM. Enda just had one handy. Wasn't that interesting? Good evening, Father. I'm sorry for your trouble, Mrs Murray. He was a great hero. And to be blown to bits in his own meadow.

ENDA. (*Shaking hands.*) Tragic. We were just saying . . . it was tragic.

RHODA. (*Inspecting range.*) Oh, it's working. Look, Father Dan, he has it fixed. Isn't that marvellous.

GENE. Isn't that marvellous, Father Dan. The wonders of modern technology.

RHODA. Well, you're the playboy, Enda.

GENE. I'm the playboy, Rhoda. He's the cowboy.

RHODA. What do I owe you Enda?

PHEILIM. Now, sure, Enda wouldn't dream of charging you at a time like this. God knows you have enough worries. Come on, Enda; we're going.

BOYLE. Don't you want to finish your drink Pheilim?

PHEILIM. Sickens me, Father. Even the smell of it. Just took it as a mark of respect. Come on, you. Good night, now. (*They exit. Boyle and Rhoda become closer, and fall into whisperings.*)

BOYLE. Rhoda, will you listen to me. (*Hugh beings to exit.*)

GENE. (*To Hugh. Shouts after him as Hugh is exiting.*) You never suspected Monsignor Danny Boyle? You know the whole country-side knew it. (*Turns to the couple.*) And you know, Rhoda, I often asked myself, you know, how he actually does it. How you could end up having an affair with a bottle of after-shave lotion.

RHODA. Because, for the last time, you . . . weren't . . . here. What am I supposed to do? Keep chaste for you?

BOYLE. Rhoda, will you listen to me?

RHODA. I don't think now is the time to talk, Dan.

GENE. Bloody sure it isn't.

BOYLE. No, no, don't mind Gene. Eugene is a man of the modern world. Aren't you, Gene? We can talk openly in front of you, can't we?

GENE. Oh, go right ahead, Your Reverence. Just allow me to be Santa Claus at the children's Christmas party this year.

BOYLE. I beg your pardon?

GENE. Wouldn't it be a wonderful way of engaging the entire population of the Catholic school, one at a time, to tell them that Santa was a Protestant?

RHODA. Gene, your manners.

BOYLE. No, no, I see the joke. Yes, very funny. What are we if we can't have a joke across the religious divide? But just sit down for a minute. Just sit. I have something to discuss with Mrs Murray.

GENE. (*Laughs.*) Something to discuss. The politeness of it all. Why don't you lean her against the table maybe, and have a lep at her, for all I care. Maybe I could watch, how you manage it, and still remain celibate. (*He sits, looking across at where Hugh has just entered with an orange and is eating.*)

RHODA. (*After looking with some frustration at Gene, and then to Boyle.*) I don't think this is such a good idea.

GENE. For he that would lust after a woman, hath even then committed the sin with her in his heart.

HUGH. You should know.

BOYLE. Are you alright, Gene?

GENE. Ah, sure; since I saw the light few nights ago, I does be confused, Your Reverence, with the tablets.

RHODA. Just go away, Gene, please, we can talk later.

BOYLE. He's on tablets again?

GENE. The ten commandments, Your Reverence. But sure yous don't heed all that fundamental biblical stuff, sure yis don't.

HUGH. Funny, aren't we? My funeral seems to have made you hysterical . . . .

GENE. It was a joke.

HUGH. A ball of laughs. There's a word for people like you. We call them mavericks.

GENE. Yeah?

HUGH. One minute you're with Sinn Fein. The next, you're preaching Jesus. No predictability. No pattern. Dangerous.

GENE. Is that so?

HUGH. Yeah.

GENE. Well, maybe you should know that there was plenty of pattern to my behaviour. Okay. I wanted Rhoda. That's all. I'm not afraid to say it. I came home here with one single intention.

To let her see what I had seen. To take her out of the hole where
you kept her.

HUGH. A hole?

GENE. A hole. A miserable hole of a life, where she ended up
chasing after the local priest for some pathetic semblance of
tenderness.

BOYLE. Rhoda, it was you started the argument.

RHODA. Me?

BOYLE. Yes, you.

RHODA. You were the one made a show of yourself in the front
room. And by the way. I think it is . . . just . . . simple . . .
outrageous, the way you used the word 'convenient'. About
Hubert's death.

BOYLE. But it is. For us. Convenient.

GENE. There's the maverick for you, Mr Murray.

RHODA. He was blown to bits, Danny, that's not convenient.

BOYLE. We know that.

RHODA. Without me hearing as much as a whimper? A big
bomb, outside the door? You see what I mean?

BOYLE. I'm sure it was the SAS. Everybody says so. You'll find
they will have a statement out in a few hours.

GENE. Sherlock bloody Holmes.

BOYLE. You shut up for a minute.

GENE. Ah, shut up yourself.

RHODA. Look, maybe it was someone around here got rid of
him. Did you think of that? Someone on our side.

GENE. Much more likely.

RHODA. And maybe they'll say it was me; that I got it done.

GENE. Entirely plausible. A crime of passion. The withered
old man, no offence, Mr Murray, done to death by young wife
who sought a lunch box elsewhere. And covered her tracks with
the thick smoke of political terrorism. Ah, ha.

BOYLE. Gene, my friend. Either you have been watching too
much American television, or taking too many drugs over there,
but things are not like that around here.

RHODA. Are they not?

BOYLE. No one is going to point a finger at you. The whole
community has compassion for a widow. It's the way it is. As they
had with Iris Caffrey . . . and Dolores Reilly . . . and Susan
Worth . . . and the woman in Belmore who found her husband

cut to bits and vacuum-packed in his own freezer. They had compassion. I'm telling you, this is a caring community. This is not America, Gene. We shed tear for tear with the widow and the orphan. We don't point fingers.

GENE. Spare us, oh Lord, from the whores of Rome.

BOYLE. God knows, there's been too much bloodshed.

GENE. Ah, put a tune to it, will ye?

BOYLE. As I said to the newspaper man, earlier in my statement, there's been . . . too much . . . on all sides. What does it matter who did it?

GENE. (*To Hugh.*) Not exactly your sentiments, I imagine.

HUGH. No.

RHODA. Look, thanks for the sermon, but can't you see the danger? Saying it was convenient? Have you any sense of what you say sometimes, Father?

BOYLE. You're over reacting. I know you never loved him.

GENE. You see what we are dealing with here, Mr Murray?

HUGH. I see you connived your way into things, made things that were harmless seem worse than they were.

GENE. You fooled yourself. The story about them was all over the place.

HUGH. No. No. It was you I hadn't figured on. Returning like a mongrel dog. What may have been between them was past. I know it. Maybe I misjudged the priest. He was weak. And that can happen. We understand our priests. But Rhoda swore to me it was over. Rhoda stood by me. Me.

RHODA. You know we're having a Republican funeral.

BOYLE. Nonsense. They can't have that. We're handling it, and there'll be no paramilitary trappings whatsoever. None.

RHODA. Tricolour on the coffin. Black berets. Shots over the grave. The lot.

BOYLE. No way. Sorry. They're not going to muscle in on this one.

RHODA. He was a soldier of the IRA, Father. And he died in action.

HUGH. You see. You see that, boy? At the end of it all, there were a few things about her I could be proud of.

BOYLE. No, I'm sorry. They won't be let. Anyway, they haven't asked.

HUGH. Listen to this.

RHODA. I'm asking.

BOYLE. What are you talking about?

RHODA. I want him to have a Republican funeral.

GENE. Oh, you're such a blind fool, Mr Murray. What you don't realize is that we were planning things. Rhoda and me. She wasn't doing anything for you. She just didn't want to let that pair of clerical pygamas ride roughshod over her.

RHODA. Nobody rides roughshod over Rhoda Murray.

BOYLE. You want a Republican funeral. You? A Republican funeral?

GENE. Oh, shut up, ye self-righteous, middle-class, pair of alter boy's knickers.

BOYLE. You. Don't make me laugh, Rhoda. In all the funerals in this county, and you never pulled with Hubert about one of them. You were never done getting up his nose about politics.

GENE. Right. Is he right, Mr Murray?

RHODA. It's for Hubert.

BOYLE. Well, I just give up on you altogether.

GENE. Good. And I'm telling you, Mr Murray, I planned it with her. We had our tidy little plan from the beginning. So there's something you didn't know before.

HUGH. Anything else?

GENE. Plenty. You said she swore it was over with the priest. Yeah?

HUGH. You're missing the point, Eugene.

GENE. Was it? Was it really?

BOYLE. And what about us?

RHODA. Us?

BOYLE. Me.

RHODA. You're joking.

HUGH. (*Taking out dollar.*) See that? That's about all you are worth (*Exits.*)

GENE. Where are you going . . . . . Mr Murray!

BOYLE. I am the youngest monsignor in Ireland you know.

RHODA. Why did you not come round last night?

JENNY. Rhoda. Rhoda.

RHODA. Just a minute.

BOYLE. Who's that?

RHODA. Who do you think it is? It's my dear sister, Jennifer.

JENNY. Joseph, don't go in there.

RHODA. And her dear, sweet, loving husband.

JENNY. Rhoda. For God's sake. Where the hell are you?

RHODA. I'll have to go.

GENE. Ah, Rhoda, we planned to be alone here, you and me, tonight, I'm going crazy. We've things to talk about. To plan.

JENNY. Rhoda.

RHODA. What do you expect at a wake? Later, Gene. Later.

BOYLE. Rhoda, I just want to hold you, I want to see you through this, to be there for you . . . to, to, to, to be a strength for you.

GENE. He . . . means . . . well . . . Rhoda, but . . . we . . . have . . . business . . . to discuss. Business. Remember?

JENNY. Is there anybody in there? Rhoda. Rhoda.

RHODA. Two minutes, Jennifer. I'll be out in two minutes.

BOYLE. Oh, well, go on then. You've no time for me. Go on. Go out to them.

RHODA. I've another bone to pluck with you.

BOYLE. What?

RHODA. Did you phone my brother-in-law today?

BOYLE. Who?

RHODA. Joe Culleton. Did you phone him?

BOYLE. I don't know. What are you talking about?

RHODA. Did you?

BOYLE. Maybe.

RHODA. Did you?

BOYLE. I wanted to know would he or Jenny do a reading at the funeral. What the hell is up with you?

RHODA. I'll tell you what is up with me. Joseph Culleton happened to marry my sister and ruin her life. Now he wants to interfere with everybody else's. Now, I don't give tuppence what he thinks. But I don't discuss you with him; and you are certainly not to discuss me with him. Is that clear?

BOYLE. What you might not appreciate, Rhoda, is that I have been under a bit of stress lately as well. I'm trying to do a very important job in the diocese, and I'm . . . trying . . . to look after us, as well. And you are not helping. I . . . am . . . doing . . . my best. And you are not helping. That's all I have to say about it. Now, look. You see? You've got me all annoyed again. (*Exits.*)

GENE. Good Christ.

RHODA. Stand beside me, Eugene. Here. Come here. And say nothing. We can talk later.

GENE. Rhoda. It is vital that we stick together. Tonight.

RHODA. Gene.

GENE. You've gotta get rid of all these relations. So that you, me, and the local heroes can arrange things.

RHODA. Gene.

GENE. (*To audience.*) Unfortunately, it wasn't that easy getting rid of them. And that's when things started to go wrong.

RHODA. Gene, what are you doing?

GENE. I'm talking to the wall. (*Joe enters, knocking as he does.*)

JOE. Sorry. Can we come in? (*Jenny whizzes past to embrace Rhoda.*)

JENNY. Rhoda, you dear, ohhhh, . . . it's just . . . awful.

JOE. Terrible. Terrible.

JENNY. They're . . . animals . . . bastards . . . Rhoda . . . I'm soooo sorry.

JENNY. I've been over at the chapel. I insisted. Wanted to light a candle for you. For you both. For you and poor Hubert.

GENE. A wonder the chapel didn't burn down.

JOE. Sorry?

GENE. Nothing.

JOE. (*Finally moving from door from where he has been watching Gene.*) Rhoda. Sorry. Sis. Didn't want to push in there. When I heard the voices. We're not disturbing . . . are we?

JENNY. I brought you this. Got it today from the Friary. It's the glove of Padre Pio.

GENE. Far out, man.

RHODA. Oh, I'm sorry, I didn't introduce . . . this is my sister, Jennifer, and her husband, Joe, they've come all the way from Dublin.

RHODA. Eh, this is Detective Inspector Brady.

GENE. Pardon.

RHODA. He's from the RUC.

JOE. Of course.

JENNY. Of course.

RHODA. They want someone to stay very close to me, for the next few days.

Pauline McLynn, Patrick Dawson, and Gabrielle Reidy in *Hubert Murray's Widow,* by Michael Harding.

JOE. Of course.

GENE. Of course. Yes. Security. But eh . . . don't mention it to anyone else. Eh? I don't want to get shot, do I? (*Laughs. The others force a polite laugh.*)

JENNY. Woke up this morning, Rhoda, quarter to seven.

GENE. Is that a fact?

RHODA. How are you, Joseph?

JOE. Say nothing. Say nothing. I was talking to Monsignor Boyle on the phone today.

RHODA. Yes. I know.

JOE. The question is . . . how are you?

RHODA. Getting through. Getting through.

JENNY. Anyway. Woke up in a terrible state. Cold shivers. Took out my rosary beads. Knew something was wrong. Never slept a wink afterwards. Ohhhh, Rhoda.

GENE. You see, with a wrong identity, I have been effectively immobilized.

JOE. Do you think there's any threat, sergeant, to our sister's life.

GENE. (*After an abrupt nervous laugh.*) Well, ah, now, we're . . . keeping an eye on it. Just, you know, practical things.

JOE. Really?

GENE. Yes. Leave light on in your bedroom, but sleep under the stairs; that sort of thing. Just advice. But please, keep it to yourself. (*All.*) Of course. (*Rhoda, who has been amused by this, can no longer repress her laughter. She covers the outburst by faking tears.*)

RHODA. I'm sorry. I'm sorry, everyone. Do you mind if I go upstairs, for a moment? I want to get some blankets out of the hotpress, for . . . the sergeant.

JOE. Of course, pet, of course.

GENE. (*To audience.*) Well, there you are. It wasn't all my doing. She was turning his wake into a friggin' circus.

JENNY. She can't go on like this. She can't. Really. She can't. Put herself in an early grave she will.

GENE. (*To audience.*) Jesus. Look at them. Trinity College Catholics. Upwardly mobile peasants. (*Joe is inquisitive and inspects cupboards, the mobile range, anything he finds about him.*)

JENNY. How do you do? Joe leave that hot plate alone.

JOE. Just looking.

JENNY. God almighty, I can't take you anywhere. Hello. My name is Jennifer.

GENE. Yes, you already told me that.

JENNY. Of course. I should have known.

GENE. Known what?

JENNY. You're so observant. The memory. I suppose you have to be.

GENE. I'd say you're a dab hand with a golf club yourself.

JENNY. Really? My goodness. How interesting.

JOE. Leave him, Jenny. I don't think we're supposed to be talking to them up here. If you get my meaning. This is not Dublin, officer, is it?

GENE. No, that's true. This is not Dublin. This is Fermanagh.

JOE. Yes. What I meant was . . . . . . oh, never mind.

GENE. I do blame the phobia myself.

JENNY. This is my husband.

GENE. Joe.

JOE. Yes. You have a good memory.

JENNY. What's the phobia?

GENE. Well, now, if I said it was a complicated condition, a desire for the presence of the beloved, which I am not enjoying right at this moment . . . if I were to say that the presence of all others, save only her, sometimes brings me out in a violent rash, you'd hardly believe me, would you? (*Laughs.*) No. But on the other hand, if I were to tell you that the phobia (fo-be-a) is the particular paramilitary organization which rubbed out Mr Murray, then, sir, I think you would know what I was talking about. Man to man.

JOE. Absolutely. Down in Dublin, we follow . . . the whole . . . politic . . . political thing. Of course.

GENE. Of course.

JENNY. We're all very concerned, aren't we, about poor Mrs Murray.

JOE. Oh, give over, Jennifer.

JENNY. Oh, but we are, truly we are.

GENE. I'd say yis are both powerful golfers.

JENNY. Joe, leave those cupboards alone.

JOE. I'm only looking.

JENNY. Well, you're in someone else's house. (*She slams cupboard closed.*) You've no business poking in other people's things.

JOE. Give me a break, will you?

GENE. Oh, your husband knows how to get on. Poke. That's how you do it. Actually there's a crate of Kalashnikov rifles out in the pantry, if you'd care to poke far enough. You might give yourself a respectable fright. (*They force a polite laugh. Jenny is fussily replacing all the things that Joe handles or pokes into.*)

JOE. The women are extremely fussy, at times, do you find?

GENE. I'm not married. Maybe they only fuss with their husbands.

JOE. Fussing.

JENNY. For the last time, Joe, nobody is fussing. I told you in the car, the remains will be coming here, to the house. Are you expecting the remains soon, sergeant?

GENE. Any minute now, madame, any minute now.

JOE. Not that there's much remains. I heard that they had to scrape bits of gristle from the front of the house this morning, officer.

JENNY. Joe.

JOE. So. The lord of the manor returns for the last time; and all his minions are fussing. What's new? I still can't understand why they come here, instead of bringing the thing straight to the church.

JENNY. They bring the thing here, as you call it, because it happens to be the custom.

GENE. Oh, yes. Remains directly to the home first. Two or three hours in the front room, before going to the church. Sort of a mini lying in state.

JENNY. Don't mind my husband, sergeant. It's just that he had very little time for Mr Murray's politics.

GENE. You can't make a silk purse out of a pig's ear.

JENNY. Well, perhaps that's a bit harsh. I mean, Mr Murray was very good to Rhoda after all.

GENE. I was speaking of your husband, madame.

JOE. You said it yourself. She won't last if she's going to carry on like this. Besides, I find it very peculiar, dragging the remains in here for two hours like a bloody mascot, instead of going straight from the hospital to the church.

JENNY. Don't be so naïve all the time, Joe, he was blown to bits for Christ sake. He has neighbours. This is Northern Ireland.

JOE. So what are you saying? That I don't understand some of the more subtle traditions relating to how you treat dead gunmen.

JENNY. He wasn't a gunman. And mind your tongue in public. (*Whispers.*) Do you want to get us all arrested?

GENE. 'Xcuse me for moment. Think I should check the roof. Case someone might come down the chimney. (*Gene exits to backyard.*)

JOE. He was a gunman, Jennifer. He talked nothing else.

JENNY. Don't you realize you were speaking in front of one of them?

JOE. Good God, woman. He's a policeman. He would have known all about Hubert and his sordid little world. That man is risking his life for you and me. In fact, I am ashamed, having to meet him in circumstances like this; where he must be associating me with . . . terrorists. Me. Me.

JENNY. I knew you couldn't let this pass, without casting politics up again.

JOE. Pardon me, but you're living in cloud cookoo land, Jennifer. You know what went on in this house. She covered up for him for years. I'm damned if I'm going to shed crocodile tears for him now.

JENNY. So why did you come? Why did you come then? If you're going to turn everything into a political argument. And leave that fucking press alone, Joe Culleton. (*She slams it again.*)

JOE. Language, Jennifer, language. (*Rhoda enters in a state of shock.*)

JENNY. What is it love?

RHODA. The police. (*Gene enters from back door.*)

GENE. Yes. The RUC.

RHODA. They're at the front door.

GENE. They're at the back door as well.

RHODA. They've brought the body.

JENNY. Oh, Rhoda. (*Hugh slips in again.*)

RHODA. They're brought him home, Jennifer.

JENNY. Oh, Rhoda. (*As she takes Rhoda back out to hall, Joe follows solemnly.*)

GENE. (*To Hugh.*) Maybe you would like to come out and look at the little bits of you that are left? (*Hugh nods negative.*) No. Neither would I. (*Talks to Joe out in hall.*) I'll be here, if you don't mind, back door, you can never be too careful. (*All exit. Gene remains with Hugh.*)

GENE. (*Singing to pass the time.*)

I have come from the grave, I have been there forever
and if you lie with me, I can promise we'll not sever
my appletree, my brightness, tis time we were together
for I smell of the earth . . .

(*Looks to exit and then to Hugh.*) There was very little of you left, I might say. Big explosion. You must have been lying right over it. (*Pause.*) Okay. I'll level with you, do you agree?

HUGH. What?

GENE. Level. I'll be totally honest with you, you just fuckin' tell me how I died.

HUGH. You don't ask the right questions, and your manner is beginning to irritate me.

GENE. I know, I know, I annoy you, I always did.

HUGH. Perhaps there were times I saw the good in you, though they were seldom.

GENE. I am lost, Mr Murray.

HUGH. I'll . . . promise . . . you . . . this . . . Mr Brady, you'll . . . work . . . it . . . out eventually. Even if I have to spell it out for you myself. (*Hugh exits again.*)

GENE. Ah, fuck you. (*Continues his song, taunting.*)
When people tell our story, they shall whisper it in dread
that she could not love her husband, until he was dead
so they searched every graveyard, through rain and
through storm
till they found here a cold corpse, to keep her old bones
warm.

(*During this verse, he moves about, careful of not being overheard, but he does not hear the knocking on door from yard, until end of song. It frightens him. He sits immediately, motionless, putting his finger to lips to indicate to Hugh to be silent. Jenny enters, distressed, and places kettle on range.*)

JENNY. They're keeping everyone away from the coffin. It's all closed. Sealed. But the men are trying to open it. Oh, my God, I don't know, I just don't know.

GENE. Excuse me, excuse me, but there is someone at the door. (*Jenny rushes and opens it.*)

BOYLE. Ah, feic me, I'm drenched.

JENNY. Monsignor Boyle, I'm terribly sorry, I didn't hear you.

BOYLE. Alright, alright, where's Rhoda? I nearly fell over Hubert's diesel drums in the dark.

JENNY. I'm awfully sorry, Monsignor.

BOYLE. Okay, okay. Now where is she? I gotta warn her. Some IRA people are coming round here; they want to stick a guard of honour into the house. With the coffin.

GENE. Jesus.

JENNY. I'm afraid you're too late. They're already in the front room with those woollie things on their faces.

BOYLE. Sweet Christ, she's being so bloody stupid.

JENNY. I don't understand.

BOYLE. When someone admits they killed him, whoever it is, she will be looking for compensation. On the grounds that Hubert had nothing to do with anything.

GENE. And having masked men with Kalashnikovs standing vigil in the sitting room, could be construed as more than a passing sympathy with Republicanism.

BOYLE. Why don't you go into the parlour with the rest, instead of slouching around here all the time?

JENNY. Oh, forgive me, Monsignor, haven't you met Detective Inspector Bradley; he's Rhoda's bodyguard, for the few days.

BOYLE. Bodyguard. Inspector Bradley.

GENE. Brady, actually.

BOYLE. How fascinating.

JENNY. Isn't it. Royal Ulster Constabulary.

BOYLE. Royal Ulster Constabulary. No less. (*Joe and Pheilim enter.*)

JOE. Sergeant. I can't believe this is happening. I mean, it's an outrage. You're supposed to be looking after this funeral aren't you? Can't you get them out?

GENE. Oh, now, wait a minute.

JOE. Sergeant, there are two men with masks in the front room; terrorists. Now, you better go in there.

BOYLE. Wait a minute, Joe, wait a minute; settle down for God's sake.

PHEILIM. (*With crate of guns.*) Will I bring this arsenal of drink out to the mourners, Father?

BOYLE. Do, Pheilim. Do. And I think I better have a little chat with Rhoda. (*Pheilim and Boyle exit. Former to pantry, latter to hall.*)

JOE. I don't believe this. It's an obscenity.

GENE. Dastardly. Unspeakable.

JOE. Yes. I mean, how are you supposed to feel? You're probably in danger here.

GENE. (*Grins.*) Ah, now, sure, lets not think anything like that.

JOE. Two little freedom fighters. Bold as brass.

GENE. Bold as brass.

PHEILIM. (*Still in pantry.*) Three, if you count the corpse.

JENNY. Look, Joe, please. You'll give yourself blood pressure. Do you want some drinking chocolate? She has drinking chocolate.

JOE. I'm not allowed drinking chocolate.

JENNY. If the sergeant here is able to live with it, I don't see why we should get over excited. It's just a custom.

GENE. True. True.

PHEILIM. Did you say sergeant?

JENNY. Yes. (*Whispers.*) RUC. Rhoda's bodyguard. But I'm not supposed to tell you.

PHEILIM. (*Still operating in pantry area.*) I see. (*Pause.*) Mrs Culleton. He's not right in the head. Got damaged be drugs in New York. Used to be a farm hand about here, till Hubert showed him the door. Couple of years ago. Been in America ever since. Not right. In the head.

JOE. I've never seen such necrophilia in my life.

PHEILIM. (*Dragging crate across stage to other door.*) Jesus, such words. A glass of whiskey the man needs. After the fright he got. It was them masks. Sure they should have given you a five minute warning. (*Pheilim exits with crate of guns.*)

JENNY. Joe, could I have a word with you in private?

GENE. (*To Hugh.*) You had one hell of a confused wake, Mr Murray.

HUGH. The only confused one around here, was you. Inspector Bradley, indeed.

GENE. it was her put me up to it.

HUGH. And you planned it well, didn't you, the pair of yis. Help Pheilim and Enda get a few guns over the border. Did you really think they would pay you that much money for such a small job?

GENE. If we were going to fill the coffin with guns and dump your body down a bog hole, it was work enough. It was dangerous enough.

HUGH. Yes. And all on the premise that I was dead.

GENE. I wanted her. I couldn't bear to be without her. Why should I see her pulled and dragged this way and that. I loved her.

RHODA. (*Screams off stage.*) Take your hands off me. Leave me alone. (*All rush out except Gene, who continues as the screams continue.*)

GENE. I was asking myself . . . what sort of shit am I getting into here; I'm only a couple of days back in Ireland, and it makes Manhattan look like an old people's bingo party.

RHODA. (*Off.*) I said let me go.

GENE. All I wanted was Rhoda.

HUGH. (*Angry.*) All you wanted was my wife.

GENE. Yeah, sure. So don't get yourself in a knot about it. I wanted none of your politics. I just wanted her.

HUGH. My Rhoda. My wife.

GENE. Hi, don't be fucking melodramatic with me now. Like you said, we're both beyond emotions as trivial as annoyance. It was me and her; nothing else. (*Rhoda enters.*)

RHODA. Hubert was a freedom fighter; what sort of treacherous bitch do they take me for?

GENE. Why did you have this . . . don't spoil our plan.

RHODA. Don't you see what I'm caught in? I could never betray Hubert.

HUGH. Not for men ten times your better. But certainly not for the likes of you.

GENE. (*To Hugh.*) You're sadly misreading the situation.

HUGH. Am I?

GENE. Yes. Are you forgetting why you ran out of here? Are we forgetting her peculiarly private devotions with His Eminence. (*He turns.*) Rhoda, don't lose control. Not now. Remember what we promised each other.

RHODA. I remember the time he beat you.

GENE. And you watched. I know. But stop bringing in things that are irrelevant. I'm older now. Just play along with the funeral for our sake. We've got a deal, Rhoda, you and me.

RHODA. Jesus, life could be so sweet. With just a bit of luck.

GENE. Remember, my little sexbomb, in the back of the Hiace van exploding like a firecracker about freedom. (*Sings.*) Come, oh my tootsie, Liberty, from all this shit, I'll set you free.

RHODA. (*Breaking away.*) Oh, not now, Gene.

GENE. You said it was like living in a graveyard Rhoda. Rhoda.

RHODA. Stop it.

GENE. Rhoda. One twenty-year-long funeral, and you were stuck forever howling in the graveyard. That's what we're gonna change. I'm your saviour. Your liberator.

RHODA. No. Why do you keep going on with that born-again stuff; telling everyone you saw the light in a tent? It's so stupid.

GENE. It's a joke. For public consumption.

RHODA. You're crazy.

GENE. I'm crazy. Who introduced me as the singing detective? You could have me shot. Look Rhoda. I've found the solution. The answer to the great question of life and death in Northern Ireland. I've found the answer.

HUGH. The question is, when you finally stop summersaulting, will we know which side of you is up . . . your head or your arse.

GENE. She likes my arse.

RHODA. Pardon?

GENE. Don't you . . . . . . like my arse.

RHODA. Yes, of course, I like your ass.

GENE. So, what's the problem? We've made our plan. We just follow it, calmly and quietly, and this time tomorrow it will all be over.

RHODA. Damn it, Gene, sometimes I hate you. (*She exits.*)

GENE. The solution, Rhoda. I've figured it out. I've got the answer.

HUGH. So you had it planned.

GENE. We had it planned.

HUGH. You had it planned.

GENE. And we very nearly got away with it. Fact is, I don't see what went wrong.

HUGH. There's a lot you don't know.

GENE. And you do.

HUGH. Of course, I do. You and your smart-aleck cynicism. I couldn't get rid of you, could I? You kepp coming back, turning up in the wood pile like a relentless little rat. That's what you are.

GENE. Am I?

HUGH. Yes.

GENE. It was simple. A simple little plan, Mr Murray . . . . It was a way out. It was our passport. (*Hugh has gone.*) Hubert. Mr Murray. (*As Gene starts to go for door, looking for Hugh, there is a scuffle, and Rhoda pushes back in, Joe forcing her without handling her, followed by Jenny, Boyle, and Pheilim.*)

JOE. Don't panic. Don't panic, anyone. Easy now, Rhoda. Cool it.

RHODA. (*Scornfully.*) Leave me alone, Joe Culleton.

JENNY. Just calm down, Rhoda. We're only trying to help.

RHODA. Your Reverence. You put them up to it, didn't you?

JENNY. Please, Rhoda, not now.

RHODA. How dare you interfere with the way I conduct my husband's funeral?

BOYLE. I did nothing.

RHODA. And you know full well, Jennifer, what I think of your Joseph.

JENNY. Oh, that's it, that's it, out with it now.

RHODA. And I know what you and him thought of my Hubert.

JENNY. That's it, go on, blame Joe. Blame Joe. Yous all blame Joe.

RHODA. Ah, don't start whining now, Jennifer. Your bladder was always behind your eyeballs.

BOYLE. Rhoda, you're making a complete fool of yourself.

RHODA. Am I, indeed? You call him a terrorist if you want, but not in this house. He was a Republican. Right? Right, Father Boyle?

BOYLE. They're just labels, Rhoda.

JOE. You know, Father, I'm being very patient; but someone is gonna have to do something here.

RHODA. I may have let him down in the past. But not now.

BOYLE. Rhoda, will you, for God's sake, shut up shut up.

RHODA. Then, of course, you wouldn't know about loyalty anyhow. With your political gymnastics, you're on every side of the fence, depending whose gin and tonic you happen to be drinking at the time. Go on, Danny, are you gonna thump me?

JENNY. Oh, Jesus. Sacred Heart of Jesus. There's going to be a row. Give her something. Where's the policeman? Someone give her something.

JOE. You give her something. You're the one with the chemist's shop in your handbag.

RHODA. Yeah, give me something, Jennifer, one of your little pills.

BOYLE. Maybe you should, Rhoda. Let Jenny give you something.

RHODA. (*Sarcastically.*) Oh, do you really think so, Father? Well alright. If Father says so. It might calm me down. Father knows best in these matters. Jennifer. (*Jenny is already dropping tablets in a glass of water.*)

GENE. She's putting an awful lot of little white things in that glass of water, Mrs Murray.

BOYLE. Would you ever keep your mouth shut for once. This is a family affair.

JOE. Father Boyle, he *is* a member of the forces.

JENNY. Joe, have nothing to do with that policeman. Apparently he's not the full shilling.

JOE. I beg your pardon? (*Rhoda is drinking, being attended by Boyle and watched by Gene.*)

JENNY. It's the truth; he's mental.

JOE. You telling me that an inspector of the Royal Ulster Constabulary is a lunatic?

JENNY. Totally. Ask the monsignor.

JOE. This is typical Republican propaganda, Father. Father Dan. Our friend here. What's the story?

GENE. Well, now, isn't it the truth, Father, about the Irish? Always fighting among ourselves.

BOYLE. A total air head. Lives in a fantasy world. Don't mind him.

JOE. Jesus Christ.

JENNY. Now, Rhoda, you'll feel better in an hour or so. Come on pet, upsee daisy, give me a hand till we put her to bed.

BOYLE. No, wait. Leave her here.

JOE. Shouldn't we get her lying down first?

BOYLE. All in its time. After we've got rid of the vigilantes in the front room. (*Pheilim attempts to slip out.*) Could you just stay for a moment, Pheilim, thank you.

JOE. I'm not quite with you.

BOYLE. We can send a message into the front room; no guns, no flags, no military display of any sort, not here, not tomorrow, not at the grave, nowhere . . . . . . Rhoda has changed her mind. Isn't that right?

JENNY. But isn't that a lie?

JOE. Congratulations, Jennifer.

BOYLE. If they think she had been knocked out, they'll not budge.

JOE. Do you think we could do that officer?

GENE. It's ice cool with me, friend. (*Noises from yard.*)

JOE. Jennifer, did you lock the car? (*Noises from yard.*)

JENNY. Well, don't be looking at me, Joe. (*Noises from yard.*)

PHEILIM. That'll be Enda. I tould him to clane up them barrels that were lying around the yard. Before someone got hurted.

EDNA. Good night again.

BOYLE. Ah, Enda. Come in. (*Pause.*) We were just wondering actually, Enda, that is, I was thinking, eh, the grave, tomorrow. We were wondering. Is it dug yet?

ENDA. Aye, it's dug this three hours.

RHODA. (*Singing.*) I am stretched on your grave, I will lie there for ever.

JENNY. Jesus, Mary, and Joseph.

RHODA. And if you lie with me, I'll promise we'll not sever.

JENNY. I think we could all do with a cup of tea.

ENDA. What happened to her? A say, what happened to this bird?

JENNY. Would you take a mug of tea in your hand, Enda. Everybody. There's plenty of everything. Apple tarts. Scones. Coffee log. Scones. Any amount of scones. You couldn't ask for better neighbours.

ENDA. A say, what happened to this bird?

BOYLE. Oh, ah, she was a bit upset. Jenny gave her something. But listen, Enda.

ENDA. Be jeepers, ye must have given her a dose fit for a bull.

RHODA. And if you lie with me, I can promise we'll not sever.

ENDA. Are you a nurse or a vet?

BOYLE. Enda, there's a guard of honour in the front room.

ENDA. So.

BOYLE. They'll have to go.

ENDA. Tell them that.

BOYLE. It's the family's wishes. Rhoda included.

JOE. Dash it, Father. There's no use mincing words here. You and the policeman here will have to go up and tell them to leave. On behalf of the family.

ENDA. What fucking policeman?

JOE. This one.

GENE. Oh, now, it's the truth. Always fighting among ourselves.

ENDA. Jesus, Joe, you're a bigger eegid than I thought you were.

JOE. How do you know my name?

ENDA. I know more than your name.

JOE. Do you now? And I suppose that's part of your snide, smarmy, water-in-the-river stuff, is it.

ENDA. You're talking horse shite.

JOE. You know what I mean. You know what I mean. You know. Oh, yes. I know you know.

BOYLE. Now, now, now, boys. We're making the mistake here of getting into polemics.

JOE. I know what I'm talking about, Father.

ENDA. You're talking through your hole.

JOE. I'll ignore that. It's the fish-in-the-water syndrome, Father, isn't it? The terrorists are the fish. People like the Maguires here, are the river. The necessary environment. Don't think I haven't studied all that. Mao Tse Tung. And all that. (*Points.*) And I have you marked, me boy. I have your card marked.

ENDA. What about Nelson Mandela?

BOYLE. Ah, for Christ's sake, Enda, give over.

JOE. (*Staggered.*) Nelson Mandela? Nelson Mandela? What are you talking about? What has Nelson Mandela got to do with it? This has nothing to do with South Africa.

ENDA. And what about the Palestinians on the West Bank? Like, do you study the ANC position on armed struggle, Professor Culleton, in the course of your intellectual political wanking?

JOE. (*Screams.*) There are terrorists in the front room, Father. Give me a tablet, Jennifer. Mad, sick terrorists.

ENDA. In the name of Jaysus, Father, where does he think he is, the Phoenix Park?

JENNY. Ignore him, Joe, don't answer him.

BOYLE. Look, I've had enough of this.

ENDA. You've had enough? Where does he think he is?

JOE. Oh, yes, let him go on. I know. I know the script. Bitch about Protestants, the British, the middle classes, the whole bloody world. You're the only ones with the right to blow people's legs off, I suppose.

JENNY. If you don't stop, Joe, I'm leaving the house, this minute.

JOE. Not such a bad idea, and you might leave on your own.

JENNY. He'll have a heart attack, Father. I know it.

ENDA. You're getting very rude, Mr Culleton.

JOE. United Ireland my arse. Do they blow up the soccer pitches? Oh, no. Not bloody likely.

ENDA. If the people inside hear you, they're going to take a dim view of it.

JOE. Is that a threat?

ENDA. No, its not a threat.

JOE. I don't give a curse who hears me. (*Shouts very loud.*) I shall not be silenced by the likes of you.

RHODA. What the feic is going on? (*After a final note there is a long, embarrassed silence.*) Sorry. I'm sorry. I apologize.

PHEILIM. Ah, Mrs Murray, are ye coming round yet? Ye missed a powerful debate. It was as good as the television.

JENNY. (*With tea.*) Best thing is to leave politics out of it. Tea everybody?

JOE. Leave politics out of it? There are two teenagers with machine guns slouching over the corpse in the front room, and you want to leave politics out of it?

JENNY. Sugar, Sergeant. How many? Five. My goodness, you have a sweet tooth.

BOYLE. Wait a minute, wait a minute, why is everyone addressing him as sergeant?

JENNY. A sandwich, Monsignor?

BOYLE. No, thanks. Look, Enda, please, for my sake, tell them to go.

GENE. Begging your pardon, Reverence, but by the grace of God I am a member of the Forty-Seventh Division, Borough of Queens, New York City, Salvation Army, rank sergeant, praise Jesus. Would that satisfy your curiosity?

BOYLE. Nothing out of your mouth would satisfy me.

GENE. Now, now, let's not be sectarian, Your Reverence. Will we tell Enda what happened to poor Mrs Murray?

BOYLE. Nothing happened to Mrs Murray. Mrs Murray was tired.

JOE. Which is hardly surprising.

GENE. (*To Joe.*) My real identity, confidential now, between you and me, secret, undercover . . . . . . I'm Mickey Mouse . . . . Okay?

ENDA. Is that what happened, Daddy?

PHEILIM. Ahhhhh, well . . . more or less. I suppose.

JOE. (*To Jenny.*) He's insane.

JOE. He is insane. In fact, I think he may be dangerous.

GENE. I was here.

ENDA. Is that what happened?

GENE. Now, there was a shocking rumpus.

BOYLE. Don't do this, Eugene, don't meddle in this family a second time around.

GENE. (*Offended.*) Oh, I see. I see. (*Pause.*) Don't meddle in this family a second time around.

BOYLE. That's what I said.

GENE. She was squealing like a pig.

JENNY. She was a bit distressed, that's all. Because everyone was telling her that the Republicans in the font room would have to go. And she particularly . . . wanted them . . . to stay.

JOE. Do you ever open your mouth without making a fool of yourself?

JENNY. Well, I'm sorry, Joe, but I'm beginning to find the whole thing a bit distasteful.

JOE. Shite.

BOYLE. Enda. We'll have to talk.

ENDA. Hang on a minute now, Father. We'll talk alright. But I didn't come back here just to listen to family squabbles.

JENNY. Oh, this is not a family squabble, Enda Maguire.

ENDA. Would you shut up for a second.

JOE. How dare you?

ENDA. Shut up. I can't get a word in edgeways with yis. Now. Eugene. Eugene.

GENE. Mr Maguire.

ENDA. Well, go on, Gene. It's all yours. You're on.

GENE. I'm on. And that's it, isn't it? Out of the emotional chaos, someone has to fashion order. We didn't plan for all these relatives to be hanging on. We certainly didn't wish to involve them. But that's the way it is. You can't plan everything in life. And there's so much quarrelling, arguing. Relentless. Obsessive. And every so often it all comes together, coheres, in one beautiful, creative act of violence. I understood that a long time ago about Ulster. The problem has no solution. Violence is just a way of imposing order on the chaos. The problem itself . . . is the solution. So why shouldn't I in my own cynical way take some advantage from it. I get the spotlight for once? I'm taken seriously. It's almost beautiful. It's almost like sex.

ENDA. Eugene. Get on with it.

GENE. What?

ENDA. Bring out what's left in the pantry.

GENE. Certainly, Mr Maguire, certainly.

PHEILIM. You see, now, the way yis were getting yourselves all excited over nothing.

ENDA. Tomorrow we'll have a Republican funeral, and there's nothing you, Father, nor anyone else, is going to do about that matter. (*Gene is dragging out the remaining crate of guns, and assembling an AK-47 in front of them.*)

PHEILIM. They're all gone from inside. Except for the colour party. Will I tell them to open the coffin, son?

ENDA. Do. And tell them to hurry. Only thing is; Hubert is going to be buried tonight.

JENNY. Mother of Jesus.

ENDA. Tomorrow, Father Boyle, not only will you be honouring Hubert, but you'll also be presiding over twenty Kalashnikov rifles, which we urgently need to get across the border, and Hubert's coffin is about our only means of transport.

JENNY. Joe, do something. Hit him.

JOE. Oh, for Christ's sake, shut up.

BOYLE. And if I say no?

ENDA. Oh, you won't say no, Father.

BOYLE. I will.

ENDA. You won't. (*Pause.*) Look, there's certain matters, which I don't wish to bring out here, Father. Look on it as a favour, to Hubert, and, eh, to Rhoda. We didn't want to involve you all, but since you are all having such a family reunion, we had no choice. What we'll do is this. Rhoda will be too ill to go to the funeral. Mr and Mrs Culleton here can stay with her. And Eugene will look after everything. When the funeral has reached its destination, in Cavan, we'll make sure that these people get back to Dublin, safely.

GENE. And that's where I come in, Your Reverence. (*Gun assembled and in hand.*) As Enda says, Eugene will look after everything. What did ye think? I'm doing a little favour for old friends. And you thought I was just two and sixpence. When in fact I'm not. I'm, half a crown. (*He laughs and cheers.*) Yahoo. (*Etc. Pheilim enters dragging a body bag behind him.*)

PHEILIM. Excuse me. Excuse me. Would you mind where you're pointing that thing. Thank you. (*Dragging and exasperated.*) Enda. Will you for Jesus' sake give me a hand with this thing. (*He leaves it.*)

ENDA. There's no rush, Daddy. Just leave it to me. Alright?

PHEILIM. (*Stares at him for a moment.*) Right. I will then so. I'll leave it to you. We'll all leave it to you. (*Exits in temper.*)

ENDA. Are ye with us, Father? We'll drive up the mountain, and give him a Christian burial.

GENE. (*Laughs, and hits a rapid beat on the floor with his feet.*) Yahoo. Up the Republic. Yahoo.

END OF ACT I

ACT II

Both Jenny and Rhoda are from the beginning under stress. Jenny's consistent strategy to deflect Rhoda's aggression is to constantly busy herself with the task of packing clothes into suitcases for Rhoda. Jenny enters, folding clothes, and placing them in suitcases. Rhoda looks at her, affecting to be in a slight trance. Jenny is fussing, hyperactive.

JENNY. Honest to God, Rhoda, I was driving up here yesterday morning, after you telephoned, and it was such a bright spring morning, and I thought . . . how long is it now . . . since the funeral. Two months. Almost two months. And you've been here all the time on your own. Sure it's not right.

RHODA. Jennifer.

JENNY. Well, of course, I couldn't get up to see you. But honestly, do we ever realize how suddenly our lives can change? Just two short months. Less. Less. Yes.

RHODA. Oh, Jennifer. (*Rhoda searches for something.*)

JENNY. I mean, there I was, happily married, or so I thought, and then suddenly, puff, I'm practically a divorced woman. Oh, now. It's an old saying and a true one. There is no life that is without its little twists and surprises.

RHODA. You know, I was just thinking, you know, that cat. She used to cry at the back door. All the time. Right? Well, you see I know why she cried now. Yes. I do. It's because she was left outside the door. (*Laughs.*) And when the cat is away, the rats return. (*Laughs.*)

JENNY. Rhoda. There is no cat in the house. If it's anywhere, I'm sure it's outside.

RHODA. They won't come inside when there is somebody dead in the house. Have you never heard that? (*Mimics the sound of cat.*) Jennifer. (*Mimics.*) I'm asking you a question, Jennifer. Have you never heard that?

JENNY. No. I haven't . . . . I don't know anything about cats. Now stop it.

RHODA. Probably don't have them in Dublin. Died out did they?

JENNY. Rhoda, you're not being fair.

RHODA. Died out. Like the corncrakes. And the house mouse. What are you doing?

JENNY. Rhoda. I have told you half a dozen times. I'm packing a few things for you.

RHODA. Oh. Am I going somewhere?

JENNY. Of course, you are. Now look, Rhoda, just stop it. We've been through this with the doctor. Now, you can stay with Enda's wife, or you can go to the hopsital. It's only for a couple of weeks. I'm doing my best for you.

RHODA. (*Screams.*) That's the way they do it.

JENNY. Do what?

RHODA. That's the way it wails. The cat. When someone dies.

JENNY. Honestly, Rhoda, you're being very selfish. Mummy always said you were selfish. I've had my troubles too, don't forget, these past six weeks. (*Rhoda wails again. Pause. And again.*)

JENNY. For Jesus' sake.

RHODA. You can hear him in the sheds sometimes. Middle of the night. Sometimes I think it's the sound of the mountain ash, shaking its branches against the galvinized roof on the granary. But it's not. It's him. I know it. I know it's him.

JENNY. Pet. Listen to me. Listen. Listen. You can't go on here on your own. The house locked up. Never going out. Not when you're unwell.

RHODA. So. I listen to the radio don't I? Isn't that what sick people are supposed to spend the day at?

JENNY. Rhoda, please, for God's sake, stop it.

RHODA. Sorry. Sorry. Sorry. I suppose you're right. We're sisters aren't we? I suppose there's no point in me taking it out on you. Is there?

JENNY. No. None in the world.

RHODA. I'll stop then, I promise. I will. Honest. (*Pause.*) Okay. Tell me about Joe. Tell me about it. How you come to leave him, all of a sudden.

JENNY. I told you. I left him. That's it. I don't want to talk about it.

RHODA. You left him.

JENNY. I left him.

RHODA. Very nice for you. Is this an epidemic in the South or what? You just leave your husband. Is that it? Everyone doing it. Like a fashion. I can't leave my husband, can I? Nearly two months since his funeral, and I still can't get away from him.

JENNY. I'm saying nothing if you're going to be like that.

RHODA. Oh, please, Jenny, little pretty Jenny. You think I'm depressed. Don't you? (*Careful not to be overheard.*) It's just that I'm afraid. Around here. Sushhhh. Listen. Don't you hear anything? Do you think I am going mad?

JENNY. That's for other people to decide. Professional people.

RHODA. You left him. Why? How? How did you leave him for Christ's sake? Did he not mind? Was he not annoyed?

JENNY. I've told you.

RHODA. Was it my fault?

JENNY. Nothing was your fault.

RHODA. Please, Jennifer, please go over it again with me. You know what the doctor said, I need to go to the hospital.

JENNY. He didn't say that. He said 'maybe.' He said, Enda's wife, or 'maybe' the hospital.

RHODA. You know, of course, I won't go to Enda's. I'm frightened. That's all. If you want the truth, that's all. Nothing wrong with me. Just frightened. There are things around here, things that go on, around here, which I have good cause to be frightened of. Do you realize that? (*Another furtive glance, continues again, as if afraid of being overheard.*) There's a lot of killing goes on up here, Jennifer. You know? On average about one killing every fortnight in this county for the last twenty years. Everybody is at it. It's all over the place. But you don't know when you're going to go out into a field and step over a corpse. Is there any possibility you could understand that?

JENNY. Okay. I'll say it again. Sit down. Sit down for God's sake. Now. Joseph and I have separated because I decided so. And anyway, I think it was the best thing for him. It was the night we were here. With that animal. Eugene.

RHODA. No, Jennifer, no, don't say that.

JENNY. Maybe it was the way Joseph was behaving. Maybe I just saw through Joseph for the very first time in my life. Saw the impotent little coward he had become. He wasn't always like that, Rhoda. I just, I just, I just . . . . I don't know . . . . I just had to leave him. That's all.

RHODA. Maybe you should have shot him.

JENNY. I beg your pardon?

RHODA. Or strangled him.

JENNY. Rhoda.

RHODA. Maybe you should have mashed up light bulbs and fed them to him in his porridge.

JENNY. Why would I interfere with his porridge?

RHODA. It might have been more fun. Than a divorce. (*Laughs.*) Do you not remember the way Eugene treated him that night?

JENNY. Of course, I remember.

RHODA. He humiliated Joe. When he wanted to go to the toilet. And Eugene insisted on going with him. Made him keep the door open. Joe didn't like that did he?

JENNY. No, he didn't.

RHODA. Well, that was the stuff for him, wasn't it? (*Shouts.*) Wasn't it? Wasn't it the stuff for your Joe, Jennifer?

JENNY. Yes. Okay. Perhaps it was. (*Enter Gene, with gun trained on Joe, who is still fixing his trouser fly.*)

GENE. Now, Mrs Culleton. Anyone else for a trip to the toilet?

JOE. Minute they release us, I'm going straight to the police.

JENNY. Don't say that to him, Joe, he could shoot you.

GENE. Oh, you're missing the whole point, arsehole. Look. Mrs Murray. Explain it to him.

RHODA. They won't bury the guns, Joe. So there would be no point in going to the police.

GENE. You see the difference between you and me, Joe, is that you are stupid, and I . . . am smart. You think that we would take a coffin load of guns. Hard-got machinery, for the struggle. And bury them? Those guns are needed all the time. Stupid. So our little funeral will go to Ballyconell, where the graveyard is, but on its way, it will stop for two or three minutes. Make a little detour. Quiet little laneway. Where the guns are taken out again, for use somewhere else. It's a war. Joe. A war. It goes on.

JOE. And why can't you just leave the guns here? Why can't you bury the man properly and not behave like barbarians?

GENE. Because the moment the hearse leaves from here, this place will be crawling with Brits. So they find nothing, okay? A corpse, believe it or not, is very disposable. Degradable. Ecologically friendly. Guns are different. The only way to get our machinery out of this security net is in that coffin. But between here and the grave, they will be moved again. For the struggle, Joe. Are you with me? The struggle.

JOE. You took a dead man from his coffin and buried him out there, somewhere in the middle of the night. I can give evidence of that. And I will.

GENE. You could. And you'd be compromising our dear Monsignor Boyle. Who's compromised far enough as it is. No. Look. I know you're stupid, Culleton, but try to understand me. I'm a will o' the wisp. See? You might as well prove Santa Claus was here. Dig up a grave on your cock and bull story? Not bloody likely. But then, on the other hand . . . your personal health would be at risk for years. Not worth it.

JOE. Oh, you're so wrong, sir. You misjudge me. It would be worth it. And I'll do it. By God, I'll do it, first thing when I leave this house; mark my words.

GENE. And compromise your own sister-in-law into the bargain? You're own little sister-in-law, that you're so fond of?

JENNY. And just what do you mean by that? (*Rhoda staggers to pantry, then looks, then continues.*)

RHODA. How much are we getting for this, Eugene?

EUGENE. Enough. (*Laughs.*) Just enough, Mr Culleton, to get Rhoda and me a new life far away from here.

JOE. You knew about this?

RHODA. Yes. I knew about this.

JOE. But, Rhoda. I thought you were totally against violence. You never pulled with Hubert. You were a thorn in his side. I always admired you for that.

RHODA. So, what's the big objection to shoving him down a boghole?

JOE. Well, you must be totally loosing your senses.

RHODA. We wouldn't have all this trouble, Joe, if it hadn't been for you. Causing such a fuss.

JOE. You're blaming me? Rhoda, I am the one you could have turned to.

RHODA. Turn to you? Don't make me laugh.

GENE. Joseph Culleton. Superman.

RHODA. Would have been all smooth and simple. Not even the priest would have known. If it hadn't been for you, shouting and roaring.

JENNY. But you're letting them get away with something awful, Rhoda.

RHODA. No. You're wrong there. For once, it's me that's getting away with it. Me. You think I could ever interfere with what Hubert did in the middle of the night, between here and Belfast? Do you? Do you? So what's one more night. They owned him. They might as well have the carcass. (*Shock of what she has said frightens her. Jenny goes to her and holds her face in her hands.*) Hubert. Hubert heard me say that, Jenny. I said . . . . . . let them have the carcass. And Hubert heard me.

JENNY. Of course, he didn't.

RHODA. It's not fair, Jennifer. Gene used to say it wasn't fair. I deserved a chance. Like everyone else. Everyone deserves at least one break.

JENNY. Yes. Yes. You're right, Rhoda. Everyone deserves a chance.

GENE. Me and Rhoda here are lovers. She's coming to America with me.

RHODA. Are you serious, Jennifer? Are you serious? You thought I was right?

GENE. Let them know it. Dick heads.

RHODA. We're not lovers. You're getting too American in your talk.

JOE. You're in very grave trouble, Rhoda, I only hope you realize that.

JENNY. You know it's what it brought out in Joe that alarmed me.

JOE. You're in very grave trouble, Rhoda, I only hope you realize that.

JENNY. You know what I wanted to say to him?

RHODA. What?

JENNY. You know when he said that, all pomp and arrogance? And I thought now, now, that's it, that's it, now. I can see it.

RHODA. See what?

JENNY. The person he had become. His arrogance. His pomposity. And behind all the huffing and puffing was nothing more than a desire to get on slightly more intimate terms . . . . . . with you.

JOE. You're in very grave trouble, my dear Rhoda, I only hope you realize that.

JENNY. I just wanted to stick my nose in his face and tell him to fuck off.

JOE. A time comes when someone has to make a stand. Draw the line. Family or not.

GENE. Shut up, dick head. Here. Rhoda. Tell us what the priest was like for a ride. Eh?

RHODA. You shut up, Gene.

JENNY. We all seem to have nothing to do except tell each other to shut up.

GENE. And I said, shut up. Did you know she was fucking the priest? (*Whisper.*) Whisper, whisper, whisper.

JENNY. I just had no idea the things that seem to have been going on.

RHODA. You had no idea, Jenny. No. Marvellous. Of course you hadn't. And if I sit here now and say . . . tell you something awful, you don't think I'm saying anything to you. You don't think, maybe now, there's something I need to tell someone but am too scared to. Here. That doesn't cross your mind? For Jesus' sake, do you ever listen?

JENNY. Rhoda, I didn't have to come up here you know. I didn't have to. I've about enough worries of my own with solicitors, and houses, and Joe. And I'm beginning to think they're right about you. You're not well. Now, what are you talking about?

RHODA. You just won't believe anything I say. And I was never, ever, intimate with your husband. So don't blame me for that one.

JENNY. I'm blaming Joe, you thick. Joe, and Eugene, and Hubert . . . . . and all the rest of them . . . . . bullies. They're all the same. Except that Eugene Brady was the cream of them all. I saw the way he was carrying on with you. I saw.

RHODA. Never ever, never once, was I intimate, never once, not me, no, not me and your Joseph, thank you very much.

JENNY. Oh, make no mistake. If you were with that fella in America for a couple of months, you'd be singing a different tune. I saw him I did. I saw the way he was . . . . . . carrying on.

RHODA. Jennifer.

JENNY. I saw it all.

RHODA. Eugene didn't go back to America without me.

JENNY. Not that I haven't seen it before with some of Joe's friends.

RHODA. That's a lie.

JENNY. Sex mad whelps.

RHODA. I'm telling you now, straight out; he didn't.

JENNY. I saw the way he was carrying on with you that time, Rhoda. I did. I did. And it was not a pretty sight.

GENE. Hi, Rhoda, tell your family, here, how Hubert died. (*Rhoda squirms.*)

GENE. Rhoda. Rhoda. I'm talking to you.

JOE. They're all the same. All bitter and twisted.

JENNY. At least it's bringing you out in your true colours.

GENE. Rhoda, I'm talking to you.

RHODA. What?

GENE. Tell them.

RHODA. No.

GENE. I said tell them.

RHODA. I don't want to, Eugene.

GENE. Tell them.

RHODA. Okay. (*Pause.*) He was sitting in the corner. Sat for nearly two hours. Wouldn't let me turn on the television. Just sat. About a quarter to twelve, 'I'm going out', says he. 'To the pub?' says I. 'No', says he. 'Just out'. I told the police that I was in bed. That I had taken sleeping tablets. Well, I didn't. I was sitting here. I heard the explosion. I even went to the front door. With the lights off. And opened it a bit. I . . . I . . . thought I could hear him . . . moaning sort of.

JENNY. Why don't we all go to bed now.

JOE. Go on, Rhoda.

RHODA. I closed the door. Just sat. Then about four o'clock, I listened to the news on the world service and went up to bed. Slept like a baby.

GENE. He was an ugly man, your Mr Murray.

RHODA. Gene knew Hubert very well. Didn't you, Gene? (*Gene rubs his fingers in Rhoda's hair. He is behind her, looking over her shoulder at Joe. Rhoda responds, catlike, with pleasure to the massage.*)

JOE. For Christ's sake, leave her alone.

GENE. (*With gun.*) Easy. Easy.

JOE. How dare you? How dare you, sir? In front of me and my wife.

JENNY. Oh, Joseph, easy on.

JOE. And you shut up, too, Jennifer, for once in your life. Just look at this mess. A young thug, an ignorant, uneducated thug, who, who, who, thinks because he has a gun in his hand that he is somebody. Well, I am not a man to stay silent. Joe Culleton is not a man you can cow into silence.

JENNY. As we all know.

JOE. And you, Rhoda. You. You. (*Pointing finger at her.*) How many times over the years? Did we meet? Did we ever speak? Yet I could have been everything you needed. I could have had the solutions. Had you bothered to knock on our door. But no. Oh, no. You knew it all, Rhoda, didn't you? Nothing but Mr Murray for you. I said it years ago. But that's past history now. Yes. The older the fiddle the sweeter the tune, as your sister said more than

Miche Doherty and Gabrielle Reidy in *Hubert Murray's Widow*,
by Michael Harding.
Courtesy Tom Lawlor.

once in the good man's defence. Well, she didn't seem to realize
that you were playing with an entire orchestra of fiddles up here.
Or perhaps she did. You're cheap, Rhoda. You know that? Cheap.
I didn't realize that. And remember we were family. Me. You.

Jennifer. Never say there was no one around to help. All the time. If only you had asked. If only you had come to me. (*He begins to leave, very upset. Gene trains gun on him. Is about to escort him from room.*)

GENE. Out, ye windbag. Come on. It's up them stairs. Beddy bye-byes. (*Gene forces him out first.*)

JOE. No, I'm not surprised you're doing this. If it's not one sort of bang it's the other. That's all either of yous want. Bang. Bang bang, bang. (*They both exit.*)

RHODA. Oh, Jennifer, I'm sorry.

JENNY. You see, he's better off without me. That's I suppose, what's so . . . . . . hurtful. Now.

RHODA. He was a fucking bastard.

JENNY. I miss him. I miss him. I miss him. I do. It's just. Oh, God, why does it have to be like this? I'm sorry. Do you mind? Do you mind if I . . . can I tell you something . . . you know . . . just about the way . . . you know . . . the way he could be.

RHODA. Oh, Jennifer. If only you would. This is what we should do. We're sisters. We should be able to talk to one another. To listen. Please. Come on.

JENNY. Well . . . that night . . . after Eugene had locked the two of us in the front bedroom. . . . . . (*She can't go on.*)

RHODA. He didn't . . . . . . do anything unpleasant, did he?

JENNY. Well, what would you expect? You could see what was in his mind. And then, what with you entertaining a murdering terrorist at your husband's funeral, didn't really help.

RHODA. Oh, yes, Jennifer. I see. I'm sorry.

JENNY. If your partner can't touch you at a time like that, when you really need to be touched. And there's dangers every-where. Then how could you imagine that there could be the slightest shred of love left between you? That's what I saw.

RHODA. He didn't touch you?

JENNY. No. No. It was me. Don't you see? It was me couldn't touch him. When he came close to me. I could smell him. And, God forgive me, but I just, nearly, wanted to puke. It wasn't at all pleasant, Rhoda. You know. The way he undressed me. Stitch by stitch. Throwing everything on the floor. He seemed as if he were moving in slow motion. Passionless. I thought. At first. I was so rigid. Well. I couldn't move. Then after a while I could see that he was full of passion alright. Oh, yes, he was full of it alright. Full of hatred. For me. Hatred. Hold me, Rhoda. (*They embrace.*)

RHODA. There, there. Poor Jenny. I'm so glad. I'm so glad. I'm so glad you told me. We must talk. We have to. Don't we? It's good. Oh, yes. And I have so much . . . . . to tell you. (*Laughs.*) So much to say (*Laughs*), Jennifer.

JENNY. Yes.

RHODA. Where am I going, Jenny?

JENNY. Well, at least you didn't go back to America with that lunatic.

RHODA. What? For Jesus' sake, Jenny, he didn't go back to America.

JENNY. Of course he did.

RHODA. He didn't.

JENNY. He let you down. And I want to hear absolutely nothing more about him.

RHODA. I'm not mad, you know. I'm not raving. I know what happened. I can't tell everyone. But you are the one who should listen. And you won't.

JENNY. I won't. If you persist in talking like you were away with the fairies.

RHODA. You're a bloody fool, Jennifer. You always were.

JENNY. That's not a very nice thing to say.

RHODA. You didn't see what went on here between me and Hubert. Years of it. Eugene was my passport.

JENNY. Look, you're my sister. I love you. We just want you to get well again. Don't destroy yourself.

RHODA. Nor have you the remotest idea what it was like to live with Hubert all those years. From the very beginning. He never trusted me. And all I could do was retaliate any clever little way I could, because there was no getting out. If I had left him and gone back to Dublin, yous would have all laughed and said I told you so. I had nothing with that man for twenty years but a cold war, Jennifer. And you. You . . . never . . . even . . . bothered . . . to find out. (*Upset.*)

JENNY. Of all the things you have ever said to me, that is the most outrageous. I know you're not well. I know you're on tablets. You need a rest. You need the hospital. Bla, bla, bla. But I'll tell you this. Hubert is nearly two months in his grave . . .

RHODA. He's not in his grave.

JENNY. Well, he's in some fucking grave, up the mountain, or out in the fields, or wherever he is, what do I care? But I don't want to hear his name again. Because I am not the one to blame for your predicament. And all I can say is I don't want to hear his name again. Good. (*Exit.*)

RHODA. I had nothing, Jenny. (*Shouting.*) From the beginning. Nothing. Just a fish. Slithering in and out. Coming and going from his meetings. Always creeping up from behind, when you least expected him. (*Hugh enters behind Rhoda and startles her.*)

HUGH. Well, what's wrong with you?

RHODA. Oh, Hubert, it's you. I'm just off to bed.

HUGH. Take your time. There's no one with me.

RHODA. There's letters there for you.

HUGH. (*A glance for letters.*) Did your sister arrive?

RHODA. She's gone to bed. She was tired. After the travelling. We thought you might have been in earlier.

HUGH. There was a meeting in the hall. The civil rights crowd are marching again. A Saturday. I had to go to the pub afterwards. There was people up from Dublin.

RHODA. That Mona Gillespie one is gone to the hospital again.

HUGH. Yeah?

RHODA. She was seeing ghosts.

HUGH. To the mental?

RHODA. Aye. Her brother drove her to Omagh.

HUGH. All the women round here seem to be going strange.

RHODA. I was very fond of Mona. She was company.

HUGH. You're depressed again.

RHODA. I'm worried, Hughie.

HUGH. Look, that woman is in and out of the mental like a yoyo.

RHODA. It's not that.

HUGH. Rhoda.

RHODA. It's not Mona Gillespie. It's other things.

HUGH. Rhoda, I've told you before. I swear. I'm not in anything illegal. Besides. There's nothing to be in. All that guff about the IRA being started up again, it's all shit. That's the past.

RHODA. I think I'll sleep in Jennifer's room tonight.

HUGH. She's a bit long in the tooth to be sleeping with her sister.

RHODA. She's very tired. And anyway. You know how nervous she gets coming across the border. I don't want her wakening. In the night.

HUGH. Jesus. Sleeping with her is hardly gonna stop her wakening.

RHODA. I'll be there if she needs me.

HUGH. Oh, you will? Yeah. Have it your own way, then. It hardly affects me. So how is the Gillespie woman, anyway?

RHODA. I told you. She's seeing ghosts. A crucifix fell off the wall in the kitchen. (*Hugh exits.*) She claims she saw a gloved hand lift it off and throw it at her. The Maguires noticed she wasn't at first mass on Sunday, and when they went round, she was hiding in the coal shed. (*She is frightened, and when she looks around, finds herself alone.*)

JENNY. (*Entering with dressing gown.*) I found this upstairs. You might as well take it. You need to keep up appearances. And it's lovely. I never saw this before, Rhoda. Where did you get it?

RHODA. Why won't you listen to me?

JENNY. Maybe we should pack a few towels as well.

RHODA. You were able to shake off Joseph. Weren't you? Simple as that. Just shake him off. I have my rights, too, you know.

JENNY. I'll go up and get you towels in the hotpress. (*Hugh and Gene enter. Gene is afraid of Hugh. She notices them.*)

RHODA. Oh, Jesus. Oh, Jesus.

JENNY. What is it, Rhoda?

RHODA. Nothing. It's just funny I suppose. Just you and me in the house. It's so empty.

JENNY. Well, Enda said he would drive you to the hospital. But I don't see any sign of him. But you're not alone, pet. I'm here. Oh, Rhoda, I've upset you again.

RHODA. Just the two of us.

JENNY. Rhoda, I'm sorry if I lost my temper. Now, don't be upset. Come along. You can help me get towels from the hotpress. Come on. That's the girl.

RHODA. Just the two of us. Now. That's right. There's just the two of us now. (*They exit.*)

HUGH. Stand there. Straight. (*Gene stands to attention.*) You were so sure of yourself. Weren't you? So high and mighty. Once you had that thing in your hand again.

GENE. Begging your pardon, Mr Murray, but . . . I was only doing what was best.

HUGH. Shut up. (*Pause. Hugh paces. Circles him.*) All cock sure of yourself. Yes, I can see you now alright. I can see you with your long hair, and your unmarried mothers, and what sort of an Ireland you'd make. You look more like a film star. (*Laughing.*) You were a buck lepper, not a soldier. And you didn't see the distinction. That was your problem. You thought the gun in your hand was a sexual organ. You would have been safer if you stayed in New York, on a picket line, with homosexuals, for some exotic human rights issue. But not here, me boy.

GENE. Mr Murray, with all due respect, you were always a bit narrow-minded, if you don't mind me saying so.

HUGH. Cast you mind back again. To that night. When my coffin had been opened, and the remains disposed of. You were here.

GENE. Correct. We had put everyone to bed with a dose of tranquilizers. The only ones left up were me and Rhoda. Then she went to bed. I stayed here. On duty, so to speak.

HUGH. Go on. Try to remember.

GENE. Well, let me see. She came back down. Rhoda. (*Rhoda enters.*)

GENE. Shhhhhh. They're all asleep?

RHODA. Yeah. (*They stare at each other.*)

HUGH. You think we're no good don't you? Think we're just cantankerous little peasants. Think you can come back here with your smart-aleck ways from America. You're just like the crowd in Dublin. Too much sex and discotecs, and too little backbone. By Jesus you surely danced on my coffin alright, till you realized I wasn't in it, ye little scumbag.

GENE. I can't dance. Look. (*Shuffles.*) Could never dance.

RHODA. Gene, stop it.

GENE. Can I dance?

RHODA. No, you can't dance. Have you been drinking?

GENE. And you love me. You need me. You'll come to America with me.

RHODA. Gene, I'd go anywhere with you.

GENE. Let's do it.

RHODA. Do what?

GENE. Do it. Make love.

RHODA. Where.

GENE. Here. Here and now.

RHODA. Gene, Gene. Easy on. Don't get so sweaty. For God's sake. You're supposed to be on duty, remember?

GENE. So what's the problem?

RHODA. Come on, Gene, sorry . . . . . I don't feel like it.

HUGH. (*Amused.*) You've a lot to learn about that too, boy.

GENE. I mean, what dye mean, I mean, like, you don't feel like it; that's it?

RHODA. Of course that's it. I'll go back up and lie down for another while.

GENE. Wait a minute. Wait a minute. So we don't do anything. Right? Because you suddenly don't feel like it?

HUGH. Women are not televisions, boy; you don't turn them on and off when you feel like it.

GENE. Rhoda; you do want to do this; I mean, we are going ahead with it, aren't we.

RHODA. Yes, of course. You're the man in my life. You're my freedom fighter. My liberator. My tootsie wootsie in American tee shirts. Okay? Now, good night. (*Kiss. She exits.*)

HUGH. Now, sir. Explain to me. What exactly you thought you might get away with.

GENE. Explain?

HUGH. Yes. Explain.

GENE. To you?

HUGH. Explain. Right now. To me.

GENE. Well. Jesus. I thought. You know. All this politics . . . . . . you know? . . . . . . it's not freedom.

HUGH. I see. Go on.

GENE. All this religion. You know? It's not freedom.

HUGH. Go on.

GENE. As long as one small corner of the heart is unfree, then nothing is free.

HUGH. And what precise freedom were you talking about?

GENE. Ah, ye know. Liberation. That sort of thing.

HUGH. Sexual?

GENE. No, Jesus, don't reduce it all to fucking sex, man. Liberation. Spiritual. Human. Call it what you want. Sexual. Sexual, yeah. That, too.

HUGH. This is something you learned in America?

GENE. You see I saw this play in Manhattan one night. In the Irish Arts Centre. There were these two lovers in it, and he says to her, 'We are the new Republicans. We should declare an independent republic of love. Between us. A republic of tenderness, affection, love, and openness'. Then she threw her arms around him, and he ravished her.

HUGH. Openness, indeed. You weren't so successful a few moments ago, before she went to bed, were you?

GENE. I need no lectures about women from you. She's exactly the one who needed some freedom, from the likes of Volunteer Hubert Murray, and the likes of Monsignor Boyle, with his designer morality.

HUGH. And you were the self-appointed liberator of my Rhoda. Is that it?

GENE. Why shouldn't we have what we want? We were gonna get on a plane to New York, and just live, be, for a change.

HUGH. And it was all based on the premise, the presumption that I was in that coffin.

GENE. Well shit, how the fuck was I to know?

HUGH. Because you should never presume anyone is dead around here unless you've checked their teeth fillings and seen the flesh on the bum putrefy.

GENE. You never cared a shit for Rhoda. I just wanted to be with her, to make her laugh, to take her to New York.

HUGH. And not a cloud in the sky I suppose. Except the one the orchestra was playing on. (*He sits. Pause.*) You're a bad breed, Eugene. Let me assure you that your death wasn't the slightest loss to humanity. (*Pause.*)

GENE. So what death is?

HUGH. Rhoda's perhaps.

GENE. You're joking.

HUGH. Brady, listen to me. We are going where the dead must go. We hover for a while. But eventually we are enveloped by darkness.

GENE. What happened to Rhoda?

HUGH. What happened to you? See? Your dollar.

GENE. I thought you said you were in hell.

HUGH. And I wasn't lying. The dollar, Eugene. You may have it back.

GENE. I remember now. I got into the car with Enda. It was dark. Middle of the night. Me hands were tied behind me back, and Enda had me by the hair, and he was dragging me from the car. He was dragging me into the forest, and I thought, Jesus, Jesus, I thought, he's gonna shoot me, the Lord is my shepherd, there is nothing I shall want, I thought, Jesus, he's gonna do it, Enda. Like he's done before, and then go home and demolish a bottle of whiskey, there was only me and him, this is more intimate than sex I thought. I'm with this man and he is going to blow me brains out, 'Our help is in the name of the Lord', I said, out loud, 'Shut up', says he. 'A, Jesus, Enda. Don't', says I. Pulling me hair. 'For the Lord shall be with us in the day of tribulation', I says. 'Fuck up', says he, 'ye mad bastard'. 'Can I not pray?' I said. Oh, Jesus, he won't even let me pray. And then I thought of that single dollar note, I brought it with me from New York. It was me good luck charm. I changed everything for sterling at the airport, but I kept this dollar, lucky charm, it meant I would be going back again. It was my promise to Manhattan. Me hands were tied. Enda was emptying me pockets. I was crying. I kept praying he wouldn't find the dollar note. And then I seen him hold it. And laughing. And he was saying, 'You won't be needing this anymore'. And then

HUGH. And then . . . . . and then.

GENE. And then I seen you. (*Kneels.*) And I says, 'Ah, Jesus, Mr Murray, don't shoot me. No. You wouldn't shoot poor Eugene would you? I'm sorry. I'm sorry. I'm so sorry'. And I kept thinking about me lucky charm. Me dollar. I wanted to hold it. If I could just have that I wouldn't mind. A Jesus Mr Murray.

HUGH. (*Hugging and embracing him.*) Shhhhhhhh . . . . . . shhhhhhhhh, here, here, stop, shhhh, here. It's okay. It's alright. It's alright.

GENE. (*After some time begins to break away. Withdraws.*) No. No. I hated you. I always hated you. Rhoda. Rhoda. (*He runs off. Hugh paces for a while. Looks at watch. Makes phone call.*)

HUGH. Hello.

PHONE. 673.

HUGH. It's me.

PHONE. Right.

HUGH. We can go on with the funeral. The priest knows no difference. (*Knock on door.*) I'll talk to you later. (*Hangs up. Enda enters.*)

ENDA. Dirty business, Mr Murray. I can tell ye I didn't like doing that to Eugene.

HUGH. You got rid of our mysterious bomb victim? The unknown soldier?

ENDA. Aye. We did like you said. Jesus, I never knew you could do that with a corpse.

HUGH. And Eugene?

ENDA. All sealed up in the coffin.

HUGH. Good.

ENDA. I'm bollixed. With all that lifting and digging, and . . . Jesus, I never knew you could get rid of a body like that.

HUGH. You'll learn. You're all done then?

ENDA. All done. 'Cept for to kill a bottle of whiskey when I get home.

HUGH. Good.

ENDA. We put him in the coffin, right? No one knows different. We'll have to find another way for shifting the weapons.

HUGH. You will.

ENDA. Mind you, washing machines aren't that difficult to get across the border.

HUGH. That's good. Pheilim was here earlier. He brought the Culletons to the mass. Took them out the front door. They'll not be any the wiser. Better like that.

ENDA. (*Handing over papers.*) There's the stuff. I.D. Tickets. Cash. Good luck. (*Shaking hands.*) I've always admired you, Mr Murray. (*Rhoda's voice off.*)

HUGH. You're a good lad, Enda. Look after your daddy. (*They shake hands and Enda leaves.*)

RHODA. (*Off.*) Gene, Gene. Eugene. Joseph. Jennifer. (*She enters.*) Hubert. Christ. Hubert. You're alive. Thank God.

HUGH. Don't pretend, Rhoda. It makes you look ridiculous.

RHODA. But you're alive. What happened?

HUGH. Someone tried to kill me. It didn't work.

RHODA. But the explosion. The body.

HUGH. I was heading down the meadow, when I noticed someone up ahead. Just over the septic tank cover. Where we usually hide things. I decided to bide me time. Then puff. It went up with a bang. I was a good five hundred yards away at the time.

RHODA. Oh, Jesus.

HUGH. We genuinely don't know who it was. It must have gone up in his face. When he was priming it.

RHODA. You didn't come back to the house. Why?

HUGH. I went over to Enda. It seemed a good moment to disappear. I can operate more effectively for a while if they think I'm six feet under. All I needed was Pheilim to go in and identify the body as mine.

RHODA. But why didn't you tell me? Why didn't somebody tell me?

HUGH. Things seem to happen very fast.

RHODA. But all last night, this funeral thing, it's been a nightmare.

HUGH. Speaking of which, you'll be late.

RHODA. I beg your pardon?

HUGH. It's a quarter to ten. You'll be late for the funeral. The rest have gone on ahead. Enda is outside. He'll drive you.

RHODA. Where's Eugene?

HUGH. I'm sorry things seem to have worked out so badly between us. I suppose a lot of the fault over the years must have been mine.

RHODA. Hubert. I'm your wife. This is terrible. But . . . you're alive. And I'm your wife. I love . . .

HUGH. Dont lie to me, woman.

RHODA. I don't understand. I'm Rhoda, amn't I? You're alive. It's a miracle.

HUGH. I was here all night, Rhoda. In the house. (*Pointing.*) In there.

RHODA. Where's Eugene?

HUGH. You're late as it is.

RHODA. Yes. I'm going.

HUGH. I'll always be around, Rhoda. You may not see much of me for a couple of months. Just a bit of a shadow. But I'll be in and out. So mind yourself. I'll always be watching.

RHODA. Why didn't you tell me, why didn't someone tell me, Jesus Christ, what have you done with Eugene?

HUGH. The funeral Rhoda. You can't be late.

RHODA. No. No, no.

HUGH. You can whine all you like at the graveside; for your tootsie wootsie in American tee shirts. (*He exits.*)

RHODA. (*Deeply anguished.*) No, no, no.

GENE. This grief of ours was not made any lighter by the memory of how we had parted the previous night. A lovers' quarrel which fate had determined would be our last words together. When everyone had been . . . put to bed. When she rejected my approaches in the kitchen, I followed up to her bedroom. (*He turns toward her. She notices him, slightly startled.*)

GENE. What's wrong?

RHODA. Nothing.

GENE. You're shivering.

RHODA. I'm cold.

GENE. You're cold.

RHODA. Just leave me alone. Please.

GENE. Why?

RHODA. Why? Why? Just do. That's all.

GENE. I don't like this, Rhoda. You're giving me the shivers.

RHODA. Don't be so suspicious.

GENE. I'm not suspicious. I just want to hold you.

RHODA. Hold me then. Later.

GENE. For Jesus' sake, what's up?

RHODA. You'll wake the others.

GENE. I don't give a fuck if I wake the others. I've a gun. Anyhow. They're all drugged.

RHODA. Well, that's just marvellous.

GENE. What is?

RHODA. You have a gun. Great. That's just great. Get out of your box, yes?

GENE. I thought we had an agreement. I thought you loved me.

RHODA. Jesus, Gene, an agreement and love are not the same thing.

GENE. You said you loved me.

RHODA. Don't push it too far.

GENE. You said it.

RHODA. What the fuck do you want? Written assurances? That you're loved?

GENE. Well, do you or don't you?

RHODA. Don't push it, Gene.

GENE. Do you?

RHODA. Black or white. That's you, isn't it? Black or white.

GENE. What the fuck is that supposed to mean?

RHODA. You're too black and white all the time for me.

GENE. Oh, is that a fact? Is that a fact? Fine. And you're still a bit green yourself by the looks of things.

RHODA. Fuck off.

GENE. I will. Don't worry.

RHODA. What do you mean by the looks of things?

GENE. Well why did you have to rise the fuss over the funeral? Insisting on tricolours and all that shit.

RHODA. The tricolour is not shit.

GENE. We wouldn't have all this baby sitting to do if you had kept your mouth shut.

RHODA. I'm not going over it again. Okay?

GENE. You still actually support the fuckers. Don't you?

RHODA. And you still hate them. You dropped me and feiced off to New York the last time. Then you come mooning back, swaning around like some, some god, some saviour; as if you were going to rescue me from the ignorant little Catholic Republican gutter.

GENE. That's not how I see it at all. How can you say that?

RHODA. Well, if we don't understand each other, then I hardly think screwing is appropriate.

GENE. I'm not looking for a screw, you bitch.

RHODA. You hate me. Go on. Admit it. You hate me. You just dress it up as salvation. I'm some little . . . some pathetic little woman whining away in the middle of the night and you're gonna save me. Well, let me tell you here and now. I'll go through this with you. I'll take the money and the airplane ticket. But the minute we set foot in New York, it's good-bye Rhoda. Because I don't love you. You were never one of us. Mister high and mighty.

Mister superiority. Saviour of the world. I'll find someone else, thank you very much. Now, why don't you go back down to the kitchen and try to stay awake for a few hours. I'll be having a long day tomorrow acting in the chapel. (*Gene walks downstage.*)

GENE. (*To audience.*) And there it ends. On a sunny spring morning. She went to the funeral. And the congregation were very moved by the depth of love she had for her husband. Her hero. It was quite apparent from her uncontrolled anguish at the graveside. They were not to know of her tootsie wootsie from the USA. (*She attends the grave and is assisted by Pheilim, Enda, Jenny, and Joe.*)

RHODA. Eugene. Eugene. I'm sorry. Eugene. I'm sorry. (*He turns on her.*)

GENE. Of course, all those heroes don't really exist, do they? They're just fantasies. Just a myth. Just something out of history books.

RHODA. Stop it.

GENE. And yet the heroes always seem to win. That's the point. And people like you and me. We lose. You see we live in the midst of death as scripture says.

RHODA. Stop it.

GENE. Sorry, but it's true about those heroes; eroticism for them is to take the chaos and fashion a little violence out of it. It's called history.

RHODA. I am Hubert Murray's widow.

GENE. History, Rhoda. Things happen. Things proceed. Ha, ha. And only we die. The mythmakers never die. They just get into the history books, eventually.

RHODA. Leave me alone.

GENE. Oh, I'll leave you alone, Rhoda. You know, I still had a lifetime to spend with you. But I will, I will, I'll leave you alright. We didn't have enough magic between us, did we, enough myth, to survive? Look at me. Look down into the grave, Rhoda. I don't even get my name on the tombstone.

RHODA. I am Hubert Murray's widow.

GENE. Look at me. A real little speck of confused history. That's me. Pity we never made it together. Yeah. A real tragedy that.

RHODA. For the last time, I said leave me alone.

GENE. I can leave you alone. I can. But they won't. No.

They'll never leave you alone now. See where you've ended up? You're haunted by them. Haunted by something far worse than ghosts. Something much more terrible than the dead. You're haunted by the living. That's it. By everything. They have got you all wrapped up and fucked up in some other man's myth.

RHODA. I am Hubert Murray's widow.

GENE. It's checkmate. Under the watchful gaze of your menfolk. Your family. Your neighbours. Your friends. Your community. Your God forsaken little arse hole of a nation. They got you. They got you. As sure as they got me. (*The funeral party begins to leave. To audience.*) And that was the truth. The weeks passed. Pheilim and Enda kept a watchful eye, and true to his word, Hubert made fleeting appearances at the gable of the house, in the sheds out the back, sometimes even venturing into the kitchen. When he wasn't otherwise occupied up and down the countryside blowing up policemen. (*Exits.*)

RHODA. Well, what do you want, Eugene? Are you saying it's a pity that I didn't love you? And I did. That is, I would have. I would have loved you. And I would have skipped off to America with you. Oh, yes. Brooklyn Bridge. Manhattan. Disneyland maybe. Would have been better than this place. Even that cat was smart enough to leave this place. (*Rhoda laughs. Jenny enters.*)

JENNY. They're here. Enda and Pheilim. Are you not ready? Oh, Rhoda.

RHODA. Jennifer, there were no guns in that coffin. And there was no Hubert in it either. I was tricked, Jennifer. I was tricked. Now, can you not put two and two together for yourself? Or do I have to spell it out for you in black and white?

JENNY. Jesus, give me patience with you.

RHODA. (*Whispers.*) It was Eugene they buried. Not Hubert.

JENNY. Oh, God, not again, Rhoda, will you not be so silly.

RHODA. Silly? Silly is it? (*Staggered.*)

PHEILIM. (*Entering.*) What's up. Ahhhhhh, is she alright?

ENDA. Car is ready. We'll drive you over to our place.

RHODA. No. No thanks. I'm going to Omagh.

JENNY. You don't have to go to the hospital, Rhoda.

RHODA. Of course I do. I'm mad.

PHEILIM. Come on, Mrs Murray, whatever you want. Upsee daisy.

ENDA. Are yis right now? Time's getting on a bit. (*She gets up. Laughs.*)

RHODA. Where's Father Boyle?

PHEILIM. He had a funeral.

ENDA. Are yis right?

RHODA. A funeral. (*Laughs.*) A funeral. (*Laughs.*)
 Of all the men I've ever known
 I've never known a one so sad
 as he who sucks his chicken bones
(*Spoken.*) . . . Leave me alone. (*And returns to song.*)
 As he who sucks his chicken bones
 and chains his dogs till they go mad.
(*She whines the last line, laughs, and then stops abruptly.*) I'll be fine now, thank you. Poor Rhoda is sick. Must go away and get better. Let me know if Eugene sends any postcards from New York. Won't you Pheilim?

PHEILIM. I will surely, Mrs Murray.

JENNY. Come on, I'll help you to the car. (*Almost gone.*)

RHODA. Oh, and Enda, if you're hungry; Hubert . . . . that is . . . my late husband . . . you'll find in the freezer. (*Laughs. She exits helped by Jenny. Enda and Pheilim stare at each other.*)

ENDA. It's a pity about her.

PHEILIM. Aye. It is.

ENDA. I mean, there's no sense to anything she says.

PHEILIM. Oh, not a bit. (*Pause.*) Go on, don't keep them waiting. I'll lock up here.

ENDA. (*Going.*) I'll just drive her over to our place, for the minute. She does have a freezer.

PHEILIM. Aye, she does. Out the back there.

ENDA. Ye better have a look. Just in case. (*Exits.*)

PHEILIM. Aye. Aye. Sure thing. No, she wouldn't . . . she couldn't. (*Pause.*) The fucking rat poison. (*Gene enters. He does not see him nor hear him.*)

GENE. You better have a look. Just in case.

PHEILIM. I better have a look. Just in case. No, no. No. She wouldn't.

GENE. She might.

PHEILIM. But there's been no trace of Hubert for the past fortnight.

GENE. Exactly.

PHEILIM. Ah, no. No. I mean, why? Why, why, why, would she do a thing like that? I better just check. Jesus Christ, but you can never be sure of anything. (*Gene watches as Pheilim exits. He is in profile. Behind him Hugh returns. Stands close.*)

GENE. Mr Murray.

HUGH. yes.

GENE. D'ye think anyone will ever remember us?

HUGH. I doubt it. (*Fade.*)

END OF PLAY

Tom Mac Intyre.

Sheep's Milk on the Boil

TOM MAC INTYRE

1994

Deirdre Molloy   Michael Collins
Pat Kinevane   Miriam Delahunt
Owen Roe   Bongi McDermott
Joan Sheehy   Tommy Hayes
Olwen Fouere   Sean Keane
Kathryn O'Boyle   Liz Keller
Jasmine Russell
Director: Tom Hickey

Characters

BIDDY
MATT
THE VISITOR
MAGGIE FRIDAY
THE INSPECTOR OF WRACK
TWO BOOKKEEPERS
LOCAL GHOSTS:
    AMELIA LUNDQUIST
    THE BLACKSMITH
    MISS URSULA
THREE MUSICIANS, a SINGER among them: position on stage or
    adjacent, as suits.

Scene

*Primitive abode. Fireplace, stage right. Door, stage left. Table, chairs,
midstage. Downstage left, exterior, a log, wedges in it, mallet handy.
The exterior, in broad terms, will gradually impinge. The vicinity is
rocky, with seaglimpses.*

ACT I

Scene 1

*Biddy in the kitchen, restive. Goes outside, looks for signs of traffic. Has
a got at the log, checks again. He's coming. Flies to the kitchen, makes
preparations, milk, bread, so on. Matt arrives, in high fettle. Nod for
her. He sits, eats, drinks.*

72

BIDDY. Well?

MATT. Well what?

BIDDY. How was it?

MATT. Like anywhere else.

BIDDY. Like anywhere else?

MATT. That's it now.

BIDDY. Was it worth your while going to see it then?

MATT. To be sure it was.

BIDDY. You went to the mainland and saw nothing?

MATT. Didn't say that.

BIDDY. Ye did see something?

MATT. I was in a shop.

BIDDY. A shop?

MATT. Ye never saw the like.

BIDDY. A bazaar, yer tellin' me?

MATT. Ye'd want to bring home the whole place. (*Matt rises, roots in a bag, takes out another bag, hands it to her, air of 'here's your present'. She opens the bag, takes out a small parcel, unwraps it. A clock, old style. She looks at it, shakes it, fiddles with it, alarm goes off, she drops it, alarm stops. Hiatus. Matt Rises, picks up the clock, tries it for signs of life. No go.*)

MATT. There y'are now . . . (*He dumps the clock on the table.*) Wonderful the works of a wheelbarra.

BIDDY. (*Ruffled.*) Shure that's grand then. (*Exit Biddy with bucket.*

MATT. To life. (*Takes out a purse, to audience.*)

MATT. There was everything you'd wish for in that place. I only wanted the one thing. The man told me what they call it. . . . What did he say? It's called a . . . it'll come again. . . . I looked, I said, 'All the treasure's not under the ground'. It was goin' for half nothing'. I bought it. And now it's mine. And mine only. (*Looks into the purse, gurgles delight, resumes.*) It was a meetin' like no other ever happened. You see more with the glimpse, it's true what they say. I wasn't lookin' when I saw it, not the colour of me. Then it happened. I walked out of the shabby hour and into a wide secret with a bay beyond. (*Biddy arrives back. Matt transforms to innocent. Sits, well-behaved. Biddy sets down the bucket, studies him.*)

BIDDY. Did you take drink on yer travels?

MATT. And have the crack
With Paddy Mack
The hackler from Grousehall . . .

BIDDY. (*To audience.*) So he goes. And comes back . . . with a lie on his smig a qualified amadhán could put a tune to. Alright, me boyo, Ill finaygle yer foosther from under yer oxter.

MATT. Divil the drink.

BIDDY. No man gets drunk on saltwater.

MATT. I'm not drunk.

BIDDY. If yer not drunk, what are ye?

MATT. Sober. (*She sniffs him. Takes up his cap, 'searches' it. Matt plays with a crust, smile just under his face.*

BIDDY. So ye went?

MATT. And came back.

BIDDY. And brought home a clock.

MATT. Brought home that article.

BIDDY. And that's yer story?

MATT. It's not a story.

BIDDY. If it's not a story, why're ye drunk?

MATT. I'm not drunk. I'm graveyard-spade sober.

BIDDY. Alright. If that's yer story, good luck to ye. (*Matt now free to rise, exits, singing to himself.*)

Scene 2

Matt to stage left, exterior. Glee coming off him.

MATT. I had a grandfather used to say all the time, 'Know what I have in here?' (*Right hand darting to breast-pocket area, it becomes a tic.*) 'Know what I have in here? A bone for me dog, a bone for me dog, a bone for me dog'. And he would too, go nowhere unless he had, even if it was only an ould bit of a thing fried on the rock. 'A bone for me dog, a bone for me dog'. That's what left him contented. A delicate man all his life . . . and yet verra healthy, verra healthy. (*Now, hand to pocket. Crisis. Can't find the purse. Mad search, eventually finds it.*) Aren't ye the little divil? (*Settles, opens the purse, takes out looking glass, polishes it, studies himself happily in it.*) I'd hardly know ye . . . but I *do* know ye . . . I *will* know ye . . . we'll know each other comin' or goin', sleep or wakin', over the work or busy idlin'. I'll learn all your bountiful tricks . . . till, no time, you'll *squeal* when ye find me comin' . . . won't ye, won't ye? O me sweet, and o me swanky! (*Starts playing games with the looking glass. Places it on the log, downstage left, covers it with cap, retreats, returns stealthily, whips off the cap, stares. He's still there. Jubilate! Now, the looking glass directly behind his head, he counts five beats, whips the looking glass to viewing position, quizzes, gesturally, the looking glass happily. Next, closes one eye, holds the looking glass at a distance, brings it closer and closer to the open eye until the two are intimately close. Goes still, shakes free.*) Like steppin' outa the March shadda and being blinded by the glare. (*Effortlessly, he finds another routine.*) Now will you listen to something? (*He places the looking glass under his shirt so's it can listen to his heartbeat. . . . Takes it out.*) That was no cuckoo ye heard, nor no corncrake neither. That was the whip of the blood ye commenced from a corner of that shop the day . . . *your* tune, your reel and roam lickin's my veins and windin' my chalk bones. . . . We're like the pair o' dancers just brought toe to toe. The best dancer's the one dances with the eyes. . . . That was in you from the first, wasn't it? (*He now has, downstage right, the looking glass propped at eye level and decorated with bits of rag—a shrine of sorts. He moves back, and whirls into a primitive dance of worship/celebration. Stops. Collects looking glass, kisses it, back to purse, hides purse in that area, scatters the shrine, gets out of there.*)

Scene 3

Kitchen alive again. Biddy checking his overcoat, that sack. No good. Takes up a poker, goes for a couple of mice playing on the hearth.)

BIDDY. Bad cess to the little bastards. . . . (*More hammering.*) Comin' in here lookin' for their soda bread . . . (*Matt, meanwhile, is downstage left, walloping the wedge. The walloping within tangles with the walloping without. Biddy catches this, tests it, elicits a 'divilment' counterpoint from Matt at the log. Biddy out to confront him.*) Where were you?

MATT. Up the fields.

BIDDY. Doin' what?

MATT. Gatherin' stones.

BIDDY. Were you now?

MATT. The big and the small.

BIDDY. What for?

MATT. For luck.

BIDDY. Did they bring ye luck?

MATT. Lashin's. (*Biddy, inside, gets holy-water bottle, blesses her-self, now outside, splashes him with the remaining water.*)

MATT. What was that for?

BIDDY. For more luck. (*Biddy, back inside, Matt follows.*) I know what yer at.

MATT. What am I at?

BIDDY. And what has ye the way y'are.

MATT. What way's that?

BIDDY. The grin stuck to yer puss.

MATT. Droves'd be glad of a grin.

BIDDY. D'ye think I'm slow?

MATT. I think yer woeful quick at times.

BIDDY. Take off that coat. (*Matt obeys, gives her the coat, goes, jocose, 'after the mice' while she checks the garment.*)

MATT. Now are ye happy?

BIDDY. No.

MATT. Well, there's few happy.

BIDDY. The boots and the britches. . . . (*He'll go with that, but not without speechifying.*)

MATT. I met me bucko from over the hill. 'Burn you', says he, 'they'll have wise ashes'. 'Right', says I, 'I don't belong to the troop with the square heads'. 'We've enough of those', says he. 'Too many', says I, 'and more comin'. 'Ye had a great day on the mainland', says he. 'Any day ye get home safe is a great day', I told him.

BIDDY. But ye didn't get home safe. (*She returns the boots.*)

MATT. Then he started on about the mother that has to pull on her socks with the tongs . . . or the craythur'd get trapped in a hoop.

BIDDY. (*Examining the britches.*) You're the one trapped in a hoop.

MATT. What hoop'd that be?

BIDDY. The hoop in the gut leaves lots in a hobble and more in convulsions. (*She returns the britches.*)

MATT. (*Cooly provocative, boots on knees.*) Aren't boots strange objects too? Did y'ever look at a boot of a mornin'—an ordinary boot with its tongue hangin' out—look too long and ye'll see the tongue move, sway a bit. . . . Look the piece longer, Christ, it's talkin' to ye in its own peculiar language.

BIDDY. You had an uncle—Hughie the Boot, didn't ye? So called because he was ignorant as a kish o' brogues. Where'd ye lave it, I'd like to know?

MATT. 'Lave it'?

BIDDY. Ye had it with ye goin' out that door. . . . I could tell by the slope o' ye. It's not on ye now. Hide it in the fields, did ye? Along the stream? Up a tree?

MATT. (*Play-acting.*) No (*pointing*) I hid it in that pot there. Hold on a minute, hould yer hoult till we see here. (*Making a meal of it, he plunges his hand into the pot and comes up with a potato.*) Begod! The lone Aran Banner . . . but aren't they champion . . . and their blossoms sailin' in the breeze!

BIDDY. I know what came over ye on the mainland.

MATT. Someone threw salt on me tail.

BIDDY. I know what happened.

MATT. God bless yer wit.

BIDDY. And what ye came home with.

MATT. I came home with Ould Maggie Doyle and her sister and a child from the bog.

BIDDY. Give it to me now, and there's no harm done. We'll peg it in the fire and forget about it.

MATT. 'Peg it in the fire'?

BIDDY. But if ye keep it from me, if ye want war, then war ye'll have.

MATT. War, begod, 'When Johnny comes marchin' home, hurrah'.

BIDDY. I know yer badger's grip, but ye won't best me. I'll find it if ye hid it in the clouds, I'll find it if ye bury it in the bog, I'll find it if ye parcel it in the wave. I'm tellin' ye now.

MATT. It? It? It? Out with yer eye-tee *it*? As well spit it as chew it . . .

BIDDY. The picture of yer trollop, yer Judy, yer fancy woman that has ye runnin' up an' down like a tinker's apprentice since the hour ye got back here. (*Exit Biddy. A wooden mug lands in the kitchen, from wherever, Matt, puzzled, looks up the chimney. A panel flips high in the back wall. The Bookkeepers' faces appear.*)

BOOKKEEPERS. 'When Johnny comes marchin' home, hurrah . . .' (*Panel flips shut. Matt, emerging from the fireplace, looks about, further puzzled. Gathers himself, however, tastes developments, elation takes him.*)

MATT. Yer trollop. . . . And yer Judy. . . . And yer fancy woman too. (*Smiles to himself.*) And a bone for me dog. . . . A bone for me dog. . . . A bone for me dog . . .

Scene 4

Biddy in the kitchen, adrift. The Visitor and Maggie arrive.

VISITOR. I met a child on the road that I never saw in these parts before. 'She's there', says he, 'and tired waitin'. Tell her', says he, 'don't darn your cobwebs'. He unvisibled while I looked. That height. (*Maggie gestures.*) Tow-haired. Independent eyes.

BIDDY. What'd the child say to ye?

MAGGIE. 'Don't darn your cobwebs'. (*Maggie boldly rearranges the chairs, the Visitor settles magisterially.*)

VISITOR. Tell me your story.

BIDDY. It's not a story.

VISITOR. What's it then? A roar, a shout, a whine, a whirr in the head?

MAGGIE. Or a whizz in the breast?

BIDDY. It's none o' those.

VISITOR. No?

BIDDY. It's the truth.

VISITOR. I never heard the truth yet.

BIDDY. Well, ye'll hear it now.

VISITOR. Wait a minute. . . . (*Visitor to fireplace, hand into chimney zone, emerges in a flash with wriggling fish.*) There's the truth (*bangs fish head against table edge, tosses the fish there.*) . . . have it for your dinner.

BIDDY. He came home drunk in himself.

VISITOR. So I believe.

BIDDY. And he's worse by the day.

VISITOR. From the look of him.

BIDDY. Ye saw him?

VISITOR. Driftin' in a field.

MAGGIE. Next minute leppin' out of his skin.

VISITOR. I thought, 'He's bringing the clouds close, take care he doesn't go off with them'.

BIDDY. It's a woman.

VISITOR. If it's not a woman, it's a man. You'd be afraid to step outside the door. (*Visitor and Maggie share wild laughter.*) If it's not a woman and it's not a man, it's a bit of a woman or a bit of a man. Locks of hair . . .

MAGGIE. Ribbons . . .

VISITOR. Letters . . .

MAGGIE. Pictures . . .

VISITOR. Geegaws . . .

MAGGIE. Ring-a-rosies . . .

VISITOR. I knew a man hanged himself with a shining lock of woman's hair, that length (*Maggie supplies the gesture*), butter blonde to catch the sun. Plaited human hair'll never break, you could anchor the fleet with it. Found a kickie wickie on his expedition?

BIDDY. Came home with her picture.

VISITOR. And that (*pointing*) clock . . .

MAGGIE. That won't work. (*The Visitor collects the clock, whispers to it, pets it. Alarm goes off. Pure health. The Visitor sets down the clock. Miss Ursula and the Blacksmith have arrived.*)

VISITOR. They're very like horses when all's said and done.

BIDDY. Who are ye? Who are ye? (*An imperious gesture from the Visitor dismisses the intruders.*)

VISITOR. We never land but a posse of local ghosts arrive to share the action. And can you blame them?

MAGGIE. It's a lonesome road.

VISITOR. You were saying?

BIDDY. No talkin' to him since he landed back.

VISITOR. Don't bother talking to him.

BIDDY. I'll take strips off him.

VISITOR. More likely he'll evaporate before you'll shine a blade. Men either evaporate or turn pudding. He's on the airy side. Find the picture.

MAGGIE. Burn it.

VISITOR. Scatter the remains.

BIDDY. I can't find it.

VISITOR. Plague him, follow him, search him night and day.

Possessed, he's on the slope, next thing he slips and he's lost. Deprive him of his pictured kickie wickie and he'll coast to level ground in anvil time.

MAGGIE. Get hold of it. Burn it.

VISITOR. And quick. Or you'll get caught on the slope with him. Easy to rescue one. Two a fret.

MAGGIE. Three the shambles.

VISITOR. I've counted the bones, returned them to terra sometimes firma. Burn that item, fair flame or foul.

MAGGIE. White ash, white ash!

VISITOR. And while I'm at it (*sudden sexual charge*), you're an amiable body, if ever I live to meet one, and you sail sweet in my regard—from the cradle I might rightly say. If that latchicoe doesn't come back to earth fast, let me know—for wider remedies. And if the clouds take him, good luck to him in the high-rise regions, and may his lovely poppy left behind among us breathe sonsy like many another widow warbling weeds and woebegones. (*The Visitor and Maggie sweep out. . . . In dim light, the cottage trembles. . . . Midsection of the back wall on the move. Biddy flees.*)

Scene 5

Midsection of the backwall gone to reveal landscape and the Inspector plus the Bookkeepers (twin figures, female, diminutive) arriving. The three advance into the kitchen zone, focussing rapidly on Matt, who has surfaced downstage left exterior, and is happily make-believing that he can't find the locking glass. Where's it hiding?

MATT. None of yer play-actin' with me now, none of yer jigantics. (*He finds it quickly—hidden in whatever crevice—playfully remonstrates.*)

MATT. Aren't ye the little divil. (*He moves to serious conversation with it, studying it intently the while.*) And how are ye doin' since I saw ye last? Did ye miss me at all? Well, I missed you . . . but I knew where ye were, and waitin'. . . . And here's something I've been wishin' to tell you—are ye listenin'? Right. . . . The man that waits for it'll always get fair wind and good tide. Wouldn't ye say that's gospel? Wouldn't ye say we're the livin' proof? Wouldn't ye now?

Jasmine Russell, Kathryn O'Boyle, Pat Kinevane, and Olwen Fouere in
Sheep's Milk on the Boil, by Tom Mac Intyre.
Courtesy Amelia Stein.

INSPECTOR. Yer no daw, are ye? And a fine speech too. . . .
(*Matt takes in the three, remains calm—just about.*)

MATT. Any business o' yours?

INSPECTOR. Yer right, what's more. The man that waits for
it'll always get fair wind and good tide. I've seen that proved ten
times over.

BOOKKEEPERS. At a cost . . .

INSPECTOR. To be sure. But proved, proved. Can I have this?
(*In advance of the question, she has already taken from Matt a strip of
rag {shrinal geegaw}, which she proceeds to tie about her upper thigh as*

decorative garter.) I collect bits and pieces. Your father—may he rest undisturbed—christened me the Inspector of Wrack.

BOOKKEEPERS. And him runnin' for his mammy . . .

INSPECTOR. And she dancin' on his thrapple . . .

BOOKKEEPERS. Perched thereon! (*The Bookkeepers whirl into wild laughter at the sally.*)

INSPECTOR. It's the one thing there's never any scarcity of—bits and pieces (*displaying the garter, Matt gawking*), so I'm always provided for. That's something in a hasky world. (*Inviting Matt to gawk his fill.*) Not many I'd show that amount to, I'll warrant ye, and processions walloping the door. (*On door, a tremendous walloping is heard.*)

MATT. Who's at that?

INSPECTOR. A few of me extended family—blackguardin' to pass the time—don't even your wit to them.

BOOKKEEPERS. Ye'll know them soon enough, Matt.

MATT. What's their game?

BOOKKEEPERS. No prisoners taken. (*Again the Bookkeepers erupt into peals of laughter. The Inspector cooly takes Matt's cap from his head, settles.*)

BOOKKEEPERS. Stay with yer find. Slide down into it. The lesson bought's worth twenty taught. You'll track more in it than just the dancy eyes. Everything comes out if it's asked out. Trouble is most wait for the sound of the carpenter over the deal planks.

BOOKKEEPERS. The timber suit! (*The Inspector now taking Matt by the hand, magically drawing him into the kitchen {direct route}. Biddy has returned and is sleeping in a chair, upstage left.*)

INSPECTOR. Too late askin' then. Lick it, lolly it, enquire it. It met you, you met it. Never be surprised by what it shows you. Great weather for pup seals.

MATT. What are ye tellin' me?

INSPECTOR. I'm tellin' ye, *listen* . . .

MATT. Listen to what . . . to you, is it?

INSPECTOR. *Whist* . . . (*We hear from the sound track {the Inspector and the Bookkeepers bow to the incursion} the potent din of a waterfall, music mingling with that. The din recedes. The Inspector and the Bookeepers exit through the back-wall gap. Matt rushes to that point.*)

MATT. Come back here with you . . . come back a minute.

. . . Come back, will you? . . . Come back, woman . . . (*The Inspector reappears from the door, stage left.*)

INSPECTOR. I love to be shouted back . . . and slowly whispered forward.

MATT. What in Christ's name are ye lookin' for?

INSPECTOR. Everything.

MATT. What's everything?

INSPECTOR. Every hairy acre. The birthmark before and the birthmark behind . . . that's lonesome for lack of endearments. The sour in yer sweat, the groan in yer sigh, the dunt in yer eye. I'm here to collect the entire cargo your silvered father—tight as Christy's britches—wouldn't loose, and my red information is— tell me if I took the losing bend—my red information is (*She has seated Matt at the table and is about to straddle his thigh*) one right splash of the dew in the cup just under the curly bush and you'll stream the sweets I'm after like the mushroom droves of mornin'. (*She returns the cap to his head.*) Dream me tonight, handsome, and track me tomorrow. (*Exit Inspector.*)

MATT. There's an apparition . . . if it's apparitions yer after . . . with her sootherin' and her colloguin' and straddlin' me thigh like she owned it from the cradle. I'm steeped she didn't strip. I was apple sure she was goin' to strip to her belongin's and come through me for a short cut.

Scene 6

Lighting change sends Matt to sleeping position downstage left, exterior. The Visitor and the Inspector, with Maggie and the Bookkeepers, sweep in. The Visitor is in a rage. The Inspector seats herself and, aided by the Bookkeepers, sees to her toilette.

VISITOR. Keep your hands off my lovely damson . . .

MAGGIE. Off the grass, please . . .

VISITOR. Lay a single tickle finger on Biddy, and . . .

INSPECTOR. I wouldn't dream, sir.

VISITOR. You would dream . . . and you would pooch . . .

INSPECTOR. *Pour la cause* . . . always. Meanwhile, I'm well aware you've been eyeing my laddy-o . . . you're tomcat to your remnant tail.

Pat Kinevane in *Sheep's Milk on the Boil,* by Tom Mac Intyre.
Courtesy Amelia Stein.

VISITOR. Watch it, Prancy . . . hold your simple tongue . . .
INSPECTOR. You'd tip the crack o' dawn, all know it.
VISITOR. Now it's comin' out . . . now the spiky truth in the
mug with the broken handle.

INSPECTOR. Your point, sir?

VISITOR. I desire an arrangement . . .

MAGGIE. *Ma'sé do thoil é* . . .

INSPECTOR. Another one?

VISITOR. This one to stick.

INSPECTOR. Spill it.

VISITOR. I've changed my mind . . . I won't bother, you can't be trusted . . . the dog's hind leg's *your* compass.

INSPECTOR. Jealousy . . . that splits the stone!

VISITOR. I will not have you plunder my juicy winnings for the pure bite o' bestin'.

INSPECTOR. I *need* the bite o' bestin' . . . takes years off me.

VISITOR. You, madame, are a tyrant, and the breed of tyrants, you'll spawn tyrants to create a weather and a world of tyrants where it's raining crowbars and hammer after the hatchet for breakfast, dinner, and tay.

INSPECTOR. Wear a hard hat. Take out insurance. Australian holiday?

VISITOR. Thailand. Valparaiso. Ultima benighted Thule.

INSPECTOR. And the penguins snorin'. And the fire out. (*They've let it all out. Now, rapprochment, embraces, soothings.*)

INSPECTOR. You know I . . .

VISITOR. Course I do. . . . And don't you know . . .

INSPECTOR. To be sure I do . . .

VISITOR. No need for this blathering . . .

INSPECTOR. We've more to do . . . we've better occupation . . .

VISITOR. Right . . . so I promise not to . . .

INSPECTOR. Cross me heart . . . the same do I . . . (*The two sit. The Visitor takes out the therapeutic hip flask. They both drink to peace. They relax.*)

INSPECTOR. And how's the bold Biddy comin'?

VISITOR. Pulsin' . . . in my conjecture . . . pulsin' like the long grass on the blue-eyed hills of will-and-won't-and-have-it-after. *Your* candidate?

INSPECTOR. I'll tell ye what ye know. I could see that boyo lower every stitch and frisk the pool beyond the weir. (*They rise for departure. More soothing.*)

INSPECTOR. I love a good spat at regular intervals.

VISITOR. Clear the liver, don't they? Rinse the kidneys good and proper . . . (*Exit the lot. Miss Ursula and the Blacksmith wander on—hungrily—at some point during the above. As the scene concludes, Maggie hooshes them from the space.)*

Scene 7

Biddy comes alive in the kitchen, busies herself, essentially tidying and prettifying herself. Meanwhile, Amelia Lundquist has come on in aviator gear, lost figure with map, binoculars, speaking in Swedish—or German—or Dutch—she addresses the landscape, howls distress at her fate, and exits. Biddy takes over.

BIDDY. When all the traffic's said and done, it's the two of us'll break or mend it. And if I don't know him . . . and know him better nor any strap of a lately met . . . then woe betide me. And so. . . . And so I'll venture what I have . . . and what I haven't I'll say prayers for. *(She has by now done herself up. And she has milk and bread parcelled, ready to go. As she's about to exit 'normally' {door, stage left}, the Singer among the Musicians {assume they're positioned off but visible, downstage, right zone} gets her attention. The song draws her directly, magically, towards him.)*

SINGER. As I went out one morning in the month of sweet
　　　　July
　　　I spied a damsel coming and she made to pass me by
　　　'Hold on, my winsome pretty, I would not with you
　　　　make free
　　　but I bring you gifts of the summer and your
　　　　meadows by the sea'. I could see distress upon her
　　　　as she made to pass me by
　　　her cheeks bespoke the lonesome and the grief was in
　　　　her eye
　　　Then cried the sorrow damsel, 'My love made free
　　　　with me
　　　There are no gifts of summer, no meadows by the
　　　　sea'.

(On that last line, the Singer presents her with a posy of flowers, purple flowers. She takes it wonderingly. Now directs her attention to the sleeping Matt. Matt stirs in his sleep, sits up.)

MATT. Riddle-me, riddle-me, randy-row
　　　me father gave me seeds to sow

Riddle-me, riddle-me, randy-row
the mother gave me weeds to hoe . . .
(*He subsides. Biddy has settled beside him. Again he stirs, sits up.*)
To be sure . . .
Because you've the heart o' corn . . .
That's the why, that's the why and that's the
wherefore
That's the bed that Paddy prayed for . . .
(*And back to slumber. Biddy to work. She touches him tenderly until he comes awake.*)

BIDDY. Well?

MATT. Well what?

BIDDY. Isn't that a grand day? I brought (*gesturing*) these for ye. And brought meself while I was as it.

MATT. And the ribbon. . . . And the shawl . . .

BIDDY. Yes, I did meself up, y'see. (*Biddy closes on him, playful. Tickles him, moves to a vehement kiss. Matt revolts, to his feet, distances himself.*)

MATT. I heard ye a mile off, heard that thumpety-thump under yer ribs.

BIDDY. I only came to see ye . . .

MATT. Ye won't get yer paws on it . . .

BIDDY. And be with ye . . .

MATT. Not while I gasp will you lay an eye on it.

BIDDY. So you admit it now?

MATT. I never denied it . . . if ye listened to me at all.

BIDDY. Now yer in the open.

MATT. Where I can get a breath of air.

BIDDY. Were ye stuck for air?

MATT. No . . . but *fresh* air . . .

BIDDY. I won't have ye play with me.

MATT. Not with you I'm playin'.

BIDDY. O, I know that . . .

MATT. (*Punitive/inflated.*) I'm playin' with me trollop . . . and me Judy . . . and me fancy woman too.

BIDDY. Mind they're not all a dose for ye.

MATT. Or for you, more likely.

BIDDY. It's true what they say of ye.

MATT. 'They' . . . who's 'they' when they're lickin' plates?

BIDDY. But I never had the wit to listen.

MATT. Ye'd rather be talkin'.

BIDDY. Till I had to listen.

MATT. And what did ye hear?

BIDDY. Like all your crowd, the fog brought ye . . . and the fog'll take ye . . . and in between times, flat or stannin', yer full o' wind and piss as a tanyard cat. (*Exit Biddy. Matt, impermeable, plants the posy in his breast pocket, digs into the bread and milk, reflects.*)

MATT. Well now, Biddy, the lump of it is this. I'm best left alone while I'm at the business. You'll be let know what ye need to know when the need and the know come together. Till then, if it's things to be doin' yer lost for, there's always mindin' the tongs from the fire.

Scene 8

The ensemble (of intruders), plus local ghosts, take over the house, the Visitor and the Inspector in charge. Matt is roughly plonked on a chair downstage right. The ensemble, with back-up gestural score, loose a blast of 'Riddle-me, riddle-me, randy row', *and add, as a note,* 'Now for sip, now for suck / Now for nip and now for tuck . . .' *Biddy arrives.*

BIDDY. Not much for knocking on doors, are ye?

VISITOR. True, Biddy . . . but we never linger if we don't feel wanted.

INSPECTOR. And where we feel we're wanted . . .

BIDDY. Ye pitch yeer tent.

MAGGIE. Correct! Correct! (*Maggie speaks from sleep. The support group have gone off into a standing doze.*)

BIDDY. I suppose I've lave to rest me bones for five minutes in what's left of the place? (*The Visitor waves her to a chair downstage left.*)

VISITOR. Take breath, Biddy, warm your toes there by the piquant fires of l'aventure et l'avenir.

INSPECTOR. L'aventure et l'avenir . . . (*Biddy sits, fretful. Matt makes a break for it. The Visitor collars him. The Visitor and the Inspector whirl him into a hand-shake sequence, Matt the one caught in the middle. That cameo springs the support group to echo the idiom, marionette style, shaking hands with invisible others. And, that done, they flip back to their standing doze. Next, Biddy to her feet and 'going' for Matt.*

BIDDY. Did you ask this pack here? (*No response.*) I said, did you ask this pack here?

MATT. Don't bar the teeth at me, me lady . . .

BIDDY. Answer what was put up to ye . . .

MATT. Maybe I did . . . and maybe I didn't . . . what's it to anyone . . . the pair of us bargin' won't shift them.

BIDDY. Who's at the bargin'?

MATT. Makin' an ass's backside of yourself in public . . .

BIDDY. I'm enquirin' who invisited the congregation into what's left of the dwellin'. What do ye want me to do? Stick a spud in me mouth and stare the hob, is it?

MATT. I don't know who they are or where they came from or who asked them, but for God Almighty's sake can ye not even let on a welcome when they're this far? If ye can't be nice be civil, I was always tould.

VISITOR. Just one moment . . . there's no puzzle as to why we're here or who asked us . . .

INSPECTOR. You could say the bird, the bullock, or the bumblebee . . .

VISITOR. Never mind, we're here to smooth the cobbles and capsize the load . . .

INSPECTOR. Sieve the smoke and jump the flames . . .

VISITOR. But I'll clear the house this blistered second, *I will do it* . . .

INSPECTOR. And you'll see nothing of us again this side Gazebo, and not a screech of hair on yeer heads . . .

VISITOR. Unless you find the bevelled manners to lift a glass and sip yeer sup . . .

INSPECTOR. The sup about to be offered . . . our prime distillation on your dusted hearthstone . . .

VISITOR. Offered in a spirit of rest aisy . . .

INSPECTOR. And if ye can't be aisy, be as asisy as ye can. (*Maggie appears with a tray on which two christening cups glitter. One to Biddy, one to Matt.*)

MAGGIE. Down them drinks . . . (*Biddy and Matt face each*

*other. Will they? Hesitations. They dive. They do it together. Acclama-
tion. The Visitor takes charge of Biddy, leads her downstage left. The
Inspector takes Matt downstage right.)*

VISITOR. Sing your song, Biddy . . .

BIDDY. I've no song in the world . . .

VISITOR. No one has . . . until they loose it.

BIDDY. How'm I to loose it, the head bothered, and that fella
twistin' in on himself in the long grass . . .

VISITOR. Air it, Biddy, whatever the flight . . .

INSPECTOR. Peg it in the fire. I only want the quiet we had
before this lit on us.

VISITOR. Ahh! Still after the quiet . . . hard to beat the quiet
life and the chimney smokin'!

BIDDY. *(Turns on him.)* Don't imagine we're chickens ripe for
the pluckin'. In my belief, ye might be on the dacent side . . . or
ye might be with the crowd lave the scorch marks in the meadow
. . . I'll let ye know when I've settled the matter for meself.
Between times, mind what yeer at.

VISITOR. Ye have heard the maiden signing . . . *(Responsive
outburst of caw-caws from the support groups.)*

VISITOR. *(To Inspector.)* You have the floor. *(Biddy is dumped on
'her' chair downstage left. The Inspector and Matt go to it.)*

INSPECTOR. Now, child o' grace, quench one eye, pull the
rope, whirl the clapper, and see how peal the bells. *(A blast of
belfry caw-caws from the support group.)*

MATT. Bells? What bells is it?

INSPECTOR. *(Derisive.)* 'Bells? What bells is it?' Were ye reared
on the hind-tit, achree?

MATT. Maybe I was as well reared as lots . . . *(The Inspector has
possession of the posy from the preceding scene. She hoists her skirt, busies
herself twirling the posy in the crotch area.)*

INSPECTOR. Matt, it's late in the day. Sometimes we pass . . .
and don't return.

MAGGIE. Stir yerself, Fusty-Nuts . . .

BOOKKEEPERS. Lick o' the relic, Inspector . . .

MATT. Ye Jezebel, ye . . . *(The Inspector annoints Matt back,
belly, and sides; climactically in the crotch zone. Matt goes down as
though felled by lightning. Acclamation. Matt, dizzily, to his feet again.
We can see him drawing sustenance from being the centre of attention.*

Biddy watches in disbelief. And he and the Inspector are into a flirty gestural score even as he delivers the speech below.)

MATT. Alright so . . . I bid ye welcome. I'd say I know why yeer here and the good weather with ye. And my question is, has no one the start of a song, rosin for fiddlers, and long until mornin'? (*Shyly, he plays with the opening lines of 'Brian O Linn', vide infra. The space empties, but for Matt and Biddy, who're left to stare at each other.*)

BIDDY. Now are ye contented, ye cloosachawn?

MATT. Y'oul Snarly-Gob . . . (*A low chant—breath-sounds, essentially—sinister/minatory—and the troop are back on. They chant to climax, at speed; and as the Singer comes in with the start of 'Brian O Linn', the Visitor and the Inspector commandeer Matt. Biddy is, peremptorily, banished to spectator position.*)

SINGER. Brian O Linn had no britches to wear
He got an ould sheepskin to make him a pair
With the fleshy side out and the wooly side in
'They'll be pelasant and cool', says Brian O Linn.

(*The Visitor and the Inspector have slipped a portion of sheepskin on Matt, and, along with the support group, they're chanting/goading him on—to wherever he'll go, basically. The obvious route has to do with inflation, and Matt's in the vein for the obvious.*)

SINGER. Brian O Linn had no hat to put on
So he got an ould beaver to make him a one
There was none of the crown left and less of the
brim
'Shure there's fine ventilation', says Brian O Linn.

(*The Visitor claps his hat—grotesquely out of shape—on Matt's head. The chanting/goading continues. Matt's fever is rising by the second.*)

SINGER. Brian O Linn was hard up for a coat
He borrowed the skin of a neighbouring goat
With the horns sticking out from his oxters, and
then
'Shure they'll take them for pistols', says Brian O
Linn . . .
Brian O Linn, his wife and wife's mother
They all lay down in the bed together
The sheets they were old and the blankets were thin
'Lie close to the wall', says Brian O Linn.

(*Matt, by now, has been supplied with another skelp of animal skin, and with a torn sheet. The goading/chanting drives him into full gear. He takes to the table, and there does his nut, to the increasingly ambiguous chanting of the ensemble. To climax. Cut. Matt left marooned on the table. Biddy, primrose-pale, staring at these developments. The ensemble wickedly exit, switching back to the sinister breath-chant of earlier in the scene. They're offstage as that hits climax. Black-out.*)

END OF ACT I

ACT II

Scene 1

Stage right wall (including fireplace) and entire back wall now gone. The Inspector and the Bookkeepers on, the Inspector in the lead, they're dowsing. Foot movement to carry the divining rod. To see if they can locate the hidden looking glass. The Inspector finds it downstage right, where Matt has stowed it. That done, she turns to entertaining the audience.

INSPECTOR. Isn't it one of the suprayme monkey puzzles, if you're to be swept away by the wave, you'll go the spot, that one rock, and perch there, and wait for the paw to come and take you . . . if you were a cripple you'd do it. Knew a man did it from his wheelchair. Paw took him, left the chair. I have it at home. I have it hanging from the ceiling for less wear and tear on the tyres that smell of the brine. (*Back to the looking glass. Plays Matt's game of closing one eye and placing the other in the looking glass. Resumes her verbal jig.*) And if you're to be drowned in a bog hole, it's no different. You'll drop what you're at, take the bog road, find the bog hole, and fall in . . . like it was a tub o' butter you'd been after all your days, there bubble your last, bog cotton lilting candled prayers for your damp departin'. (*The Bookkeepers are staring mesmerically into the imaginary bog hole. As the above speech reaches climax, they spit a benediction on the deceased. Matt has come on, upstage left. The Inspector spots him in the looking glass and commences sexy games with the glass, playing it against various parts of her body.*)

INSPECTOR. Come on down here, will you . . . and stop looking at me like a Jackaroo with the mange.

BOOKKEEPER 1. Shift it, laddy-o . . .

BOOKKEEPER 2. If she bites, she'll bite ye where it sings . . .
(*Matt comes downstage in a fury, goes for the Inspector. She, with the
Musicians contributing, magics him into falling in a heap. The Book-
keepers squeal delight.*)

INSPECTOR. You met it, it met you. Everything either growing or withering, did ye never hear? Only two trees in the wood,
and meaning ample everywhere. You don't want the change . . .
you're too lazy to lift the skin off potatoes. Get up off your crucified back now and come over here and see how peal the bells.

MATT. I'll do no such a thing . . . let me have it now . . .
(*Again he rushes her, is again magicked to immobility. Again the Bookkeepers squeal delight.*)

INSPECTOR. He's full o' jangle-jumps and hopalongs, God
bless him. Take care you don't meet yourself comin' back and
damage your comestibles with a baw-ways socdollogher. (*She closes
on him, arm-locks him, presents the looking glass to them both, his face
beside hers.*) What did I tell ye, ye thullabawn? Look at that pair
looking at ye? Your wide secret and your bay beyond, she grows,
she gapes, she's broad as all outdoors . . . now let the jant commence and the seesaw with it and you tell me who'll cross us on
the slopes of sweet renown? (*Teasingly, she slips the looking glass
away. Matt breaks from her.*)

MATT. Yev all the words, haven't ye . . . and a gradle o' stories
. . . but I'll tell you, you've no place where I'm goin'.

INSPECTOR. Haven't I though?

MATT. There's one there before ye . . . and long before ye . . .

INSPECTOR. Who might she be when her washin's out?

BOOKKEEPERS. And her freckles lotioned . . .

MATT. Well, you know who she is . . .

INSPECTOR. I half know . . . but I'd like to hear it spelt out
. . . for the music in the undulations.

MATT. Me trollop . . . me Judy . . . me fancy woman too . . .

KOOKKEEPER 1. His kickie wickie . . .

BOOKKEEPER 2. Across the waves . . .

MATT. Now are ye contented?

INSPECTOR. As the cow on the cock o' hay . . .

MATT. She's there . . . and me with her . . . on your slopes o' sweet renown.

INSPECTOR. She's there . . . and you're here . . . and I'm here with you . . .

BOOKKEEPERS. And we're here as witness to the union . . .

INSPECTOR. Don't despise the givin' hand. There's a shut fist in every bush, y'know, and a knife in every haystack.

MATT. Ye streel ye, yer out to do away with me, aren't ye?

INSPECTOR. D'ye sing a song at all? I love the raw bar . . . 'In came her sister, steppin' on the floor.' (*The Inspector chants the above, with provocative choreography, and the Bookkeepers join her, con moto.*)

INSPECTOR/BOOKKEEPERS. It's tell' me, my sister, that you're
become a whore . . .
A whore, sister, a whore, sister,
that's what I'll never be
I'm not so great a whore, sister, as
liars does on me lee . . .

(*Again, this time decisively, the Inspector collars Matt, offering him the looking glass, rather as a toxic lollipop. The Bookkeepers are energetic in support.*)

INSPECTOR. Now take your fill . . . (*She allows him another taste of the two faces in the glass, the two of them sway into the image.*) People meet and the hills don't, a sailor sang me once. . . . Lick it . . .

BOOKKEEPERS. Lick-an'-learn. . . . Lick-an'-learn . . .

INSPECTOR. Lick it, Sunshine, taste it. . . . Lolly it, enquire it . . .

BOOKKEEPERS. Sook-sook-sook. . . . Sook-sook-sook. . . . Sooky-sook-sook . . . (*Matt yields.*)

INSPECTOR. Come on now, let travels commence . . .

BOOKEEPERS. Swing yer clapper, Sonny . . . (*The Inspector and Matt licking the glass in turn, the bunch exiting. The Inspector and the Bookkeepers 'sook-sooking' triumphantly. Matt subservient, in swithers and swives.*)

Scene 2

Biddy has surfaced again in the kitchen. The Visitor and Maggie sweep in. they're in hilarious mid-conversation.

VISITOR. (*Laughing.*) Again . . . give it to me again . . .

MAGGIE. (*Milking it.*) 'You never wear a coat?' 'No, I never was.' (*Raising the volume they go through that again, enjoying themselves no end. The Blacksmith and Miss Ursula appear.*)

VISITOR. (*Turning on them.*) Go back to your stations. You'll be told when you're wanted.

MAGGIE. And come when you're wanted.

VISITOR. There's some abroad and they'd rush the growth of an oak at the butt of the lane. (*Turning to Biddy.*) Well, my beauty, tell me your now story.

BIDDY. Will someone take this knife from my heart?

MAGGIE. Now d'ye mind?

BIDDY. (a la derive.) Now d'ye mind? (*The Visitor takes a knife from his pocket, liturgically hurls it at, and beds it in, the table surface.*)

VISITOR. I was out fishing, the calmest day. The sea turned tough. A big wave swept down on the boat. I took off a shoe, flung it at the wave, and the wave fell away. Minutes later, the bigger wave. I took the other shoe, flung it at the wave, the wave fell away. In no time, the biggest wave. I grapped the bait knife, flung it at the wave, and the whole sea calmed. That evening's there's a knock at the door. A stranger on the doorstep. 'Will you come with me and take from my sister's heart the knife you flung there today?' 'Alright . . . but no harm to me nor any of mine'. We spun through the air, landed before a door in the side of the mountain. We entered. A fine castle before us, set among trees. He took me inside and upstairs to a bedroom where a beautiful young woman was lying with a bait knife stuck in her heart. 'Will you come and take this knife from my heart that you flung there today?' 'Alright . . . but no harm to me nor any of mine'. I drew out the knife. She was healed. 'Why did you try to drown me today?' I asked her. 'I love you and want you'. 'And you'd take me under to have me?' 'I love you and want you'. 'That can't be'. In seconds I was home again. Next time that woman and I met it was a different story, a warmer and a wiser. (*Pause. Turns to Maggie.*) Stories only happen to those that have the knack of tellin' them, anyone ever learn you that?

MAGGIE. The day you met the scholars comin' home . . .

BIDDY. That's a story from the shaddas, isn't it? Yeer from elsewhere.

VISITOR. A while back they'd the right cure for Matt's like. Take him out in a boat, give his moidhered head a good drench in saltwater.

MAGGIE. And repeat to taste . . .

VISITOR. I saw . . . and I speak truth . . . his twin afflicted come back wide-eyed and ruminant from such immersions.

BIDDY. You won't be content till you drag me under . . . amn't I right, amn't I?

VISITOR. (*Heedless.*) The shore's the place where processions meet and scatter . . . (*The Visitor, giddy, begins to lose the run of himself. Maggie, who, during the knife story, buried her gaze in the Visitor's hat {of which she's generally the custodian} as in a crystal ball, now covers her face with the hat, anticipating the reprimand from above, vide infra.*)

VISITOR. (*flashing vertigo.*) I heard the seals singing one morning on rocks by the shore. I sang back to them (*He imitates the barking of the seals.*). They listened, slipped off into the water, calling, 'You're an inland seal, come down here, child, come down and come into the sea'. (*Minatory intrusion, the sound of galloping hooves, close, intimately close, then fading. The Visitor sobers on the spot. Goes to Biddy, gives her a shot of whiskey from hip flask.*)

VISITOR. Are you in your health?

BIDDY. I'm not in meself at all.

VISITOR. Good. 'Never feel alright when you feel alright' was the sweetest counsel that ever a nipple did gift to me. (*Exit the Visitor.*)

MAGGIE. Cheer up, Biddy. Bar the sun risin' or settin', damn few arrangements that aren't provisional. (*Exit Maggie.*)

Scene 3

The Ensemble (bar the Visitor and the Inspector) appear, take over the space. Biddy is plonked downstage right. The Inspector dances in with Matt in tow with the sooky-sook choreography. She positions Matt downstage left and the Visitor surfaces, oozing ambiguities.

VISITOR. (*To Inspector.*) Ye heard the drummer tappin' and ye took the greensome road. Céad míle palpitating fáiltes.

INSPECTOR. What they call The Point of No Going Back or Who'll Find a Tune For the Thunder of the Falls . . .

VISITOR. Time now for the ABCs of the juicy abacus and the Ps and the Qs of the hindside views.

INSPECTOR. The day she hums and the night opens, sod tumbles from the fire and the stranger's at the door. (*The Visitor sits stage right, the Inspector stations herself upstage left, contemplatively smoking.*)

MAGGIE. Musical instruments . . . please! (*The Bookkeepers rush off, return at once, one with mandolin, one with guitar. These are offered to the visitor. He opts for the mandolin and commences to play. The support ensemble—Maggie, the Bookkeepers, Blacksmith, Miss Ursula, and Amelia Lundquist—flash right fists to their mouths.*)

VISITOR. Somewhere the sun is shining
    But, honey, don't you cry
    There'll be silver lining
    The clouds will soon roll by . . . (*Biddy is laughing delightedly.*)
    I hear a robin singing
    Up on the tree-top high
    To you and me he's singing
    The clouds will soon roll by . . .
    Each little tear of sorrow
    Only brings you closer to me
    Just wait until . . .

(*He leaves it there, dumps mandolin. At some point in the song we have the interpolation below by the Inspector and Maggie.*)

INSPECTOR. His mother was a blackbird . . .

MAGGIE. In the wood beyond the glen . . .

BIDDY. (*Entranced.*) I know a tune for The Thunder of The Falls . . .

VISITOR. Enough of darnin' your cobwebs, Biddy . . . (*Biddy goes, a mite solemn, and sits on the Visitor's knee. Acclamation. Now the Visitor, turning it with Maggie's aid into an event, tickles Biddy into gusts of laughter, spins her in his arms about the space.*)

MATT. Grand to see people enjoyin' themselves.

BIDDY. I've an ass-load o' tickles. How's it you could never spill them?

MATT. They were night and day thatched like an onion, that's the why, ye hussy. (*Advancing belligerently, Matt is quelled and driven back by the Bookkeepers. Abruptly, Biddy and the Visitor are isolated downstage right.*)

BIDDY. Where were you until now?

VISITOR. On my way to you . . . can't you tell?

BIDDY. And will ye stay now yer here?

VISITOR. Will you come now we're here?

BIDDY. Where are ye from, if it's not an impudent question?

VISITOR. We're travellers, Biddy, the road's our residence. We're the view before us and the dust behind us.

BIDDY. Your lashes are longer than anyone's. (*The two kiss. Exuberant caw-caw from the support group. Biddy takes the Visitor's jacket, dons it herself. Embraces him again, a tad parentally. He cools it, puts her back on her chair, sits apart himself, watches the Inspector swing into action with Matt. The Bookkeepers in attendance, she first presents him with that posy, this time ceremonially removed from her garter.*)

INSPECTOR. There's a hand (holding his hand aloft), let the past doze with the leaves, there's a hand . . . in my tasty reckoning . . . with fingers to it could stir reels yet. All it needs . . . I say it humbly . . . is the tutor with the gift and the favours of the gloaming. (*She takes Matt centre stage, starts playing sexy games with him, sniffing him, circling him.*)

VISITOR. Hard to beat the slow simmer . . .

MAGGIE. If you've no wok. (*The Inspector now into action in earnest. Closes on Matt. Punches him several times.*)

MATT. Punch me again, I'll be dug out of ye. (*She does punch him again, closes on him, tears the shirt from his back, nuzzles him. Matt, now pulled into the combat, gets a retaliatory hold on her, nuzzles in turn. Next they shift, the Inspector in the lead, to a rudimentary tango routine, which doesn't progress, can't, because Matt is suddenly crucified with cramp. He breaks from the Inspector, clutching his leg in agony.*)

MAGGIE. Ah, the poor fucker has cramp . . . (*The Inspector advances to help the sufferer.*)

MATT. *Don't touch me, don't touch me. . .* (*Exit Matt, writhing, the Bookkeepers in pursuit, the better to keep an eye. The Inspector follows them, hissing the local ghosts from the space as she does. Biddy rises, takes off the jacket, hurls it at the Visitor.*)

BIDDY. We're dacent God-fearin' people and nothin' to do with the likes of ye. (*Exit Biddy.*)

VISITOR. She would if she could . . . but she can't . . . so she don't. (*Exit Visitor and Maggie.*)

Scene 4

Biddy and Matt in the kitchen, seated by the table. Morose, long silence. Eventually, they speak together.

MATT, BIDDY. Now look at the . . .

BIDDY. Go on . . .

MATT. No, you go on . . .

BIDDY. Go on with you, I said . . .

MATT. No, you go on . . .

BIDDY. I disremember.

MATT. Say it anyway.

BIDDY. I will if it suits me.

MATT. Well, shure do if it suits you.

BIDDY. I will.

MATT. Grand. (*Pause.*) Well, does it suit ye?

BIDDY. No, it doesn't.

MATT. That's grand. (*Biddy starts to shiver. Matt goes, hesitant, to give solace. He touches her. She explodes.*)

BIDDY. You . . . and your kicky wickies . . . (*Matt goes, fetches the looking glass {in purse} from a hiding place, flings it on the table.*)

MATT. Ye know what that is?

BIDDY. A head o' cabbage.

MATT. It's what has yer bowels in an uproar since I came up from the shore that day.

BIDDY. I wouldn't take it if it was wrapped in gold, frankincense, and myrrh. (*Matt takes the looking glass from the purse and, forcibly, makes her view it. She suffers a rush of knowledge.*)

BIDDY. Someone opened a door . . .

MATT. What are y'at?

BIDDY. Someone opened a door (*Glass back into purse, leaving it on the table.*) And now the traffic's racin'.

MATT. Traffic racin'? I didn't invite that pair nor the pack at their heels.

BIDDY. No more did I.

MATT. Who then? The cat's mother?

BIDDY. I don't know. Maybe like lots in the world they come without askin', just like that, land, say their bit, and go, and never seen again.

MATT. Go? They won't stir till they're finished with us.

BIDDY. I suppose . . .

MATT. Ye 'suppose'? Ye may do more nor 'suppose'. We're up to here in their whirl . . . ye bought yer share . . . and make the best of it now, ma'am.

BIDDY. I am to . . . never fret.

MATT. All signs on it.

BIDDY. Skin yer eyes for more. A smart change to have a man with hands other than shovels tucked around me and smells like the summer growin' and can open his mouth and sing a story.

MATT. Good luck to ye. And meanwhile I won't be idle, a woman by me with a travelled tongue knows the four quarters and no way slow about showin' her learnin' either.

BIDDY. O, to be sure. I was sure she was goin' to swally ye whole once or twice.

MATT. I'd a different fear for you.

BIDDY. What was that?

MATT. I was afraid yed take fire . . . and lave only the charred remains. Did ye not get the whiff of sulphur from that ould reprobate?

BIDDY. I'll tell ye one thing . . .

MATT. Do. Tell me the one thing. Only steady yerself first . . . yev the cut of a jade with her head in a spin.

BIDDY. More than that in a spin . . . or are ye deaf as a whetstone? Can't ye hear the roar of him in me? Can't ye tell a man knows what he wants . . . and gets what he wants . . . and comes back for more in the mornin'?

MATT. Who are ye, Biddy.

BIDDY. I never met ye before in me life. (*She extends a hand to his face, as if to steady it for inspection. That done, she slaps him wickedly. Exits.*)

Scene 5

The wood by night. The ensemble, the Inspector, and the Visitor seated on a simple throne.

MAGGIE. The wood by night
A nest of spiceries
Vagrant kisses, wayward juices
shadows put to many uses . . .
Fits and seizures melt your garments
stir your limbs and ripe endowments
Farewell reins, farewell halters
strut your stuff for further orders
Prosper Jack, prosper Jill
foot the bill tomorrow morning . . .
But first, as prelude
entertainment in a lighter mode
local talent (mainly) hits the road . . . (*Drumroll.*)
Miss Amelia Lundquist . . . her recital of her
misfortunes!

(*Amelia forward, speaking in Swedish, she describes, with 'air-crash choreography', her misfortune. In the climax, she airs her sole English phrase.*)

AMELIA. And now the cold feet of the bog . . .

VISITOR. (*Greatly taken.*) And now the cold feet of the bog!
(*Reaches to console her.*)

MAGGIE. Búaladh bos, búaladh bos . . .
(*peremptorily Maggie sweeps the performer off, and the support group join in the* búaladh bos *applause system.*)

MAGGIE. (*Drumroll.*) The Blacksmith, his anvil, and Miss Ursula dancing . . . (*The pair come forward, the Blacksmith pushing a makeshift wooden anvil, hammers convenient. Wielding the hammers with zest, he bursts into song, while Miss Ursula (slow daughter of the big house) performs a simple and strikingly undistinguished set of steps.*)

BLACKSMITH. I had a little pony
We got drunk last night
drunk last night and drunk the night before
the morra we'll be sober
but not for long . . .

INSPECTOR. Enough, enough . . .

VISITOR. No, please, please . . .

INSPECTOR. Enough, *enough*. I can't stand heavy metal . . . (*Maggie leads the support group into búaladh bos, and whirls the performers to one side.*)

MAGGIE. (*Drumroll.*) Our Bookkeepers . . . a singular duet . . . (*The Bookkeepers forward.*)

BOOKKEEPER 1. I only learn this song since . . . we landed here . . . (*she proceeds to sing the opening stanza of a searingly tender love song {director's discretion}. Simultaneously, Bookkeeper 2 gives herself to a grotesque cameo, facial and body/limb contortions, while not moving from her position. Maggie again leads the búaladh bos chorus, and the space empties, bar the Inspector and the Visitor. They remain on the throne but veiled. They are also not there. Biddy and Matt on.*)

MATT. Biddy, will ye tell me something?

BIDDY. What is it ye want to be told, Matt?

MATT. Why . . . in the name of all that's holy . . . aren't the pair of us at home an' our ears to the pilla?

BIDDY. You said, 'We'll take a ramble' . . .

MATT. It was *me* said it?

BIDDY. You said it, mister.

MATT. Biddy, do you take me for a patent-leather eejit?

BIDDY. Whist, would ye . . . we're here either way, aren't we? Maybe we'd get lost . . .

MATT. We *are* lost . . . we were hardly past the Holla Lane an' we were astray, if ye didn't notice.

BIDDY. Well, we'll have to take our chance so, won't we?'

MATT. Likely we will, likely we will. (*Biddy looks about her, blesses herself idly, drifts off. Sober-puss, Matt blesses himself in turn, follows her off. Cacophony, and the two are driven back onstage by the support group. Hurled to the ground, they get up, try to escape, are again hurled to the ground. The Inspector and the Visitor 'appear' again on the throne.*)

VISITOR. Biddy, in the wilds of the woods know your friends, know your friends . . . (*Biddy is moved to express assent to that. She kisses each of the support group in turn. Matt, far less in possession of himself, is pulled into the routine. The vignette is rapid. The support group vanish.*)

BIDDY. I don't know am I goin' to be able for this at all.

MATT. Nothin' 'd do ye, nothin' 'd do ye.

BIDDY. Arrah, would ye stop yer whingin', I've bothered ears listening' to ye.

MATT. 'Shure maybe we'll take a ramble' . . .

BIDDY. Spare me yer gyernin', will ye, spare me, spare me . . . (*The Inspector and the Visitor intervene. The Inspector takes Matt's arm, leads him off.*)

INSPECTOR. It's the bones of the young do creak and groan, me mother told me what the songbirds know. (*And the Visitor leads Biddy off.*)

VISITOR. You came here with nothing, now give it back. (*Lighting change to the phantasmagoric and sound track, various voices, prolonged calling for Biddy. Maggie on, and crosses stage. She's in surplice, black tights, and carrying a large lighted candle. The Blacksmith on, in drag, and with fan. He's cruising. Amelia on with one of the Bookkeepers, as dog on leash. The dog is busy nuzzling Amelia's cunt. The latter enjoys but finally flips to vociferous reprimand. Miss Ursula, tranced, is 'making love' to a tree. The Fiddler, among the Musicians, supplies a wild accompaniment to these events. There's a freeze halfway through. Resume. and cameo over. Reenter Matt and Biddy, pell-mell. They meet 'by accident'.*)

MATT. What are they tryin' to do to us?

BIDDY. Tear us to bits.

MATT. And then what?

BIDDY. Put us together again.

MATT. If they're fit.

BIDDY. They're fit for anything. Isn't that plain as porpentine?

MATT. That man o' yours had his hands all over me up there and under a bush.

BIDDY. They're shameless, the bare naked shameless, like they only dropped into the world . . . an' never knew anything else. (*Exit Biddy.*)

MATT. Do we want it, Biddy? Do we, Biddy? (*Exit Matt.*) *Lighting change. Two ghost figures on, both female. They approach each other, tentative. Rather, one suppliant, the other tentative. The suppliant extends a hungry hand. Hesitation. The tentative one extends a hand, touches, and no more. Turns away, exits, leaving the suppliant to make do with that, exit lonesome. The note aimed for is 'lost' sex, 'cool' sex. The Bookkeepers on, cock-a-doodling, and bearing a bench {for the Inspector*

*and the Visitor, next scene}, which is placed downstage centre. Support
cock-a-doodling from off. Exit the Bookkeepers. Biddy and Matt on
again, dishevelled, in shock. They find a resting place.)*

BIDDY. Now where are we . . . now we've tipped the churn . . .

MATT. And slobbered the dairy. . . . Wherever we are, I'll tell
ye where we're goin'.

BIDDY. Home. And shut the door.

MATT. I won't be the better o' that for a decade. . . . Jesus,
the stagger of it . . .

BIDDY. Decade? I won't over it for the rest o' me days. And
beyond. *(Pause.)*

MATT. Are we for home, Biddy?

BIDDY. What brought us out?

MATT. *(Rising, exiting.)* Are we for home, Biddy? *(She follows
him off.)*

Scene 6

*The Visitor and the Inspector on. Dress and accoutrements exude depar-
ture. Both, plainly, out of sorts. The downstage bench, as indicated, is
available for them.*

INSPECTOR. What's stuck in your craw? Let it out, you've
enough foam on your bile as it is.

VISITOR. Thanks.

INSPECTOR. Not at all.

VISITOR. Thanks for putting in your perished cloot and your
famished paw so's the pot boils over and puts out the fire . . . will
you now face those above and explain why by the time my lovely
was in my arms she was whirling like the straw was in the gale
. . . will you convey that, will you?

INSPECTOR. I'll deny nothing.

VISITOR. Good woman yourself.

INSPECTOR. I'll stand over my proclivities.

VISITOR. A credit. Truly. A credit.

INSPECTOR. Am I to make no mention of your intrusions?

VISITOR. Your friend let slip he felt hooshed . . .

INSPECTOR. 'Hooshed'!

VISITOR. I was aimin' to steady the lad.

INSPECTOR. You winded the poor stumpawn . . . will you trumpet that above? Will you blow loud to them what they know of an ould date, if I plucked a nettle you'd want it for your pillow and your bolster and your feather tick, will you jingle that?

VISITOR. Down from your prosecutor's podium . . . *please* . . .

INSPECTOR. Don't podium-odium me, sir, don't you dare . . .

VISITOR. And will you, madame, stop trying to thraype down my throat that I'm the one offended.

INSPECTOR. I'll thraype down your gullet what I know to be truth. I've lied on your behalf too often. (*Pause to catch breath. Let's cool it, they decide, mutually.*)

INSPECTOR. Maybe we're well rid of them.

VISITOR. Leave them to heaven.

INSPECTOR. Nowhere near ripe.

VISITOR. Raw, raw, raw . . . (*He looses a theatrical sigh.*) Times, times I wish I was a professional golfer . . . (*The Inspector views him with suspicion.*)

INSPECTOR. Have you the colic?

VISITOR. It's a pity though . . .

INSPECTOR. What's a pity?

VISITOR. I call it one great pity. . . . Something in her step I could never quite describe, a dainty idle thing, lazy almost . . .

INSPECTOR. Christ, he's on the hook, my susceptible colleague is, once again, on the hook. We've other work to do, you may recall?

VISITOR. Touching the good Matt . . . our passing tumble . . . I have to say it, he surprised me. (*The Inspector stares at him.*) Do you care for details (*The Inspector ponders.*)

INSPECTOR. Tell the truth he would surprise you, a gentle unruly touch, asleep or half-asleep, and the breath beguiling . . . (*She faces the Visitor, seduced.*)

VISITOR. A last throw?

INSPECTOR. Don't you think?

VISITOR. Scenario?

INSPECTOR. Domestic bliss?

VISITOR. Lovey-dovey by the hob . . .

INSPECTOR. How like life, when you think of it . . .

VISITOR. You couldn't make it up . . . they'll set fire to the house . . .

INSPECTOR. Like Paddy Fitzsummonses mother . . .

VISITOR. Remember when she had the twins? (*The pair now exiting.*)

INSPECTOR. 'Sarch her well, Doktor, she's a roomy woman . . .'

Scene 7

As scene change (from the wood to the kitchen) is effected in partial black out, the Singer gives us . . .

SINGER. 0, there was a widow woman in The Westmoreland
And she never had a daughter but the one
And her only advice by day and by night
Was to never give her maidenhead to one
'O, hold your tongue, dear mother', she said,
'There was a jolly soldier of The Queen's Lifeguards,
Last night he stole my maidenhead from me . . .'
. . . 'O, go, o go, you saucy jade
and bring back the maidenhead you lost last night
Or another night you'll never lie with me . . .'

(*Here a break in the song. Matt and Biddy are back in the kitchen.*)

MATT. Now we'll throw a bit o' shape on this place, get the smell o' them outa the crockery. (*The two commence gathering bits and pieces {connected to the Inspector and the Visitor, 'the invaders' generally,} into a basket. The Singer resumes.*)

SINGER. Now she is to the soldier gone
With a heart both light and free
Saying 'Give me back the maidenhead you stole last
    night
For me manny she is angry with me' . . .
So he got her by the middle so small
And he threw her into the bed
And he turned up her heels where her head ought to
    be
And he gave her back her maidenhead . . .
Now she is to her mammy gone
With a heart both light and free . . .

(*Matt cuts across that last line.*)

MATT. Enough. That's enough of that now . . . on with the business. (*The two stand over the loaded basket.*)

BIDDY. Pitch it in the tide, I'd say . . .

MATT. The very place.

BIDDY. Back where it came from.

MATT. And the bad troop with it. (*They hug supportively.*)

BIDDY. Sup o' bainne?

MATT. I'd kill for it. (*They're at the table, seated, drinking.*)

BIDDY. Matt, I'm sorry . . . things I did . . . and said . . . whatever took over me . . .

MATT. Two of us in it . . . shure ye saw me, tremblin' like a dog in a wet sack.

BIDDY. The thing is . . . just don't let them in. If they're not let in, they'll just canter on to their next stop . . .

MATT. And the divil mend them. (*They sit there. Prolonged silence.*)

MATT. Christ, it's bog-hole quiet, isn't it? (*She looks at him.*) Is it the quiet of the day . . . or is it us that's quiet?

BIDDY. What are ye sayin', Matt?

MATT. I'm sayin' is it the quiet of the day . . . or is it us that's quiet?

BIDDY. The both. The day's quiet. And we're quiet. (*Pause.*) We've a right to be quiet. (*Pause.*) We'd our fill o' loud weather, didn't we?

MATT. That we did. (*He looks vacant. She grips his hand.*)

BIDDY. Are y'll right?

MATT. Never better. (*Pause. Biddy rises, takes the clock from its perch, and with conviction, pitches it into the basket and sits. Beat. Matt rises, fetches the looking glass from downstage right cranny, dumps it in the basket.*)

MATT. Slán abhaile . . . (*He sits again. Beat.*)

BIDDY. You know what I think?

MATT. What d'ye think, Biddy?

BIDDY. I think . . . and do believe . . .

MATT. Ye think . . . and do believe . . .

BIDDY. I think . . . and do believe I'll let a run o' buck roars outa me.

MATT. Why don't ye? And frecken the crows. (*She goes to it, leaving the table. He joins her. They whirl into a wild duet of buck roars that exhausts itself. Seated again.*)

MATT. Hard to beat the good buck roar. (*Biddy has drifted elsewhere.*)

BIDDY. Remember Bessie?

MATT. That used let the fried eggs slither off the plates?

BIDDY. She always said people should screech far more. (*Pause.*) She screeched till her windpipe ravelled. Then she shut up. And lay down. (*Shaky silence. Matt rises, wanders.*)

MATT. (*Under his breath.*) And have the crack
> With Paddy Mack
> The hackler from Grousehall . . .

(*Hiatus. Now he forces himself to the question.*) What is it ye want?

BIDDY. I don't believe I'm finished with them yet, that's all.

MATT. Are ye captive then?

BIDDY. We're all captive.

MATT. Are ye captive, Biddy?

BIDDY. I want to know.

MATT. Ye want to know?

BIDDY. Yes, Matt, I want to know.

Scene 8

Ensemble on. The Inspector collects the looking glass from the basket. Matt and Biddy still by the table, seated. The Inspector stations herself by Matt, the Visitor by Biddy.

INSPECTOR. To all the stories waiting . . .

VISITOR. And the tongues of the honey flow . . .

INSPECTOR. To the first road of all . . .

VISITOR. Forever winding back on herself because she knows just where she's going . . .

INSPECTOR. To the smell of the sea . . .

VISITOR. From your empty shore . . . (*Beat. Now, with 'farewell' patina, the ensemble move into their assertive anthem.*)

ENSEMBLE. In came her sister, steppin' on the floor
> 'It's tellin' me, my sister, and you're become a
> whore . . .'

'A whore, sister, a whore, sister, that's what I'll
never be
I'm not so great a whore, sister, as liars does on
me lee . . .'

(*And, at once, into a reprise, upping the volume. A third to halfway
through, the minatory galloping of hooves impinges. The chant ceases.
Heads bow, deferring. Beat.*)

VISITOR. We have prodigiously enjoyed our stay . . . a pleasant
part of the world, all told.

INSPECTOR. Only pressing business elsewhere would drag us
from it, departure coloured . . .

VISITOR. Tinged . . .

INSPECTOR. Tinged, coloured, coloured, tinged . . . by a certain disappointment. . . . That our endeavours have not met with
the outcome desired. . . . Sweated and prayed for . . .

VISITOR. Nothing morose . . .

INSPECTOR. Nothing sombre . . .

VISITOR. Simply a certain disappointment.

INSPECTOR. No rancour . . .

VISITOR. No recriminations . . .

INSPECTOR. Horses for coorses . . .

VISITOR. Horses for coorses. (*The Visitor moves to exit. Biddy
rushes after him.*)

BIDDY. Yer not goin'?

VISITOR. You might swear we're going.

BIDDY. Where are ye goin'?

VISITOR. Ye know where we're going.

BIDDY. Tell me a story.

VISITOR. I told you a story.

BIDDY. Tell me another.

VISITOR. There's only the one.

BIDDY. Tell it again.

VISITOR. Said the Little Red Hen. (*Exit the Visitor with Maggie.
The rest of the ensemble, bar the Inspector, are drifting off. The Inspector,
playing idly with the looking glass, circles Matt.*)

INSPECTOR. A terror how rapid men can disremember. . . .
Disremember how the shabby hour can open to the widest secret
and the bay beyond. . . . Disremember how one right splash of

the dew in the cup south of the curly bush, and sweets all yearn for straymin' like the mushroom droves . . .

MATT. (*The Visitor has surfaced again by the Inspector. Matt explodes.*) Get outa here . . . lave us alone, lave us be, can't ye see we're not for ye, nothin' to do with ye, nothin', nothin' . . .

INSPECTOR. Yer terrible big when yer out . . . like an ass's tool. I said the same words to your father the day he lost his venture.

MATT. Get out, lave us, I told ye, lave us . . . (*Biddy is motionless, fraught, downstage left.*)

INSPECTOR. Don't ballyrag me, ye scantling. I'd beat ye into an ointment if I thought there was any use for ye. (*She flings the looking glass on the table beside him.*) Hold on to that . . . so's you'll recall the Inspector of Wrack suppled you once upon a day . . . and mourn her in your dotesomes. (*The Inspector and the Visitor exit. Beat. Biddy moves to follow them. Matt, stricken, rises.*)

MATT. Biddy . . . (*She moves past him.*) Biddy . . . (*She's gone. He staggers out after her. We hear him, off.*)

MATT. Biddy . . . *Biddy . . . Biddy . . . BIDDY* . . . (*Matt returns, sits. Fade-out.*)

END OF PLAY

Donal O'Kelly.
Courtesy Denis Mortell.

Asylum! Asylum!

DONAL O'KELLY

1994

The play is constructed around two real events, with some license taken with details. One is an incident in Bucoro, Gulu District, Northern Uganda, reported in Amnesty International Report, December 1991, where five prisoners were placed in a pit, the pit covered with logs, and a fire lit on top of the logs. The second incident is the burning of the Vietnamese immigrants' hostel in Rostock, Germany, in August 1992, while police looked on.

All the action takes place in Dublin, beginning in the recent past and ending in the near future.

The settings comprise a modern-decor pub, a cell in Santry Garda Station, a visiting room in Mountjoy Jail, and the backyard of Bill Gaughran's house. All should be served by the one set without any need for scene changes.

Original Cast

Vincent McCabe	David Fishley
Conor McDermottroe	Jane Brennan
David Herlihy	Judith Ryan

Director: John Crowley

Characters
(In order of appearance)

BILL GAUGHRAN, just-retired sacristan, late sixties
PILLAR BOYLAN, Irish immigration officer, mid-thirties
LEO GAUGHRAN, immigration officer also, Bill's son
JOSEPH OMARA, from Bucoro, Gulu District, Northern Uganda
MARY GAUGHRAN, just-appointed solicitor, Bill's daughter

ACT I

Pub. Bill Gaughran sits at a bar. Pillar Boylan enters.

PILLAR. Howya Bill.
BILL. Where's Leo!?
PILLAR. He's held up.
BILL. The place he picks to meet me! Done up as if it was a clearing in the jungle!

PILLAR. Congratualations! I believe you've taken the high jump!

BILL. I didn't jump . . . I was pushed!

PILLAR. Retirement! A gentleman of leisure, what!?

BILL. Oh yeah, . . . all that, yeah.

PILLAR. The oul biddies in the church won't know what to be doing. They all fancied you in that slinky black soutane. "Big Black Bill" . . . that's what they call you.

BILL. Are you going to get yourself a drink or what!? . . .

PILLAR. Look on the bright side. Now you've all day to do whatever you like. You should be over the moon.

BILL. Wait 'til your turn comes and see how well you cope. Where's Leo!? Damn it, he's dead late.

PILLAR. He's out on a job. Bouncing business!

BILL. What!?

PILLAR. Bouncing, you know!? They try to jump in, we bounce them out again.

BILL. He sent you along to nurse me, what!?

PILLAR. Are you alright there? . . .

BILL. Yeah. Look after yourself.

PILLAR. (*To barman.*) Gimme a Grolsch . . . by the neck!

BILL. Great changes, what!? . . . (*Pause.*)

PILLAR. Tell us, Bill, did Leo mention the Europol job to you?

BILL. The what!?

PILLAR. You know he's applying for this big-time job in Europe . . . in the new FBI-type-of-yoke they're setting up in the EC . . .

BILL. No.

PILLAR. He didn't say anything to you? . . .

BILL. I never see him. Except the odd time at breakfast. Oh, he wouldn't waste his breath informing me about his plans, Pillar.

PILLAR. Would he not?

BILL. Not on your nanny! (*Leo enters.*)

BILL. Well, the dead arose!

PILLAR. Pint, Leo!? You're alright Bill? . . .

BILL. I've never been better.

LEO. Yeah. A pint, Pillar. What the hell is that?

PILLAR. Grolsch.

LEO. Grolsch!?

PILLAR. You know . . . Continental stuff . . .

LEO. What's it like?

PILLAR. Strong. Very strong.

LEO. I'll have one of those then.

PILLAR. Another Grolsch! Must have a leak. Where's the john?

BILL. You're in the jungle. Just pee against a tree! (*Pillar exits.*)

LEO. How are you?

BILL. Oh, never better!

LEO. What did you do today?

BILL. Nothing.

LEO. You're asking for trouble. You've got to keep occupied. Otherwise you'll vegetate, I'm telling you!

BILL. And merge in with the surroundings, what!?

LEO. Where are your socks?

BILL. What!?

LEO. Your socks! Why aren't you wearing your socks!?

BILL. I don't know . . . it's warm. I couldn't find a clean pair.

LEO. You've hundreds of pairs of socks!

BILL. Ah, shut up about my socks!

LEO. Don't blame me if you get pneumonia!

BILL. Your best buddy is on to you.

LEO. What!?

BILL. Pillar. He's got his knife ready for you.

LEO. Ah, would you go away out of that! God you're terrible bitter.

BILL. He was pumping me to know if you're going for the Europol job.

LEO. I was going to tell you tonight.

BILL. Oh, I'm sure. So long as I'm not the last to be told I'm happy enough . . .

LEO. I didn't want to be . . . upsetting you.

BILL. Ah, thanks, son . . .

LEO. Is he going for it too!?

BILL. Of course he is! He wants to know if he's up against you.

LEO. What did you tell him?

BILL. Do you think I came down with the last shower!?

LEO. Thanks.

BILL. Where the hell were you until now!?

LEO. The airport. Just finished. Came straight here.

BILL. Used to be tiny.

LEO. What!?

BILL. The airport. Just the little apron. With the light going around on the top. Don't tell me you forget!?

LEO. It's not like that now. You'd hardly see the apron. I don't think they even use it anymore.

BILL. Used to visit on wet Sundays. You and Mary used to wave at the planes taking off. Waving at the hands in the windows. "Bye-bye." Yiz were gas.

LEO. Please God I'll be waving from the inside soon. (*Pause.*)

BILL. What's that meant to mean!?

LEO. Nothing.

BILL. Nothing!?

LEO. Yeah nothing! This place is fit for nothing.

BILL. This place!? Or this person!?

LEO. What the blazes!? . . .

BILL. Are you going to sit and have a drink with me or are you ashamed of your old fella!

LEO. Ah, stop the messing, of course I'm having a drink.

BILL. (*To barman.*) Here! A pint for the young lad. (*To Leo.*) Grolsch my, ah! (*Pause.*)

LEO. Good news about Mary!

BILL. What about Mary!?

LEO. The parchment. She got her parchment today. Your daughter's a solicitor. Mary Gaughran, Bachelor of Law! Are you proud?

BILL. No. She never bothers with me. Why should I bother with her!? She's nothing to me. The other side, I've always said it.

LEO. Well, if I'm gone away, you might be glad of Mary.

BILL. Oh, I see. I have to hand it to you, Sherlock, . . . you're always one step ahead! (*Pillar returns. Silence. Glances.*)

PILLAR. What's new, Leo!?

LEO. Zilch! Yourself?

PILLAR. Not a sausage . . .

BILL. Yeah. The weather's been dull too . . .

PILLAR. 'See if I can shift a bit of skirt over here. (*Pillar exits.*)

LEO. If he's in for it, it's between him and me.

BILL. He's in for it. Amn't I after telling you!

LEO. He never mentioned it. Sneaky.

BILL. You never mentioned it to him!

LEO. He's younger than me. It's my last chance of a break. (*Leo's mobile blips.*)

BILL. The tom-toms are calling.

LEO. What!?

BILL. Send smoke signals back!

LEO. (*On phone.*) Shit! (*Pause.*) Okay!

BILL. What was that?

LEO. Nothing.

BILL. Nothing!?

LEO. Nothing. Just a nuisance.

BILL. What kind of a nuisance?

LEO. Ah, nothing.

BILL. Am I not worth talking to now!?

LEO. It's just work. The fella I put on the plane. He jumped.

BILL. He jumped off the plane!?

LEO. He just kicked up a fuss. The pilot threw him off.

BILL. What!?

LEO. Ah, for God's sake! It was still on the ground!

BILL. Well, thank God for that!

LEO. Speak for yourself.

BILL. What!?

LEO. Bloody messer! It could be serious for me!

BILL. All the same now! You see!? *He* doesn't want to leave!

LEO. Bloody sure he doesn't. Shag all where he came from. The arsehole of Africa.

BILL. Ah, God help him. He's banging to get in. You're banging to get out.

LEO. Nope. I'm banging to get in.

BILL. What!?

LEO. Europe. The centre. No future here. We're only an offshore rock. Clinging on for dear life. A lump of wet moss. We're pathetic.

BILL. What the hell puts you into these black moods!?

LEO. What are you talking about . . . black mood!?

BILL. Yeah. Hey . . . bring your little alien into the jungle-pub . . . he'll be more at home than me.

LEO. I have to go in to see him. Finish that quick! I'll drop you at the house on my way up to the station.

BILL. No. Go on. Pillar's minding me. He's going to fix me up with the bit-of-fluff's friend.

LEO. Don't wait up for me!

BILL. No chance! I'll have my hands full.

LEO. See you in the morning so.

BILL. Yeah. Good night, sunshine. (*Leo exits.*)

Joseph alone in Santry Garda Station interview room.

JOSEPH. Short has been the life . . .

Short has been the life . . .

Short has been the life, many the vicissitudes . . .

Short has been the life, many the vicissitudes . . .

Short has been the life, many the vicissitudes . . .

Short has been the life, many the vicissitudes, of the Uganda Railway.

(*Joseph rubs his arms gently just above the elbow. He hugs himself. Leo enters. He stands staring at Joseph.*)

LEO. Bad boy!

JOSEPH. I'm sorry, Leo, don't be angry. I don't want to make trouble for you, Leo. I'm sorry if I'm giving you trouble.

LEO. Not half the trouble I'm going to give you.

JOSEPH. Hey, Leo my friend! Leo the Lion! What's wrong? You laughed at me yesterday. We swopped stories about our mad daddies. You enjoyed that, Leo. Don't you dare deny! You had tears coming down your face. Your face changes when you laugh. You have a happy laugh, Leo.

LEO. I don't like being made to feel a fool.

JOSEPH. You're not a fool, Leo.

LEO. You're a sharp operator.

JOSEPH. Did you visit your father after the airport? How is your father, Leo?

LEO. Stop calling me Leo.

JOSEPH. What will I call you?

LEO. I've been a long time in this game. You're the worst I've ever met. I'm going to talk to you straight.

JOSEPH. Okay.

LEO. Do you know how many are out of work here? Three hundred and fifty thousand. Do you know how many are out of work in the entire European Community? Eighteen million. That's why I'm paid to keep outsiders out. There's no room for anybody else. It's obvious and it's simple. We're full up!

JOSEPH. Just one, Leo.

LEO. Look. My job is to keep a clean sheet. I'm a goalkeeper and I'm good at it and I'm going to punt you into orbit with the next kickout.

JOSEPH. Why?

LEO. Because that's the way it is, damn it!

JOSEPH. Why are you angry, Leo?

LEO. I'm not angry! I'm just trying to show you reality! You're carrying on as if you're in some kind of dream. (*Pause.*)

JOSEPH. I want to stay here, Leo. You laughed at me. Somewhere else a cop would have pulled out a gun.

LEO. Yeah. Maybe that's my mistake!

JOSEPH. Leo, Leo, Leo! Why can't you just turn around. Please. Just turn your back, look at the wall, and concentrate. When you turn around again, I'll be gone. I'll disappear into that city out there and this will be the last time your eyes will ever fall on me. I'll disappear and I'll survive, quietly, but efficiently. What do you say, Leo?

LEO. No can do. You're registered now. Alien, illegal. It's down in black and white. Out you go. Sorry. Tough. But that's the rules.

JOSEPH. Rules are made to be broken. Or at least bent.

LEO. Not this one. Cast iron. Written in stone.

JOSEPH. Leo! You could explain. One through Leo's net. The exception that proves the rule. Even Homer nods.

LEO. Not Leo.

JOSEPH. Leo the Lion never ever nods.

LEO. Now you're getting it.

JOSEPH. Hey, Leo! One last quick one before you pack me off. I know you'll laugh at this one. About my father, Leo . . .

LEO. No more daddy yarns!

JOSEPH. This one will cheer you up. I know it will. It's the kind of story you like, Leo.

LEO. How the hell do you know what kind of stories I might like!?

JOSEPH. Are you a father, Leo?

LEO. What!?

JOSEPH. Have you any children?

LEO. Look! Just drop the topic! That's my last word of warning.

JOSEPH. You know the things fathers do to put their children to sleep!? You know the games they play!? The songs they sing!? Hey, Leo, my father was the best.

LEO. Is that so!?

JOSEPH. You have children? . . . (*pause.*)

LEO. (*Quietly.*) The red choo-choo and the blue choo-choo . . .

JOSEPH. Choo-choo! That's amazing, Leo! The story I was going to tell about my father . . . trains on the railway! What a coincidence! You see!? People are the same everywhere! Always trying to get the kids to go asleep! The red choo-choo and the blue choo-choo! How many children, Leo?

LEO. One.

JOSEPH. A boy! I bet it's a boy!

LEO. Yeah. A boy.

JOSEPH. What's his name, Leo?

LEO. Bill.

JOSEPH. Bill. That's a good name, Leo.

LEO. Cut the bullshit!

JOSEPH. Tell me about the red choo-choo and the blue choo-choo.

LEO. I don't see him.

JOSEPH. You don't see him!? Why not?

LEO. I was a bad boy.

JOSEPH. A bad boy! 'Let him who is without sin cast the first stone'. What was you sin, Leo?

LEO. Long story.

JOSEPH. I've got plenty of time. (*Pause.*)

LEO. You're one clever fucking operator. But you've met your match. You'll be saying bye-bye, me bucko. You're not going to shit on my copybook. Where's your passport!?

JOSEPH. I don't know.

LEO. What do you mean you don't know!? Answer the question!

JOSEPH. Where's my passport? My passport could be any-where. . . . It smells of smoke, like me. Do you get the smell of smoke from me, Leo? It's driving me insane.

LEO. Why is it not in your possession?

JOSEPH. Crayons. I had to give it away when I was driving crayons.

LEO. Driving crayons!?

JOSEPH. Driving a truck with a load of crayons. Most of it was crayons. Education aid. World Bank stuff. I was driving it across the border where dollars are easier to get.

LEO. Smuggling!

JOSEPH. Surviving! We call it eating.

LEO. Crime! You're a goner. No fucking way. We've enough of our own, thanks very much. Jesus! The neck!

JOSEPH. Crayons, Leo!

LEO. Yeah, crayons! For kids! Not for lining your pocket! (*Leo pulls a handful of crayons out of the pocket of Joseph's baseball jacket. He slams them on the table in front of Joseph. Joseph stares at the crayons for a moment. Then he flings them across the room. They scatter on the floor.*)

JOSEPH. (*Shouts.*) They are not mine!

LEO. What the fuck is this about!?

JOSEPH. How did they get into my jacket!?

LEO. I've seen and heard it all now! You mean to say you've travelled thousands of miles and never checked your pockets!?

JOSEPH. Those crayons . . . you planted them on me!

LEO. Don't fucking start!

JOSEPH. Those broken crayons . . .

LEO. Get a grip!

JOSEPH. I had no crayons!

LEO. Liar!

JOSEPH. Those crayons . . . followed me . . . how did they follow me!?

LEO. They're your guilty conscience.

JOSEPH. Shut up, you stupid fool!

LEO. Time you learnt a lesson! (*Leo grabs Joseph from behind. he pulls his jacket down pinning his arms behind his back. He exerts pressure. Joseph screams in pain.*)

LEO. That's always the way! The hard-chaws always roar the loudest. Ordinary Joe just takes a belt on the chin and carries on. But you're no ordinary Joe. Where did you get your perfect English from? (*Pause.*)

JOSEPH. Release my arms! My arms are sore. (*Pause.*)

LEO. Jesus Christ! What happened you? What happened your

arms? (*Leo looks at Joseph's arms which are ringed with welts just above the elbows.*)

JOSEPH. Now I must speak to a solicitor. (*Pause.*)

LEO. You didn't get that here. Fuck! That didn't happen here.

JOSEPH. You refuse to let me stay the quiet way. You could have let me walk out the door and disappear. Now I must demand asylum. I want to talk to a solicitor.

LEO. How did you get those marks on your arms?

JOSEPH. No more questions. I want to see a solicitor. Asylum! Asylum!

LEO. Alright. It's the middle of the night. I'll see what I can do. (*Goes to door.*) Pick up those crayons while I'm gone. (*Joseph sits looking at the crayons. Lights fade.*)

Leo alone in outer office. Mary enters. She's wearing a sexy red dress.

MARY. What the hell is this all about? Is it Dad?

LEO. Congratulations! Mary Gaughran, Solicitor! (*Leo kisses Mary.*)

MARY. I haven't heard from you in ages, and then a call in the middle of the night!? Is there a blue moon out?

LEO. Well done, sister. I'm proud of you. And so is Dad.

MARY. He's alright then!?

LEO. He's . . . fine.

MARY. Did you see him?

LEO. Earlier tonight. He's very proud.

MARY. Yeah. I'm sure he is! I'm sure he's hanging from the ceiling shouting for joy.

LEO. Ah, don't be bitter.

MARY. He doesn't give two shits about me. And frankly, my dear Leo, I don't give a damn!

LEO. You're gas, Mary. You're just the same.

MARY. Am I!?

LEO. He's getting old, Mary. He's shuck. Retirement doesn't suit him.

MARY. He's only had a few days of it!

LEO. He's starting to go. It's sad. He's losing it. He's clinging on to me. Hanging out of me. He called me 'young lad' tonight.

MARY. That's serious.

LEO. He wasn't wearing any socks.

MARY. Why not?

LEO. I don't know! He just forgot, I think. (*Pause.*) I'm trying for a job in Europe. If things work out I won't be around much longer.

MARY. That's nice. Good luck!

LEO. You wouldn't think of moving back? . . .

MARY. Back where!?

LEO. Back in with Dad.

MARY. No.

LEO. We'll talk about it another time. You're great. Thanks for coming. Were you out?

MARY. Yeah. Celebrating! I only got in the door, got your message, and stopped the taxi before he turned. (*Pause.*)

LEO. It's awkward.

MARY. What have you done, Leo?

LEO. No, no, nothing. There's a chap inside . . .

MARY. Yeah? . . .

LEO. He's asked for a solicitor. So I called you.

MARY. For fuck's sake, Leo! I could be struck off for this!

LEO. Not at all. It's an asylum case. African. He hasn't got a bean. Legal aid doesn't cover asylum-seeker cases . . . no fees, so don't worry . . . you won't be treading on anyone's toes. You can't get solicitors to take a case like this, bar the oddballs and the zealots.

MARY. And you figure I fit both categories, right!?

LEO. That's not what I meant . . .

MARY. I'm leaving.

LEO. What about all the high-minded stuff about helping the poor and the wretched of the earth!? Here's the case you've been looking for! Beats conveyancing and contract law. Give it a shot!

MARY. I'm half-pissed and look what I'm wearing!? Don't be ridiculous!

LEO. Mary! Listen! He has marks on him. Bad bruising . . . very bad . . . on his arms. Maybe all over . . . I don't know. He's been in one hell of a scrap. That's why I rang you. He's a chancer. He might try to frame me. Police brutality . . . all that jazz. I'm going for this Euro job. I don't want to foul it up getting into that sort of shite.

MARY. You want me to fix up the mess you've got yourself into!

LEO. I thought the situation might be mutually beneficial! (*Pause.*)

MARY. The only time you ever contact me is when you're in trouble.

LEO. We're . . . that kind of family. A bit distant, I suppose. We should work on it. Try to get to know each other again. Maybe go out for a night on the town . . .

MARY. Maybe not.

LEO. Right. Maybe just one step at a time . . .

MARY. How did he get the bruises?

LEO. I don't know.

MARY. Leo!

LEO. I didn't lay a finger on him. I swear to you, Mary. I didn't touch him.

MARY. Then how did he get them?

LEO. He won't tell me.

MARY. Where's he from?

LEO. He says he's from Uganda. No documents.

MARY. What's his name?

LEO. Joseph.

MARY. Just Joseph?

LEO. He says it's Joseph Omara. No apostrophe. (*Mary has to laugh.*)

MARY. Maybe he needs to talk to someone who'll listen.

LEO. That's why I rang you.

MARY. Don't be a hypcrite! You rang me to save your skin, Leo . . . as always! (*Mary turns on her heel. Lights fade on Leo.*)

Joseph alone. Mary enters.

MARY. Hello, Joseph.

JOSEPH. Hello. Who are you?

MARY. Mary. Mary . . . Mary Ni Ghauchrain. Solicitor.

JOSEPH. You're a solicitor!? (*Pause.*)

MARY. More like soliciting. I know . . . the dress! An accident of fate! I was out. Caught unawares.

JOSEPH. Caught unawares. Me too. (*Pause.*)

MARY. I must warn you that I'm . . . not well up on Irish Immigration Law. But . . . that shortcoming can be corrected.

JOSEPH. My name is Joseph Omara, from Bucoro, Gulu province, in the north of Uganda. I'm very pleased to meet you, Mary.

MARY. I'm pleased to meet you too. Tell me your story, Joseph. (*Sees crayons.*) Where did all these crayons come from?

JOSEPH. They came from a man in Kampala who got them from a man who had a contact in the World Bank. The policeman Leo was upset when I told him this.

MARY. Don't mind him. He's a gobshit.

JOSEPH. You know him?

MARY. I've come up against him. You know the way.

JOSEPH. My job was to drive a truck. It didn't matter to me what was in the back. I didn't know. I drove the truck across the border and unloaded the stuff. Then back again for another batch. Often it was useless stuff . . . fancy chemistry equipment for schools that were now just heaps of rubble. (*Pause.*) My father was the schoolteacher in our village. He loved to teach. And he loved to talk. Does your father like to talk?

MARY. I wouldn't really know.

JOSEPH. This policeman Leo said his father talks 'until the cows come home'!

MARY. Ireland's like that . . . plenty of variety.

JOSEPH. My father . . . wait! I'm sorry . . . you asked me to tell my story, not to talk about my father.

MARY. Go ahead! It's fascinating. (*Pause. Joseph goes into a semi-trance.*)

JOSEPH. My father's chest was hard, yet gentle, loud, yet soft, his arms were warm, yet cool, close, yet loose. His shoulders were high, yet safe, sharp, yet round. My cheek rested on his shoulder. My ear rested on his chest. Spittle ran from the corner of my mouth as I closed my eyes on the setting sun and he half-said half-sang his nightly lullaby.

> Short has been the life,
> many the vic-iss-it-udes,
> of the Uganda Railway.

(*Pause.*)

MARY. Your father sounds like a beautiful man. (*Pause.*)

JOSEPH. Sometimes he was funny. Sometimes he was cruel. He

was tall and thin. Sometimes he looked like a giant. Sometimes like a leaf. When he laughed, everybody laughed, because you just bloddy well had to. When he frowned, all the kids ran to hide. He blew hot and cold. (*Pause.*) My father said the Romans invented the greatest trick of all. The trick of how to copy. (*Pause.*) 'Copy the conqueror' he used to say. Whoo-woo!

> Short has been the life,
> many the vic-iss-it-udes,
> of the Uganda Railway.

Whoo-woo! Winston Churchill was his hero. We should copy Winston Churchill, he said, for peace and prosperity. He could recite many passages from Churchill's book. He loved the bits about the railway. So did I. I was a baby-train choo-chooing through Uganda to the Land of Sleep and Dreams.

> Through the forests,
> through the ravines,
> through troops of marauding lions,
> through famine,
> through war,
> through everything,
> muddled and marched the railway.

(*Pause.*)

MARY. God. Such wonderful memories. You must love your father very much. (*Pause.*)

JOSEPH. These crayons . . . (*Pause.*) I wanted to be like the prodigal son . . . but not destitude and broken. I wanted to return home bearing gifts. The gift of crayons and paper for the children in the school. I took a detour to Bucoro. The truck kept slipping out of gear, but it didn't bother me . . . I was happy. The military stopped me before I reached Bucoro. (*Pause.*) My father was right. I should never have left Bucoro. Especially me, he said. The others . . . alright, but me . . . he said I had a nose for trouble.

MARY. These military . . . gave you trouble? . . .

JOSEPH. 'Who are you? Where do you come from?' A soldier took my passport from the dashboard. They didn't like me. Big shot, you know . . . with a passport! 'What's in the back?' 'Crayons', I said. They looked. 'Where did you get them?' 'Kampala', I said. 'From who in Kampala?' I started to shake. 'Get out' the one who took my passport said, 'we think you have been eating.'

MARY. Eating?

JOSEPH. They took me to the school. The soldier who took my passport gave a shovel. 'Dig', he said. I started digging in the schoolyard. It was hot. The military watched me from the shade. They were young. Finally they told me to stop. The pit I dug was maybe six feet deep. Then they sent me to the shed. They told me to carry logs from the shed to the pit. Many logs. I carried the logs one by one and laid them down beside the pit. (*Pause.*).

MARY. Go on, Joseph.

JOSEPH. The smell of smoke! It's coming from my clothes. Do you smell the smoke, Mary?

MARY. No.

JOSEPH. I smell smoke . . . from my clothes.

MARY. What happened then, Joseph?

JOSEPH. Bloody questions . . .

MARY. I'm sorry. Joseph, what happened to your arms? How did you get the bruising on your arms?

JOSEPH. *Kandooya?* The soldier who took my passport led me to the part of the school that still had a small piece of roof. (*Pause.*) *Kandooya* means 'briefcase'. (*Pause.*) They tied my arms, here, above the elbows . . . you can see the bruising. They tied my feet, at the ankles . . . you can see. They pushed me. I fell on the ground. Then they tied the rope on my arms and the rope on my feet . . . together. They pulled my arms and feet together behind . . . and they tied them. They picked me up like that. That's why they call it *kandooya* . . . briefcase. They carried me around like a briefcase. A screaming briefcase. Then they tied me to the one remaining rafter of the roof. They brought people in to watch. 'This is what happens when you don't obey!' (*Pause.*) But I did obey. I dug the pit. I carried the logs. (*Pause.*) I tried to keep still. But they poked me with their guns to make me swing. I thought my chest was going to rip. I thought my heart was going to burst through my chest and fall out onto the ground. (*Pause.*) They left me there. I heard the sound of burning from the direction of the pit. I wanted to die. Hanging there, I tried to make myself die. (*Pause.*) The smoke came in and collected under the small bit of roof. I tried not to cough. I tried not to cry. (*Pause. Mary walks around the table and embraces Joseph.*)

MARY. You can cry now, Joseph. You can cry now.

(Joseph and Mary embrace. They kiss. Eventually they separate. They are both a bit stunned.)

MARY. There's nothing like a good cry.

JOSEPH. Mary. Will you help me? I want to stay here. In Ireland.

MARY. I'll come back tomorrow. I'll have my act together. I'm a bit scattered tonight. *(Pause.)*.

JOSEPH. You will apply for political asylum for me?

MARY. Yes. I'll handle it. *(Mary goes to door.)* Asylum is right! . . . *(Mary exits. Lights fade on Joseph.)*

Lights up on Leo alone. Mary enters.

LEO. Well, Mary, How's Joseph?

MARY. Do you know how he got the marks?

LEO. He wouldn't tell me.

MARY. He was tortured.

LEO. Is that what he said?

MARY. It's what he described. *(Pause.)*

LEO. That's me off the hook. Of course, . . . just to put you in the picture, Mary . . . torture . . . they all say that.

MARY. Leo, the story he told . . . he couldn't have made it up.

LEO. Yes he could. The stories are always good. He's special. I bet his is the best.

MARY. I don't want to discuss it with you. I'll be back tomorrow. *(Mary makes for exit.)*

LEO. He'll be in jail tomorrow. Mountjoy.

MARY. Jail!?

LEO. The rules.

MARY. Jesus! *(Mary makes for exit.)*

LEO. Mary and Joseph! Bum-bum! Hey!? Did he like the dress?

MARY. He didn't seem to notice. *(Mary turns to exit.)*

LEO. Mary!? Be careful. That fella's hiding something. I swear to God he is.

MARY. Yeah . . . he was hiding the fact that he was tortured . . . he was so terrified of you!

LEO. He's been around. He's a smart operator. I'm telling you . . . he's far and away the smartest I ever came up against.

Dave Fishley and Jane Brennan in *Asylum! Asylum!*, by Donal O'Kelly.
Courtesy Amelia Stein.

MARY. Leo. You've developed the power to smell guilt! That's
a special skill! Be sure to mention it for the Euro job.

LEO. I smell smoke. And where there's smoke, there's fire.
(*Mary exits.*)

Mountjoy Jail. Visits room.

Joseph alone. Mary enters, wearing sober black solicitor's suit, flat heels, etc.

JOSEPH. Hey, Mary! Do you know what the warder just told
me!? Do you know how much it costs to keep me here'? One
hundred and seventy four pounds per day! One hundred and sev-
enty-four pounds! They can't keep me here for long.

MARY. They can and they will! Sit down, Joseph. First, I'm sorry for behaving unprofessionally last night. On two counts. One, I was . . . drunk, a bit, and my judgement was consequently impaired. My behaviour was not in keeping with reputable legal practice. I apologise. Two, the sergeant who called me about your case last night, Leo Gaughran, is my brother. He called me because he was afraid another solicitor would charge him with assaulting you. It's an unforgiveable denial of your right to independent legal aid. I apologise profoundly. On both these counts you are free to take legal action through the courts and to make an official complaint against me to the Law Society. I think you should, I'll understand fully if you do, and I won't appeal or contest. In any case, I've lodged an asylum application on your behalf, with no obligation on your part to retain me. It's up to you. (*Pause. Mary places a fat file on the table.*)

JOSEPH. Your brother!? That Leo is your brother!?

MARY. Yes. My only brother. We're not close. (*Pause.*) We hate the sight of each other.

JOSEPH. Then why did you come when he called you?

MARY. I only got a message. I thought something was wrong with my father.

JOSEPH. Ah! You like your father!?

MARY. No. But . . . you know, I thought maybe it was an emergency.

JOSEPH. You thought your father was dying? . . .

MARY. That's what I thought.

JOSEPH. And you found me.

MARY. I should have turned on my heel and walked out. I was drunk.

JOSEPH. And the kiss? . . .

MARY. The kiss was a result of the fact that I was drunk . . . a bit. It was my first time to drink in a long, long time, and it went to my head.

JOSEPH. Did you kiss me only because you were drunk!?

MARY. Yes. More or less. Now. You must decide, Joseph. Do you want to report me for unprofessional behaviour? Do you want me to leave? Or do you want tme to take your case? (*Mary places her hand on the fat file.*)

JOSEPH. Take my case.

MARY. Good. You won't regret it.

JOSEPH. I'm sure I won't.

MARY. Now. First we must arrange an independent medical examination. Those injuries must be recorded. Then we need to make out a deposition with the reasons why you are entitled to political asylum. I've made a synopsis of what you told me last night. I'd like you to check it. You were stopped by soldiers near Bucoro. You were forced to dig a pit. You were forced to lay logs beside the pit. Then . . . you were tied *Kandooya*. Joseph, did anything else happen after you dug the pit and laid the logs?

JOSEPH. Is it not enough that I was hung up like a dead bird!? Is that not torture!? Have the officials in the Department of Justice ever been tied up *Kandooya!?* How would Leo like it!?

MARY. I'm merely trying to get all the details in order to help you. (*Pause.*)

JOSEPH. I know they burned something. They burned the logs. They took me away and hanged me from the roof, but I could smell the smoke . . . the smell of burning. Yes, they burned the logs.

MARY. Why?

JOSEPH. Shit! To keep warm!? How the hell do I know!? I was hanging from the roof! I was trying to stop my arms from ripping out of their sockets! I was screaming for them to kill me!

MARY. Joseph! I understand how difficult this must be, but we must present the strongest case we can.

JOSEPH. There is a smell of smoke all the time in this jail. I hate it here. Get me out, Mary! Get me out of this jail! I'm suffocating here.

MARY. I'll get you out, Joseph, but you have to provide me with the weapons to fight your case. You have to tell me everything.

JOSEPH. Take me away from this smoke!

MARY. It will take some time, Joseph. But I will get you out.

JOSEPH. When?

MARY. Even if it takes a few months . . . and it might . . . there'll soon be standardised EC laws for asylum seekers. That's bound to be far more agreeable than the Law of Nod and Wink.

JOSEPH. Is it?

MARY. We're going to get you out, and we're going to get you the right to stay and live here if you want . . . permanent residency. It's the least you deserve.

ACT II

Many months later. The backyard of Bill's house. Bill, wearing pyjamas and dressing-gown, is sitting in his chair. Leo stands.

LEO. We never made enough of this yard. If this was on the Continent, there'd be flower boxes, flower beds, a patio, a paddling pool maybe . . .

BILL. It's all right the way it is. It's just a backyard. Leave it alone. (*Pause.*)

BILL. So. Tomorrow.

LEO. Yeah. Tomorrow.

BILL. Well . . . good luck, son. You've chosen it, you've worked for it, you have your heart set on it, you're my only son, so, what else can I say except . . . Good luck, Leo, I hope your dream comes true for you.

LEO. Fair play to you. Thanks. It means a lot.

BILL. It'll mean even more next time you're back.

LEO. What do you mean!?

BILL. Just what I've said. Next time you're back, remember it . . . I gave my blessing. (*Pause.*)

LEO. This barbecue yoke'll come in handy. I'll show Mary how to work it. If yiz get the weather . . . might be nice.

BILL. Oh, me and Mary'll be having midnight bonfires every chance we get. Yahoo! . . .

LEO. Well! You never know! Yiz might . . . I don't know . . . yiz might discover each other again.

BILL. Leo! Thanks very much for the lovely barbecue yoke. Now!

LEO. Mary was very enthusiastic about coming. I think she's going to make a real effort.

BILL. Maybe. Maybe. At this stage, I rule nothing out. She's late.

LEO. Yeah, well . . . she's in the High Court today.

BILL. Auh . . . higher and higher! My children are gone into orbit.

LEO. Remember the fella who jumped off the plane!?

BILL. I remember. The night we were in the jungle pub.

LEO. She's trying to get him out of jail.

BILL. What did he do!?

LEO. Nothing. Well . . . he entered illegally.

BILL. If he did nothing, why is he in jail?

LEO. That's the way the system works. It sounds more . . .
crude than it is when you actually study it.

BILL. I see. And have you got an interest in keeping this fella
behind bars!?

LEO. Not anymore. I'm beyond that now.

BILL. Bigger and better things.

LEO. That's the idea. He's Pillar's problem now.

BILL. So that's what Mary's doing. Making problems for
Pillar. God, you never know, there might be hope for Mary and
me yet. (*Pause.*)

BILL. Leo . . . tell me what you want to do, will you?

LEO. I want to get the family together for one last . . . for a
barbecue! We're desperate. There's only three of us, but we're not
like a family at all. We never do things together like other
famillies.

BILL. Okay. I'm all in favour of the barbecue. But I mean long
term . . . tell me what you want to do! (*Pause.*)

LEO. I want to get somewhere, Dad.

BILL. Where's 'somewhere'?

LEO. Somewhere I'm valued. I want to be able to look at myself and say . . . Leo, you're someone, and you're doing
something.

BILL. Why go away? Can you not get that feeling here?

LEO. No. Nobody gives you credit here. It's small, it's paro-
chial, nothing is decided on merit, everybody knows everybody's
past, everybody's out to rattle the skeleton in the other fella's
cupboard, it's all nod and wink and who does High-and-Mighty
think he is considering where he came from he's only a glorified
bouncer . . . back biting and back stabbing, I can't stick it anymore. Thank God I'm getting out. I hate it here. (*Pause.*).

BILL. Alright. That's what you're getting out of. But what are
you going into?

LEO. A life where my skills and experience will be appreciated!

BILL. What do they appreciate about you, Leo?

LEO. They've told me. Straight up. Makes a difference from
the nod and wink shit you get here.

BILL. Go on.

LEO. It's technical stuff . . . to do with the job.

BILL. I'm interested, Leo. Tell me anyway.

LEO. Well, I get inside the immigrant mind. That's what they told me. More effectively than anyone else in the force.

BILL. How did they work that out?

LEO. They put me through a test. They made me act the part of an African trying to bust his way into Europe. I acted it so well they told me . . . this was unanimous . . . they told me they'd have granted me asylum on the spot. These guys were the toughest enforcers around. I was able to soften them.

BILL. What did you do? (*pause.*)

LEO. Told them stories about my daddy.

BILL. About me!?

LEO. No. A pretend daddy.

BILL. You made it up?

LEO. Yeah. No. Not really. I . . . eh . . . I just repeated what I heard from one guy I interrogated. He told some amazing stories about his father . . . all intended to bamboozle me, of course. And I mixed in some real things that I remembered myself. Some stuff you did when I was small, some stuff I've done myself. They said I was a natural.

BILL. A natural liar!?

LEO. Ah Dad! A natural storyteller. A natural for understanding the twists and turns of the immigrant's mind when he's trying to squeeze in uninvited.

BILL. What did you tell them about me and you?

LEO. Where did you learn your interrogation technique!? Do you want a job in Europol!?

BILL. Come on, Leo. Tell me what you said.

LEO. Remember the red choo-choo and the blue choo-choo? . . .

BILL. What!? Going up to bed?

LEO. Yeah . . . up the stairs on your back. And you'd say 'Oh, the red choo-choo is running out of coal.' And I'd say 'You can have some of mine, red choo-choo' And I'd be the boy loading the coal from the blue choo-choo onto the red choo-choo and then both of us would be able to get to the top.

BILL. 'I—think I can . . . do it, I . . . think I can do it, I think I can do it, I-think-I-can-do-it, I-know-I-can-do-it, I-know-

I-can-do-it, IknowIcandoit IknowIcandoit IknowIcandoit, Whee-wee!'

LEO. 'All change for Leo's beddyhouse!'

BILL. You told them that!?

LEO. Yeah. And then I . . . I tagged on a tragic ending.

BILL. What tragic ending?

LEO. The red choo-choo . . . the father . . . gets dragged away by the army and . . . ah, you know, mutilated or something. (*Pause.*)

BILL. Mutilated!?

LEO. It's just a yarn. But it worked a dream. They were gobsmacked. Putty in my hands.

BILL. And tomorrow you're off to join them. (*Pause.*)

LEO. You know those pinky-blue paving slabs . . . with a raised flower bed along the back wall . . . I'll pay for it. Next summer it'll be in bloom. What do you say!?

BILL. Bill loves it here.

LEO. What!?

BILL. Little Bill loves it out here in the yard.

LEO. She brings him here!?

BILL. To see his grandad, yeah. Every now and then.

LEO. She never told me.

BILL. She told me not to tell you. But . . . well! He has your laugh, Leo. His face lights up.

LEO. She won't let me near him. She thinks I'm a bad influence.

BILL. I know.

LEO. Do you agree with that kind of fanaticism!?

BILL. She's bringing him up a lovely little fella. He's a joy to have around.

LEO. And he plays out here, yeah!?

BILL. He loves it out here.

LEO. My Boy Bill! It's a shocking price to pay for one mistake, Dad.

BILL. Is that why you're going, Leo? Are you trying to get away from all of that!?

LEO. No! I'm going away to advance my career! It's what everybody's meant to do in this day and age!

BILL. Alright, alright! So long as you feel you're advancing, that's alright. (*Pause.*)

LEO. All the same . . . something like that hanging over you here . . . they use it against you every chance they get. I know I was wrong and all that . . . I admit it . . . but, there's no sense of forgiveness. There's no second chance.

BILL. Well . . . not without expressing real . . . remorse.

LEO. I'm telling you . . . if you saw the weekly cheque I'm lodging . . . you'd know the pitch of my remorse. Now drop it Dad! (*Pause.*) Where the hell is Mary!?

BILL. She's always late. Always. You know that by now . . .

LEO. I'm going to start the barbecue. Otherwise we'll still be hanging around at midnight. I've an early start tomorrow. (*Mary enters.*)

MARY. Hello. The front door is open. So I came straight in.

LEO. We'd almost given up on you.

BILL. Hello, Mary.

MARY. Hiya, Dad. This is Joseph. (*Joseph enters behind Mary. Joseph stands having just entered.*)

BILL. Hello, Joseph.

JOSEPH. Hello, Mr Gaughran. I've heard so much about you.

BILL. Good, I hope.

JOSEPH. (*A glance at Mary.*) Very, very good.

MARY. How are you feeling, Dad? . . .

BILL. Oh very, very good! . . .

LEO. Is this called bringing your work home with you?

MARY. Joseph had nowhere else to go. So I thought . . . why not!?

BILL. Leo was just putting on the barbecue . . .

LEO. There. It's lit. Now we have to wait until the flames die down. That's when it's at its hottest.

MARY. Very nice. (*Pause.*)

JOSEPH. Hello, Leo.

LEO. Hello. You're out.

JOSEPH. Six months after our little chat . . .

LEO. Well, you're out legally now.

JOSEPH. Thanks to the solicitor you got me.

LEO. Yeah. Told you she was keen.

JOSEPH. I hear you're going up in the world.

LEO. Off your back anyway.

JOSEPH. I'm sure there are others to take your place.

LEO. There's one. And you'll know all about it.

JOSEPH. Yes. I know. Pillar. We met in court.

MARY. Joseph said Pillar had a forthright manner! Very good, Joseph . . . God, you have a way with words.

LEO. Say what you like, but Pillar knows the job inside out.

MARY. Oh I'm sure he does . . . and he has a liver on him now because you pipped him to the glamour job in Europe.

LEO. I don't know about that . . . but don't count your chickens before they're hatched when you're up against Pillar. You might be left with nothing but feathers.

MARY. (*To Bill.*) Isn't Leo great gas!?

BILL. Sit down, Joseph. Leo will give you a bit of barbecue when he figures out how to work it . . .

LEO. Between ourselves . . . expect things to be hotter.

JOSEPH. It's hot in Uganda, Leo.

LEO. Temperature is directly proportional to pressure . . . and the pressure is rising fast.

JOSEPH. What pressure!?

LEO. From Europe. Pressure for expulsions. Pressure for asylum rejections. Pressure to stop immigration.

MARY. Ah, will you leave him alone! His first day of freedom, and you seem hell bent on spoiling it.

LEO. I'm only telling him the truth.

MARY. There's a time and a place! Anyway, he'll get his asylum before all that.

LEO. Will he!?

MARY. Yes. He will.

BILL. Good.

JOSEPH. Will I, Leo? . . .

MARY. This is just idle speculation . . .

JOSEPH. Will I, Leo!?

LEO. Off the record . . . hard to say.

MARY. Joseph . . .

JOSEPH. Come on, Leo, tell me what you think my chances are.

LEO. The pitch is changing all the time . . .

MARY. Well of course it is when there's no legislation to cover refugees. We're reduced to the Law of Nod and Wink.

LEO. You might crave the good old days of Nod and Wink when legislation finally does come in.

MARY. It couldn't be worse than no law at all. The EC is used to legislating for hundreds of thousands of immigrants. You'll be like a dinosaur with your narrow mind. They'll be laughing at you.

LEO. Look, Mary! I've been immersed in this for the past six months. I've met the Brits, the French, the Germans, the Italians, the whole lot of them. If pressure in Europe keeps building up, the shutters will come down like a guillotine . . . and woe betide any dodgy immigrant caught beneath it, Joseph. That's how hot it's going to get.

BILL. The pair of them are creating a fair amount of heat as it is, Joseph, what!?

MARY. Well, that's a nice little piece of conjecture. Thanks very much, Leo! Just what we want to hear today!

LEO. Why shoot the messenger!?

MARY. If what you're saying is true, . . . if, I'm saying . . . then you're not the messenger. You're the enforcer.

LEO. Of policy democratically decided! No crime in that!

MARY. Well it's not. If it comes to that, it's not! It's policy decided behind closed doors! By secret meetings with no reference to any democratic forum! Let's be clear. That's what you're getting into.

LEO. You can't blame me for the way the EC runs its business.

MARY. Ah, Pontius Pilate wash your hands!

LEO. One minute you're cheering the EC, the next minute you're jeering . . .

MARY. Give me the EC, warts and all . . . at least there'll be a procedure. Better than getting the runaround from fobshites like Pillar and you who think anyone from south of Courtown is an extraterrestrial.

LEO. Only if they hadn't got a valid visa.

BILL. We have a guest here, folks, who we should be looking after . . .

MARY. Maybe we should cut the shop-talk, Leo? . . .

LEO. Yeah. Suits me. (*Pause.*)

BILL. Do you know what we were talking about, Mary? You'll remember this . . .

MARY. What!?

BILL. Putting them up to bed, Joseph, when they were small . . . (*To Mary.*) Do you remember? . . .

MARY. No. Remember what!?

LEO. Dad . . .

BILL. What?

LEO. She doesn't remember.

BILL. You *must* remember . . . the red choo-choo and the blue choo-choo.

MARY. What!?

BILL. You don't remember!? . . .

JOSEPH. I remember the red choo-choo and the blue choo-choo.

BILL. You remember them!?

MARY. What in blue blazes are you all talking about!?

LEO. (*Regarding the barbecue.*) This is getting hotter alright.

JOSEPH. Leo told me about the red choo-choo and the blue choo-choo one night in the station. We were trading stories about daddies. Isn't that so, Leo!? (*Pause.*)

BILL. Is that right?

LEO. Joseph had a way with the repartee then as much as now.

BILL. Yeah. The repartee. Daddy talk, what!? The red choo-choo and the blue choo-choo.

MARY. Excuse me . . .

BILL. Ah, of course you remember . . . going up the stairs to bed, the red choo-choo runs out of coal so the little blue choo-choo gives him some of his and they both go 'I think I can do it' and so on up the stairs to bed! (*Pause.*)

LEO. I think you only played it with me . . . for what it's worth.

MARY. On a point of information . . . yeah . . .

BILL. I played it with the two of you!

LEO. I think you'd stopped playing it when Mary came along.

MARY. Oh, that'd be it, yeah! (*Pause.*)

BILL. Well, do you want to play it now, Mary!? I would if I could! I'd carry you up on my back . . . except I can't even get myself up the stairs now!

MARY. It's alright, Dad. It's all a long time ago and it doesn't really matter anymore. It's alright.

LEO. Good. (*Pause.*)

BILL. Women, Joseph, what!?

JOSEPH. She's a very beautiful woman. (*Pause. Then Mary starts laughing. Then Bill, then Leo, and finally Joseph laughs because everybody else is.*)

LEO. This is ready for the meat. Here we go. (*Leo tends to the barbecue. Joseph gets more agitated.*)

BILL. I suppose you do a lot of this in Africa, Joseph!?

JOSEPH. A lot of what?

BILL. Cooking out of doors, eating out of doors . . . you have the weather for it.

JOSEPH. Yes.

LEO. There. Now. Three or four minutes and we'll be sucking bones.

BILL. Mmm. Nice smell, alright. Very appetising. Surprising enough!

LEO. Wait 'til you dip it in the sauce! Mwuh!!

MARY. It's very smoky! Can you not turn it down?

BILL. Does you father do the cooking, Joseph?

JOSEPH. No.

BILL. I reared the two of them alone, you know. Cooked a dinner every day.

MARY. Meatball stew.

BILL. You ate it!

LEO. Eat it or starve. Dad believed in choice.

BILL. Don't be so ungrateful. See what I'm up against, Joseph!? The prodigal son here! Wait 'til you see . . . he'll come crawling back some day feeling very chastened.

LEO. Wishful thinking, Dad, but no chance.

BILL. Mark . . . my . . . words!

MARY. Read . . . Dad's . . . lips!

LEO. This bloody thing is going haywire. The stuff is burning!

BILL. Is your father as handsome and successful a da as I obviously am?

MARY. Ah, Dad, you've let yourself go. Since you retired you've lost your holy face.

LEO. Jaysus folks! We're making a holy hames of these ribs.

BILL. Come on, Joseph. Tell us about your father.

MARY. Tell them the song he used to sing when you were a baby. (*To Bill and Leo.*) Wait 'til you hear this!

LEO. Whoa-hoa! The Uganda Choo-choo! (*Sings.*) Pardon me boys, is this the pan-Uganda Choo-choo! Aw f-iddlesticks! Barbecue my backside!

MARY. With the greatest of pleasure, Leo!

JOSEPH. After I had finished the digging . . .

LEO. Diggin' the spare ribs, geddit!!? Bum! Bum!!

MARY. What digging, Joseph?

JOSEPH. After I had finished the digging, and I had finished carrying the logs, they brought some people from behind the school. They brought them to the pit.

BILL. Who did? What's this Joseph?

JOSEPH. They told them to get into the pit. These people started to get down on their knees in order to get into the pit. There were four, and another, older man. This man looked at me. (*Pause. Joseph looks at Bill.*)

BILL. Are you alright, Joseph?

JOSEPH. Tall like a giant, thin like a leaf. His lips moved a little. No sound, but he was saying something silently. (*Pause.*) The other four got down into the pit. Then this last tall man got into the pit as well.

MARY. Joseph, you don't have to put yourself through this here.

JOSEPH. The soldier who took my passport told me to place the logs across the pit. I picked up the first log, and I placed it across the pit. Then the second. The third. The fourth. There were I think twelve logs. The men in the pit looked up at me as I placed the logs. The older man looked at me. I looked at him. Nobody spoke. (*Pause.*) When all the logs were placed, the pit was almost completely covered. There was a narrow gap at the end. The older man looked out at me through this gap. His lips were still moving silently.

> Short has been the life,
> many the vic-iss-it-udes,
> of the Uganda Railway . . .

The soldier who took my passport told me to place straw and soil onto the logs. People watching started to wail very quietly. The soldier who took my passport told me to hurry. He told two others to help me. We gathered up the straw and soil and covered the logs. (*Pause.*) Still the older man looked up through the narrow gap at the end of the logs. Once the soil and straw that I threw on the logs spilled down onto his face. The lips stopped for a second. Then started moving again.

> not a paper plan,
> or an airy dream,
> but an iron fact,
> grinding along through the jungle and the plain,
> waking with its whistles
> the silences of the Nyanza . . .

We finished covering the logs with the straw and soil. The people watching went silent again. The soldier who took my passport handed me a lighter. 'Light it', he said. 'Light the straw', he said. (*Pause.*) 'Light the straw'. 'I cannot light the straw' I said. 'Why not!? Do you know these men!?' (*Pause.*) 'No, I don't know anybody here.' (*Pause.*) The older man's eyes looked up at me through the gap at the end of the logs.

> Short has been the life,
> many the vicissitudes.

The soldier lit the straw himself. He lit it at four different points. The straw blazed. The logs began to smoke.

> Short has been the life,
> many the vicissitudes.
> Short has been the life,
> many the vicissitudes.

Lumps of burning soil fell through the logs onto the men in the pit. They screamed and coughed. Except the older man. He just moved his lips and looked at me. The prodigal son. Returning, laden with gifts. The soldier who took my passport led me to the part of the school where the roof still was. Smoke followed us. They strung me up *Kandooya* because I didn't burn the straw. (*Pause.*)

MARY. My God. Joseph! . . .

LEO. (*To Mary.*) Is this news to you as well!?

MARY. Joseph . . . why didn't you tell me? . . . (*Leo claps a small applause.*)

LEO. Six months to work on that one, Joseph. I'll hand it to

you. It's the best I've ever heard. But be warned, Joseph and Mary
. . . it won't get you asylum. Unless you can produce proof. And
that'll be impossible I'm willing to bet, isn't that right, Joseph!?

MARY. Jesus Christ! Have you no shred of humanity left!?

LEO. Have you no shred of savvy!? He's taking you for a ride.

JOSEPH. That's what happened. It's the truth.

LEO. The truth that suits. The same scam all over Europe.
Heart-wrenching stories like this being trotted out of every point
of entry. I've read them. Files full of them. With no documented
proof. Top of the hard-neck fiction list, Joseph!

MARY. What's happened to you, Leo!?

LEO. I'm trying to open your eyes to reality, Sis. You're being
used.

JOSEPH. You are the one being used, Leo. I think you know it.

LEO. He's using you for all he's worth. He may play the phi-
losopher, but his only interest is the betterment of Number One.
That's the only thing he loves, not his da, and certainly not you.
So don't fool yourself!

MARY. (To Bill.) Look at the hatred.

LEO. It's not hatred! It's ordinary streetwise commonsense!
You're so obsessed with carrying his baggage for him that you
can't even see it!

MARY. Carrying his baggage!?

LEO. It's embarassing. You want to be his mule.

MARY. I want to treat him like a human being. Is that a
crime!? Am I on a Europol suspect list for that!?

LEO. Ah, don't be hysterical!

MARY. I'm hysterical!?

LEO. You want to suffer with him . . . share his trials. It's the
worst kind of racism . . . you have him at your mercy and you
want to keep him there. He'll love it while it suits him . . . but
don't fool yourself . . . he doesn't love you.

MARY. After thirty years' experience of this family, I don't fool
myself about love. No fucking fear.

BILL. (To Leo.) You! Get out! Get out of my house! Take your
stuff and go!

LEO. (To Mary.) Now look what you've started. He's not able
for this kind of fuss. (To Bill.) It's alright. It's just an argument.

BILL. I never want to see you again. Do you understand me?
While I still breathe, I never want to set eyes on you again.

MARY. Dad, it's okay . . . I can handle him . . .

BILL. This man (*points to Joseph*) has expressed love for his father in terms like I've never heard before. My son's reaction is to seize him and try to stuff those words of love back down his throat.

LEO. Dad, you're missing the point . . .

BILL. You used this man's pain to pump your own ambition! You told me! The test! The immigrant's twists and turns. The stores about your father! How they thought you were great! Your ambition will bring you nothing but pain.

MARY. Careful, Dad, take it easy . . .

LEO. I didn't know this stuff about the burning pit . . . ah, for God's sake can't you see it's all a ploy!? Bravo Joseph, you're a maestro!

BILL. Get out! Go to Europe, go to Europol, and take your hatred with you. It's the same aggressive hatred that lost you your wife and your son.

LEO. That's enough now! Shut up!

BILL. I pray to God you didn't learn it from me.

LEO. (*To Mary, regarding Bill.*) He's all yours now. Good . . . luck! (*Leo turns on his heel and marches out.*) (*Pause. Mary throws the contents of the barbecue in the bin.*)

BILL. (*To Joseph.*) I'm sorry that my son attacked you like that. He used to be different. He's . . . I don't know . . . he's had his head turned. All I can say is . . . I apologise on account of my son's aggression.

JOSEPH. You have nothing . . . *nothing* to apologise for. I lost my father that day in Bucoro. You listened to me. You believed me.

MARY. Are you alright? . . .

JOSEPH. Am I alright!? . . . Yes. I think I'm alright. I feel . . . lighter. As if a rock has been lifted off my chest. My heart was tight. Now it feels . . . like it's loosening.

MARY. It was a heavy secret to carry around. You should have shared the burden earlier.

JOSEPH. Oh! You want to carry my baggage?

MARY. Ah shut up!

JOSEPH. You want to be my mule? . . .

MARY. Hee-haw! (*slight pause.*) So . . . what's the plan!? . . .

BILL. Joseph! Where are your bags?

JOSEPH. (*To Mary.*) Where are my bags?

MARY. They're in the hall. (*To Bill.*) Why?

BILL. (*To Joseph.*) Bring them upstairs to the empty backroom. If any of Leo's stuff is still there just dump it under the stairs.

MARY. Dad . . . are you sure? . . .

BILL. (*To Joseph.*) Go on. Get your bags.

MARY. Well, Joseph? Do you want to take up the offer? . . .

JOSEPH. You haven't lost a son, Bill. But if you want to gain a second son . . . I'm delighted to accept.

MARY. So! Hello Brother! I'm your sister! Welcome to the family!

BILL. (*To Joseph.*) Go on, will you!? What's keeping you!?

JOSEPH. There are conditions.

BILL. What conditions?

JOSEPH. I don't accept charity. We'll make a deal. I'll be your . . . your assistant, Bill. I'll be your house manager. In return you will provide me with food and lodgings. Do you accept my deal?

BILL. I accept. Now go on! (*Joseph exits. Pause.*)

MARY. That's very generous, Dad.

BILL. I left it late. It's about time I discovered how to show a bit of . . . you know . . .

MARY. Love.

BILL. Yeah. Come here, Mary. (*Mary goes to him. He embraces her and holds her for a long, long time.*)

BILL. I'm sorry about the red choo-choo and the blue choo-choo.

MARY. What I didn't know didn't hurt me.

BILL. But it's true. I only played it with Leo. What is that!? Helen used to stand at the bottom laughing at us. 'Don't let him fall', she'd say.

MARY. Well, Helen wasn't around once I arrived.

BILL. You're Helen's side, you know. The living spit.

MARY. The red choo-choo and the blue choo-choo didn't stand a chance. When you looked at me, you didn't think of play. You thought of her. And when you thought of her, it made you sad, because you thought of death.

BILL. I'm sorry, Mary.

MARY. It's alright now. I think I know that Joseph meant about his heart feeling looser. (*Kisses Bill.*) You're touching hearts, Dad!

BILL. A romantic in the end, what!? I bet Helen's having a laugh! Listen, what about Joseph!?

MARY. (*Quickly.*) He's just a client, but I do care about him.

BILL. Oh obviously, . . . but his asylum request. What happened to his father . . . that'll stand to him . . . it'd have to, wouldn't it!?

MARY. I'll have to try digging up proof . . . but it enhances his prospects.

BILL. My God! Enhances his prospects!

MARY. I know.

BILL. This crowd Leo's with are going to be aggressive.

MARY. They'll be well muzzled. Europe has a long liberal tradition. They're not going to lose it overnight.

BILL. You don't remember the bombing of the North Strand. I do. It happened overnight.

MARY. Ah, not the North Strand again, Dad! . . .

BILL. He's a grand son. God help him, it'd be awful to lose him.

MARY. You're trying, but you're still a son's father! . . . Ah well, we've come a long way in the short space of time.

BILL. Yeah.

MARY. 'Short has been the life, many the vic-iss-it-udes'.

BILL. What's that?

MARY. Of the red choo-choo and the blue choo-choo . . . (*Joseph reappears.*)

MARY. Well, Brother Joseph!? Settled in?

JOSEPH. I'm starting to feel at home, Sister Mary.

BILL. Good. (*Pause.*)

MARY. So. Do you want to go to bed, or will you accept my offer of a night on the town!?

BILL. Go on! Go out and celebrate, for God's sake! Why wouldn't you!?

JOSEPH. It's been a long time since I had a night on the town.

MARY. We better make it special then. I'll get ready. (*Mary goes upstairs.*)

BILL. That poem your father used to say . . .

JOSEPH. It wasn't a poem. It was a book. Churchill's *African Journey*.

BILL. About trains, yeah!?

JOSEPH. Some of it. The bits my father liked best. The Ugandan Railway.

BILL. The British built it!?

JOSEPH. Yeah. At the turn of the century. From Mombasa on the coast of Kenya to the shores of Lake Victoria.

BILL. Your father was a Churchill fan . . . ?

JOSEPH. My father used to fool that Churchill was his best friend. 'My friend Winston', he would say, 'was telling me the latest from the Railway . . .' and he'd begin! . . . (*Pause.*)

BILL. And was that . . . a popular thing to be saying? . . .

JOSEPH. Everybody laughed.

BILL. Everybody? . . .

JOSEPH. Bill, my father wasn't killed because he had an eccentric regard for Churchill's african journey.

BILL. Do you know why?

JOSEPH. No. (*Pause.*) They said a rebel uniform was found in his house.

BILL. Is that true?

JOSEPH. I don't know. If it is true, I don't know where the uniform came from. And I'm certain neither did he.

BILL. If you had said . . . who you were, they would have . . .

JOSEPH. Yes, Bill! They would have!

BILL. No way of explaining? . . .

JOSEPH. No. Not from a pit in the schoolyard in Bucoro. No way of explaining.

BILL. Like Saint Peter the Rock. The cock crew thrice. What could he do!? He didn't risk trying to explain.

JOSEPH. No. He didn't. (*Pillar enters.*)

PILLAR. Sorry folks. The door was open. I took the liberty.

BILL. Obviously.

PILLAR. How are you, Bill?

BILL. Not a bother.

JOSEPH. Hello, Pillar.

PILLAR. Sergeant Boylan, yeah. (*To Bill.*) I presume he's here at your behest.

BILL. He lives here.

PILLAR. (*To Joseph.*) Didn't waste time getting installed, what!?

JOSEPH. Do you have a purpose for your visit? Sergeant Boylan?

PILLAR. (*To Bill.*) Just dropped by to make sure you're alright, Bill . . . Leo going off and all that . . . I said I'd keep an eye . . .

BILL. There's no need. You're a busy man, Pillar . . .

PILLAR. Not so busy that I can't find time for the odd courtesy call. (*Mary enters, wearing red dress she wore the night she met Joseph.*)

MARY. Courtesy!? You might start by knocking before you enter.

PILLAR. Pretty dress. Nice colour. Reminds me of the good ol' Leeson Street days. Remember, Mary?

MARY. I think I prefer to forget!

JOSEPH. Good-bye, Sergeant Boylan. It's time for you to leave.

PILLAR. Working on the door . . . I'd be relatively sober, you see . . . I never forget.

BILL. Eh, Joseph, would you give me a hand up the stairs? I'm suddenly awful tired.

PILLAR. I'll do that, Bill.

JOSEPH. (*Holding Bill.*) I've got you . . . just take it step by step, (*Joseph helps Bill off.*)

PILLAR. Congratulations on the High Court win.

MARY. Thank you!

PILLAR. I couldn't believe it was the same Mary Gaughran I used to know so well.

MARY. You obviously didn't know me as well as you thought.

PILLAR. People who can advance themselves out of a rut always impress me.

MARY. I hope you meet one of them sometime.

PILLAR. I heard you gave up the jungle juice. You're wise. It never suited you. You tended to go gaga (*Pause.*) What does Leo think about him moving in?

MARY. Delighted, I'm sure.

PILLAR. It's a bit . . . compromising for Leo, isn't it!?

MARY. No. I can't see how it could be.

PILLAR. Looks bad.

MARY. How does it 'look bad'!?

PILLAR. Looks bad that you fobbed him off on your da! Why isn't he shacking up with you? You don't want him that close, what!? Look . . . don't touch!?

MARY. State your business and leave.

PILLAR. No business. Friendly call. But since you insist . . . I was on my way to deliver this to your office. Do you want to accept it now!? (*Pillar holds out an envelope. Mary takes it. She opens it and reads.*)

MARY. Rejected! On the day he's released from wrongful imprisonment, his asylum request is rejected!

PILLAR. If it was good news, you'd be waiting for years . . . it's always the way, isn't it!? . . .

MARY. No doubt your recommendation expedited the process. You can take it I'm appealing. I'll lodge it in the morning.

PILLAR. No hurry, Mary, no hurry! We're not going to expel him on the spot. Though I believe Leo's working on getting that procedure in place as soon as possible . . . (*Joseph reappears.*)

PILLAR. Sorry to burst your bubble, Mister Omara. I'm afraid you're getting the bum's rush.

MARY. Don't worry Joseph, I'm appealing it.

JOSEPH. I've been rejected!?

PILLAR. I'll bid my own adieu now if you don't mind. (*To Mary.*) Give my best to Bill. *Pillar leaves.*

PILLAR. (*Off.*) Don't let it spoil your night out, Mary! And stay away from that jungle juice . . . it's bad for you! (*Pause. Joseph and Mary slump down on the seat.*)

JOSEPH. (*Dispirited.*) Shit! (*Pause. Still dispirited.*) You look beautiful.

MARY. (*Depressed.*) So do you. You always have. From the first moment I saw you. There. I've said it. (*Pause.*)

JOSEPH. For six months in Mountjoy I kept myself alive by dreaming of spending tonight with you.

MARY. Wow! . . .

JOSEPH. I created a little fantasy in my head every night. I escaped into that fantasy . . . totally! It was as if you were there with me . . . always wearing that red dress . . .

MARY. Very honourable of you . . .

JOSEPH. . . at the beginning . . .

MARY. Auh-hauh! Well . . . I used to dream of what I'd like to do with you . . . when I'd lure you into telling me another story about when you were small. . . . . I loved the softness of the stories you told. It was far far far better than sex!

JOSEPH. Wow! . . . (*Pause.*) So who have you been having sex with!?

MARY. Ah . . . not worth remembering. (*Pause.*)

JOSEPH. What did they say?

MARY. Just grunts usually.

JOSEPH. The department, Mary . . .

MARY. Oh. No reason. They never give a reason.

JOSEPH. But the *Kandooya* marks . . . they know I was tortured.

MARY. The fruits of a life of crime, I suppose.

JOSEPH. What!?

MARY. They could argue that since you admitted to Leo you were smuggling . . . getting beaten up is a hazard of your chosen livelihood. The 'what did you expect' school of thought. Like, say, a prostitute claiming sexual harassment. That's not to say she wouldn't have a case. But how do you prove that the harassment is unconnected to the normal practice of the way she makes her living?

JOSEPH. Mary, what has my asylum case got to do with prostitutes?

MARY. It's all the same, you know!? 'What did you expect!?' Justice!? Look at Leo! Look at Pillar! Look who's calling the shots!? Oh God, Joseph, come on . . . let's go on a pub crawl and get completely rat-arsed! Then we'll take it from there!

JOSEPH. No. Let's stay here.

MARY. Why?

JOSEPH. We can look up at the stars.

MARY. In my father's backyard!?

JOSEPH. I haven't seen the stars for six months.

MARY. Okay. We'll do the stars. Any chance of a story while you're at it? . . .

JOSEPH. What kid of story would you like, Mary?

MARY. I don't mind.

JOSEPH. A story of me being small and soft and sweet . . . is that what you want?

MARY. Oh yes! That sounds wonderful!

JOSEPH. Joseph the Innocent. Joseph the Noble Savage. That's what you want, Mary. You don't want Joseph Omara the small-time smuggler who made his living out of what the fucking department calls crime.

MARY. That's where you're wrong!

JOSEPH. I've been a thief. I don't apologise. Even Christ said it is alright to steal if you're hungry. You don't want Joseph Omara the liar! You don't want Joseph Omara the coward! You don't want Joseph Omara who stayed silent hanging from a beam while my father burned alive! You only want the nice side of me . . .

MARY. That's not true!

JOSEPH. The soft side of me that makes you feel safe and a little bit superior!

MARY. Oh. And we haven't even had a drink! Well, if it comes to that, I'm not Mary the Competent Counsel twenty-four hours a day! I'm not always the Mary who listens sympathetically to your tragic past . . . and I do, Joseph, I do, and I am sympathetic and I will do anything to help you, . . . but most of the time I'm a messy kind of Mary who's actually weak sometimes in private, and who trembles inside with panic when she looks like she's at her coolest and most confident, and who cries on occasion for no fucking reason whatsoever, and who craves just the kind of gentleness that you manage to show when you tell your stories about when you were small . . . (*Pause.*)

JOSEPH. Have I told you the story my father used to tell of the time when he was a boy that a Chinaman came to Bucoro. A Chinaman with a Chinese hat and Chinese whiskers, on a bicycle. He taught my father how the Chinese fished by starlight, from a boat with a big bright dragon lantern on the back . . . to attract the fish, he said. They would tie a rope around a cormorant's neck and throw it in . . . (*Pause.*) I've always wondered how my father managed to understand such a long story from the Chinaman . . . (*Joseph and Mary almost kiss. Then they stand back from each other. Slow fade to blackout.*)

INTERVAL

ACT III

Months later. Pub.

PILLAR. A Grolsch by the neck and? . . .

MARY. Soda water.

PILLAR. Still don't trust yourself in my presence, what!? God knows what you'd do if you had a few inside you . . .

MARY. Exactly.

PILLAR. It's a pity that our encounters are always so fraught. There was a time . . .

MARY. Times change, for most of us.

PILLAR. You're telling me! (*Looks her up and down.*) Okay. I'm in an awkward situation.

MARY. You must be. Why else would you have asked to meet me?

PILLAR. Yeah, well. Leo's coming back next week . . . you know that?

MARY. No.

PILLAR. Oh. Family rift!?

MARY. No.

PILLAR. Well, I suppose I'll just barrel on with it!

MARY. Please do.

PILLAR. Off the record, right!?

MARY. As you wish.

PILLAR. Leo's coming back next week with his Europol unit. It's like they're doing a minitour of Europe, making sure that every country has the same procedures in the treatment of immigrants. Do you follow me?

MARY. (*Weary.*) Yes.

PILLAR. Right. Now you've got to start reading between the lines.

MARY. Oh, goody!

PILLAR. Mary, can I give you a tip?

MARY. By all means.

PILLAR. Learn to listen! You might be able to spare your African pal an unpleasant ordeal. (*Pause. Mary thinks about leaving, but she stays.*)

PILLAR. Read between the lines. Leo's under pressure. It only takes one leaky section in the walls of Fortress Europe and the flood of immigrants will pour in and swamp the Continent. Laugh if you like, but that's the way they think. I'm in the business. I know how it works. Europe thinks we're leaky. They want to see us plugged. They lean on Leo. Leo leans on us. The result is Operation Sweep. . . . All illegal aliens out before Leo and the Europol inspection team come next week. First priority are rejected asylum seekers. They're seen as chancers to be made an example of. They're all to be deported to country of origin, to deter any other chancers from trying the same scam. (*Pause.*) Your client Joseph is first in the exit queue.

MARY. But the appeal . . .

PILLAR. Rejected!

MARY. Jesus!

PILLAR. Leo's office sent us a list of countries they consider safe and democratic. Uganda's on it.

MARY. What list!? I'll appeal it!

PILLAR. No appeal! No further comeback!

MARY. There's got to be a comeback!

PILLAR. That list is the end of the line! He's got to go, Mary, (*Pause.*) You look like you could do with a drink.

MARY. Why are you telling me this?

PILLAR. I know your father's . . . low. I don't want to cause him unnecessary pain.

MARY. What's Dad got to do with it?

PILLAR. I have orders to forcibly deport your Ugandan. He resisted once before, you see, so that makes him a category A deportee. (*Pause.*) Do you know what that means, Mary? (*Pause.*) That means bursting into your father's house with five officers, a bodybelt, mouth tape and binding, pinning the Ugandan to the floor, parcelling him up, taking him to the airport and strapping him to a seat on a plane back home. It's a messy untidy business. (*Pause.*) I don't want to have to do that, Mary. (*Pause.*)

MARY. So what do you suggest?

PILLAR. There's another way of doing it.

MARY. What's that?

PILLAR. Quietly. Just me. I'll drive him out. No struggle. No bodybelt. No binding. Civilised behavior.

MARY. He won't go willingly. I know he won't.

PILLAR. He might if you advise him to. (*Pause.*)

MARY. There's another way. You could just fail to find him, couldn't you?

PILLAR. No way, Mary. The entire department is buzzing with the story that a rejected asylum seeker is living in Leo's father's house. Everybody knows he's there.

MARY. Yeah, but maybe he could get away before you raided the house.

PILLAR. They'd know I leaked it that he was to be deported.

I'd be accused of favouritism, I'd be blackballed, I'd be understandably annoyed, and in the end he'd get a special-treatment Category A depor-fucking-tation courtesy of Pillar Boylan! Pardon me, excuse my French! (*Pause.*) Are you reading between my lines, Mary?

MARY. I hardly need to.

PILLAR. No fancy stuff when the moment comes, okay? No injunction shit . . . if you want it quiet, it has to be clean.

MARY. Quiet and clean . . . like the best vacuum cleaners!

PILLAR. Yeah . . . Operation Sweep! (*Pause.*) You have to give me credit for leaving him alone as long as I did. I could have lifted him anytime. (*Pause.*)

MARY. Please don't take him, Pillar.

PILLAR. Poor Mary. You're a bad case.

MARY. I'm asking you for old times' sake. We must have spent a full two weeks on the skite back then. Some of it was a bloody good laugh, Pillar. Admit it, we made each other laugh.

PILLAR. You cried most of the time.

MARY. The early morning pubs always made me cry. Tired, that's all.

PILLAR. The good times weren't all they were cracked up to be.

MARY. I have some fond memories . . .

PILLAR. You've left that shite behind! Don't take me for a fool! I've seen you in court. The spirit! The fire! All that you didn't have in the messy days of six packs and naggins! You're a totally different woman!

MARY. Is that intended as a compliment?

PILLAR. What the fuck do you see in him!? Are you blind to the fact he's a chancer!?

MARY. If you're referring to my client, I think we've said enough.

PILLAR. I take it this means you want it the messy way.

MARY. Oh, no! Please! I'd much prefer the quiet and clean way! What time shall I expect you, Mr Sweep!?

PILLAR. Get a grip, for fuck's sake!

MARY. Ha-ha! Some things don't change, Pillar! People like you stay the very same!

PILLAR. Ten o'clock tonight. Ring me if you're interested. (*Pillar exits.*)

Bill's backyard. Bill is sitting over a chessboard. Mary enters.

MARY. Where's Joseph?

BILL. Gone to the shop for milk and bread. I was taking so long with my move . . . he's getting good, you know. Or maybe I'm just fading . . .

MARY. Which shop did he go to?

BILL. Down the corner, I suppose. He can't sit still. Up and down! In and out! All day every day . . . that's his way.

MARY. I know.

BILL. He'll be back in a minute. Sit down! I was telling him about the North Strand.

MARY. What?

BILL. The bombing of the North Strand.

MARY. You're obsessed with the bombing of the North Strand.

BILL. May 1941. Mammy gave me a terrible clatter for standing up at the window. The sky was lit by the flames. 'Get back in under the stairs', she said. Next morning the smell of the black smoke was everywhere. Mammy and I went down to have a look.

MARY. How long is Joseph gone?

BILL. The North Strand was gone. For a minute we couldn't figure out where the butcher's had been. It was just a jumble of burnt beams and the odd croooked girder sticking up. 'Oh, my God', Mammy said. Over and over again. 'Oh my God they never got out of that'.

MARY. I've heard it a million times, Dad . . .

BILL. Mary . . . I want to tell you this. I don't want it buried with me.

MARY. Ah, Dad!

BILL. They did, they did get out of it, because then Mammy saw Mrs Brietner up on the canal bridge with her daughter. Helen.

MARY. Helen? . . .

BILL. Helen Brietner. They were in a shocking state. 'Everything is gone', Mrs Brietner kep saying. She was going to the mater to visit the daddy. 'Would Helen like to stay with us?', Mammy said. (*Pause.*) And she did. She stayed for a week. For the first three days she was shy. She slept on the settle in the parlour. On the third night I had to get up and go down to get a drink of water. Dying with the thirst. (*Pause.*) Sitting on that settle under the window . . . whispering in the starlight, shivering, feet frozen, sharing the tablecloth, my pyjama-sleeve touching the puffed-out shoulder of her cotton nightdress every breath she took. (*Pause.*) You lot think you invented it. But you didn't. Helen did. Helen and I did, after the North Strand bombing.

MARY. Invented what?

BILL. Well, I wouldn't call it sex, because that sounds . . . rude. And I wouldn't call it love, because that sounds . . . pure. It was far beyond being either rude or pure. I don't think there's a word. Helen didn't think so either. (*Pause.*)

MARY. No wonder you loved to talk about the North Strand bombing. I always wrote it off as morbid fascination!

BILL. Now. You can tell it to yours when the time comes. So they'll know where they came from . . . out of the ashes of the North Strand fires!

MARY. Unlikely, Dad . . .

BILL. Oh, things are changing all the time. You never know what's around the next corner . . . (*Joseph enters.*)

BILL. For example . . . who would ever have thought an African would be beating Bill Gaughran at chess in his own backyard!?

JOSEPH. (*To Mary.*) He tries to goad me with the white man's wiles! He lures me into a sense of security! (*To Bill.*) It's not going to work! You have oppressed me long enough! You have defeated me for the last time! The African will rise up! His day will come! Have you made your move yet?

BILL. Just a minute now . . . burrow-wurrow . . .

MARY. What!?

JOSEPH. Don't listen to him! He's up to his tricks.

BILL. Burrulum! That's it . . . come on . . . Burrulum!

JOSEPH. Huma!

BILL. Burrulum!

JOSEPH. Huma!

MARY. Joseph . . . can I talk to you?

BILL. Just a minute! Burrulum!

JOSEPH. Huma!

MARY. What the hell is that?

BILL. Churchill in Uganda . . . tell her the story, Joseph!

JOSEPH. No! You're trying to distract me.

BILL. Churchill was carried by rickshaw from . . . where?

JOSEPH. From Entebbe to Kampala.

BILL. (*To Mary*.) Another of his da's favourites . . .

JOSEPH. Mounted in this light bicycle-wheeled carriage
      drawn by one man between the shafts
      and pushed by three more from behind,
      we were able to make more than six miles an hour
      in . . . very . . . comfortable . . . style.

BILL. Gas. The neck of it. Gas. Go on.

JOSEPH. From the moment their labour begins,
      the rickshaw boys embark
      upon an ever-varying but absolutely interminable
      . . .
      (*Joseph and Bill*.) an . . . ti . . . phony

JOSEPH. Which, if it exhausts their breath,
      serves undoubtedly to keep their spirits up.

Burrulum!

BILL. Huma!

JOSEPH. Burrulum!

BILL. Huma! (*To Mary*.) Do you know what they were saying!?

MARY. No idea.

BILL. Iron upon wood! Iron upon wood! Very, very clever!

MARY. Iron upon wood . . .

BILL. (*To Joseph*.) Explain it to Mary . . .

JOSEPH. The iron of European strength and skill . . .
      (*Joseph/Bill*.) However superior! . . .

JOSEPH. Yet cannot get along without the wood of native la-
      bour and endurance.

BILL. Burrulum!

JOSEPH. Huma!

BILL. Burrulum! (*Pause*.)

JOSEPH. (*To Mary*.) You're right. It's a stupid story.

BILL. It's a great story! Putting one over on Churchill! Four
young black lads!

JOSEPH. Bill! They were still carrying the bastard!

BILL. Still. They were making a fool of him.

JOSEPH. 'Burrulum huma! Iron upon wood . . . tee-hee-hee!
How many more miles must we carry the stupid fat bwana!?'

Churchill carved a wound through Africa on that journey, and it's still pumping blood. Funny!? It's like looking down and laughing at your own disembowelment.

BILL. I see. Not a laughing matter, what!?

JOSEPH. (*Looking at Mary.*) It's enough to make one cry! Times have changed. Europe's iron doesn't want the wood of African labour and endurance any more. Not in Europe anyway, thank you very much, isn't that right, Mary? (*Pause.*)

BILL. I think I'll go up for a lie-down . . . while I consider my next master move to bamboozle the African.

JOSEPH. I'll help you.

BILL. No. Stay here. I'll be alright. I'd rather do it myself. (*Bill stands up and moves unsteadily and slowly to the door, holding on to the wall for support.*)

BILL. We'll finish the game inside later, Joseph. (*Pause.*) You two get the last of the evening sun. (*Pause.*) The stars will be out soon. It's still warm enough to sit in the starlight. (*Bill exits, Pause.*)

JOSEPH. Stars again!

MARY. Yeah. (*Pause.*)

MARY. How's the heart, Brother Joseph!?

JOSEPH. Fast.

MARY. And loose?

JOSEPH. Yeah. Fast and loose. How's yours, Sister Mary?

MARY. Oh . . . bursting! Away beyond being either rude or pure. (*Pause.*)

JOSEPH. Mine too.

MARY. Yeah?

JOSEPH. Most definitely! (*Pause.*) We'll have the stars soon. You want to share the tablecloth in the moonlight? . . . (*Pause.*)

MARY. You've opened his heart, Joseph. He told the story so softly and sweetly it made me want to cry.

JOSEPH. You can cry now, Mary . . .

MARY. They're going to deport you back, Joseph. I was talking to Pillar. The appeal's been turned down.

JOSEPH. What!?

MARY. They're kicking out all rejected asylum seekers. Leo's ordered it.

JOSEPH. Leo's kicking me out!?

MARY. There's nothing I can do to stop it. They're within their rights in European law. I could get an injunction to delay it by a day or two, but that'll only make it worse for you.

JOSEPH. Worse!?

MARY. Pillar says he'll deport you himself if you go willingly. Otherwise they'll tie you up and gag you like a lunatic.

JOSEPH. Nobody is going to gie me up!

MARY. That's right. It's better to arrive at the other end like an ordinary passenger.

JOSEPH. An ordinary passenger!?

MARY. It's the only way, Joseph! When Pillar comes cooperate with him . . . please! (*pause.*)

JOSEPH. You've made a deal behind my back.

MARY. Joseph . . .

JOSEPH. You've made a deal on my behalf! You didn't even consult me!

MARY. No. I haven't made a deal.

JOSEPH. Your old flame Pillar's coming here expecting me to purr like a kitten on his lap all the way to the airport!

MARY. The situation has been forced on both of us. I'm giving you my best advice! Don't see me as an enemy!

JOSEPH. You've turned against me. We could have run away together.

MARY. What!? Don't make me laugh!

JOSEPH. We could have fled together to the mountains, to some wild part of the country.

MARY. I'd have done that long ago if I thought you had the slightest interest! I'd have grown wings to bear you . . .

JOSEPH. If you had thought it right to give me some control over my destiny . . . human independence . . . we could have planned a way to . . .

MARY. What!? A ride out of here on Churchill's jungle railway to the land of Love and Dreams!? Okay! Let's go! Don't worry . . . you'll merge into the background no matter where we go . . . Termonfeckin, Ballymote, Knocknagoshel, Timahoe . . . who'll ever think to look at us twice!? Joseph! You're black!

JOSEPH. I know it well!

MARY. You can't hide here!

JOSEPH. I've been hiding all my life! That's how I've survived!

MARY. Within two days Pillar will take you in, and when he does you'll realise too late the stupid mistake you've made.

JOSEPH. You want me to sit back and let myself be sent to hell!?

MARY. No! But if it means staying alive then . . .

JOSEPH. I cannot do that! It's like submitting to slavery. It's worse! Like kissing the slave trader's feet! (*Pillar enters.*)

PILLAR. Jaysus! I thought you wanted it quiet!

MARY. You said ten o'clock!

PILLAR. Sorry! Busy times! Blame Leo for the pressure!

MARY. You said . . .

PILLAR. If you want to do this quietly without upsetting Bill I'll wait in here for two minutes to let you say your good-byes. Make your mind up!

JOSEPH. (*To Pillar.*) You shut your mouth! Get out! Get out of my sight!

MARY. You'll have to wait! Wait inside! (*Pause.*)

PILLAR. Two minutes max! (*Pillar goes inside.*)

MARY. Joseph! What choice have we got!?

JOSEPH. I've been given none!

MARY. You'll go with Pillar, won't you?

JOSEPH. I did what I was told in Bucoro! I dug a pit! I covered it with logs! I looked at my father's face as if it was a stone!

MARY. Your father understood! He forgives you!

JOSEPH. I took the easy choice to save my skin.

MARY. It was your only choice, Joseph! Just like now! Do as he says!

JOSEPH. No! I will not do it!

PILLAR. (*Off.*) Make it snappy folks! I've got to move!

MARY. Listen to me, Joseph! There's a way we haven't tried. It's mad but I don't care. We make a solemn declaration that we intend to marry! Fuck it! I could get an injunction on the strength of that. What's stopping us!? To hell with dignity, propriety, and all the rest! You could stay! We'd be together! You said your heart is bursting! What do you say!? I could tell him now. Even if he takes you, I'd get an injunction to the airport before the plane takes off.

JOSEPH. I can't.

MARY. Why not!?

JOSEPH. I can't accept marriage as an act of charity from you, Mary.

MARY. Who said anything about charity!? The charity would be to me! Drop your sense of honour for a moment!

JOSEPH. I love you, Mary . . .

MARY. Then let's do it!

JOSEPH. I want to join my life to yours . . . I have dreamed about it. How I bring that about is a matter of honour to me. I will not do it with a chain around my neck . . . the bond of the slave. I want to come to you with strength, with pride, with freedom, and with a future. (*Pillar steps in.*)

PILLAR. I have to break it up, folks. Time's up . . . or I'll have to call the squad. (*Joseph and Mary kiss.*)

PILLAR. Has he any bags? I'll let him take a bag. (*Pillar takes handcuffs from his case.*)

PILLAR. Now! Come one! You've stalled long enough. I have to insist on handcuffs.

JOSEPH. Handcuffs?

PILLAR. Come on! Don't act the innocent!

JOSEPH. You will not put bonds on my wrists! I will go of my own free will.

PILLAR. (*To Mary.*) Explain to him!

JOSEPH. You will not tie my hands!

MARY. (*To Pillar.*) He's given his word of honour.

JOSEPH. Don't let him tie me *Kandooya!* Stop him, Mary! Don't let him do it to me! (*Pillar reaches for his mobile.*)

PILLAR. Right! I'll call the squad.

MARY. Joseph, it's just handcuffs. Maybe it's worth it . . .

JOSEPH. Do you think so, Mary!? Is that your considered counsel!?

MARY. I don't want to see you hurt!

PILLAR. Save yourself an ordeal, Joseph!

JOSEPH. (*To Mary.*) Don't you want to tighten them around my wrists!? Perhaps another kiss while you're doing it!?

PILLAR. Don't be toublesome! She's only trying to help you. Wasting her sweetness if you ask me!

JOSEPH. Nobody asked you!

PILLAR. Last chance! The cuffs . . . or the recommended treatment from the squad outside. (*Pillar advances. He suddenly lunges and turns Joseph face against the wall. He pins his arms high up behind him. Joseph screams. Pillar clasps the handcuffs on his wrists. Mary tries to pull Pillar off him.*)

MARY. (*Screams.*) Don't! His arms! He was tortured!

PILLAR. Nothing compared to what I'm saving him from. He should be on his knees thanking me! (*Shouts.*) For fuck's sake! I'm trying to be civilised! (*Leo enters. He carries a bodybelt with handcuffs attached and a roll of gaffer-tape binding.*)

LEO. Pillar!

MARY. Stop him, Leo! He's hurting him!

PILLAR. Jesus! The prodigal returns! I thought you weren't due 'til next week.

MARY. (*To Leo.*) This is your doing! I hope you're proud of yourself!

LEO. (*To Pillar.*) What are you doing, Pillar!?

PILLAR. Deportation.

JOSEPH. You've got blood on your hands, Leo! Send me back and you've got blood on your hands!

PILLAR. Stop the whining! Uganda's not that bad!

MARY. Leo! Even *you* can see the monstrosity of this!

JOSEPH. Leo and Pillar! Come to Uganda with me! Come to Bucoro! Come to the schoolyard. I'll show you a pit! There is a smell of smoke! Explain to the people! Tell them I didn't light the logs. Tell them I only dug the pit! Tell the brothers of the four that were burned with my father. Tell them it wasn't me who burned them! Leo, you're a big man in the Europol. Tell them and see if they believe you!

PILLAR. Nothing but the same old yarn! We don't believe you! You're a chancer!

JOSEPH. And tell the army that I never saw Bucoro in my life! I've never seen the schoolyard! Tell them I said there never was a school in Bucoro. There never was a teacher. I never knew my father! Tell them and see if they believe you!

MARY. (*Quietly.*) Help him, Leo!

LEO. Why the handcuffs Pillar!?

PILLAR. It's fucking obvious!

LEO. He's category A!

PILLAR. I know he's category A but . . .

LEO. But what!?

PILLAR. I didn't want to upset your dad by giving him the full works.

LEO. Follow regulations!

PILLAR. I love the 'old friends' attitude, Leo. I'm glad success hasn't gone to your head.

LEO. This is a category A deportee. Why is this man only in handcuffs?

MARY. Jesus!

PILLAR. Can we talk about this inside?

LEO. No. Take the handcuffs off! (*Pillar unlocks the handcuffs.*)

PILLAR. Leo . . .

MARY. What do you intend to do with my client!?

JOSEPH. Not anymore! I'm not your client anymore! Count your thirty pieces!

LEO. There are regulations governing the deportation of illegal immigrants. (*To Pillar.*) Put the bodybelt on him! (*Leo throws the bodybelt down.*)

MARY. Pillar and I have reached an agree . . .

PILLAR. Okay, Leo, I'll do it by the book.

MARY. (*To Pillar.*) We have a deal!

PILLAR. Bullshit! I follow orders.

JOSEPH. (*To Mary.*) You admit it!

LEO. And orders are given for a reason! (*Joseph spits in Mary's direction.*)

MARY. (*To Joseph.*) Damn you! I'm trying to help you! (*Mary storms inside.*)

PILLAR. (*Picking up bodybelt.*) You got this from the lads outside?

LEO. Put the bodybelt on the deportee!

PILLAR. Don't push me, Leo! I've had as much of this bullshit as I can take!

LEO. Follow regulations! You're instructed to use force!

PILLAR. Alright I'll call the squad in.

LEO. No need! There's two of us.

JOSEPH. Nobody will ever tie me up alive!

PILLAR. Leo, let me take this fella to the airport and then we'll go for a jar . . .

LEO. Maybe. Now put the bodybelt and binding on him.

PILLAR. Why not let him come quietly!? It's easier.

LEO. It makes your life easier!? Is that the criterion for enforcement of the immigration barrier in Ireland?

PILLAR. Why be deliberately aggressive!?

LEO. Because the only way to get to zero immigration is to instil fear as a deterrent. Fear! Fear of the bodybelt! Fear of the gag! Fear of being bound! Fear for your life.

PILLAR. Okay . . . in extreme cases.

LEO. He's an extreme case.

PILLAR. No, he's not.

LEO. He's resisted a deportation. He's a bogus asylum seeker. He's an extreme case.

PILLAR. I don't think it's necessary.

LEO. It is necessary. To follow policy, it's necessary.

PILLAR. It's counterproductive. Use the carrot instead of the stick.

LEO. The stick is what's required by regulation. Do it!

PILLAR. No!

LEO. Put the bodybelt on him and gag him!

PILLAR. No!

LEO. Why not!?

PILLAR. I just won't!

LEO. (*Shouts.*) You think it's cruel!

PILLAR. (*Shouts.*) Yeah I think it's cruel!

LEO. (*Shouts.*) So do I!

JOSEPH. Nobody will tie me! You will have to kill me first!

LEO. Now. Uganda is safe and democratic. There is no such thing as a Ugandan refugee. That's official. This man is not a refugee. He is a mere economic migrant. He has already resisted a deportation. He must be bound and gagged and returned to where he came from! In accordance with regulations!

PILLAR. Fuck you and your regulations!

LEO. (*Grabbing him.*) What did you say!?

PILLAR. I said 'fuck you and your regulations'. They're a heap of shite. (*Leo suddenly embraces Pillar tightly.*)

LEO. That's right, Pillar! You've said it yourself!

PILLAR. What the fuck has happened to you? (*Pause.*)

LEO. Three nights ago I was in a shitty suburb off the ringroad round Berlin. It was raining cats and dogs. A shitty night in a shitty place. I was in the surveillance van . . . all mod. cons., cameras, videos, zoom lens, telescopic sights, infrared, state of the art stuff. Jesus, Pillar, it's a branchman's dream! We were observing an immigrants' hostel . . . a grey block in the middle of mud . . . getting ready to move in and arrest the illegals. We had riot police backup just behind us.

PILLAR. Tell me over a pint later tonight. (*Pillar moves towards Joseph again. Leo steps between them.*)

LEO. The Chief was all excited . . . biggest joint operation yet . . . Europol cutting its teeth. He was shaking with excitement.

PILLAR. I don't have time to listen to this!

LEO. Next thing a noise! We swung the cameras round. A crowd of thousands was coming over the motorway bridge. I shouted at the Chief to come and look . . . I had it on my monitor. The crowd started running towards the hostel. Then a rain of bricks. Within thirty seconds every window in the hostel block was smashed. Then the petrol bombs flew. Whuh! Whuh! Whuh! Blazing curtains hanging out of windows. The lights went out. The Chief kept gawking at the monitors. I switched to infrared. Flames spread through the floors. I could see people running up the stairwell dragging children. I panned along the top floor. Through the open doors of the flats I could see them crammed in the top corridor. Two of them were trying to break through the hatch to the rooftop. They were swinging hatchets at the bolt. I could see the screams in the faces of the children watching. One girl ran to a window and jumped. Fourth floor. The crowd cheered. Six or seven of the crowd climbed the fire escape ladder onto the roof. They danced and jumped on the hatch the immigrants were trying to raise. The flames reached the top of the stairwell. I panned along the top floor again. Now the windows were packed with men, women, and children leaning out for air. The men on the roof pelted them with bricks. The Chief said nothing. We continued to gawk. I panned across to the last flat. A man stood there, looking out. I felt he was looking at me. The flames burst through the door of his flat. He still didn't move. Smoke filled his room. His lips formed words. I zoomed in. 'Short has been the life', I swear to you Joseph, 'many the vicissitudes', he spoke the words silently, 'of the Uganda Railway'.

JOSEPH. Liar!

LEO. Tall like a giant, thin like a leaf.

JOSEPH. What are you trying to tell me!? That my father isn't dead!? I know he's dead! I saw him burn!

LEO. The man I saw in the pit in Bucoro I saw again in Berlin.

JOSEPH. No you didn't!

LEO. I saw him in the burning block. Young thugs danced on the hatches over his head. I watched until the smoke engulfed him.

JOSEPH. The smoke got into your brain, you stupid fool!

PILLAR. I think you're agitating my deportee.

LEO. The riot squad formed a path through the crowd to get the hostel residents out. I watched. The tall man in the last flat never left the block (Pause.) I asked the Chief why we let it happen. He sighed. He acted sad. 'Because fear is the only deterrent', he said. 'Fear is the only thing they understand!'

PILLAR. That's very deep, Leo.

LEO. That's why you have been ordered to bind and gag this man and deport him to Uganda.

PILLAR. It's a bit late to be finding out you haven't got the bottle for the job.

LEO. Bottle!? . . .

PILLAR. Now I'm going to deport this illegal. Humanely. In the way that I intended.

JOSEPH. No!

LEO. You said the regulations were bullshit.

PILLAR. They are. That's why I'm ignoring them.

LEO. You said they were cruel. You can't turn your nose up at the regulations while you accept the basis that they're built on.

PILLAR. What's the basis?

LEO. Fear! Fear is the only deterrent! That's the basis, Pillar! That's what we're paid for! That's the basis of the whole fucking thing!

PILLAR. No, it's not! Survival is! Survival of the fittest! That's the basis! Everybody knows it's a jungle! What you have you hold! That goes for anywhere! Here! Berlin! Or fucking Omaraland-Bucoroganda! I know my job is dirty work. Keeping the streets clean . . . call a spade a spade! But it's an essential job in the running of a country! Thanks be to Jaysus for that! I'm not ashamed! (*Points at Joseph.*) And neither would he if he was me! I'm proud of my work!

LEO. Proud!? Proud that you provoke fear!? (*Leo takes up the bodybelt.*)

PILLAR. Fear my arse!

LEO. Proud to force someone into one of these!? Proud to slam gaffer tape on mouths to stifle their screams!? (*Leo makes as if to place the gaffer tape on Pillar's mouth. Pillar pushes him off.*)

PILLAR. You've hit the road to Damascus with a big fucking bang! Were you knocked off your horse!?

LEO. And I saw the flash of flame! A blazing block of flats! Kids bawled from the windows! Fucking bawled! One jumped! People stood and cheered! We're marking them! We're impounding them in camps! We're forcibly transporting them! We're calling it a solution! It's domination by fear! It happened once before . . . Dad remembers. It's happening again.

PILLAR. For fuck's sake, I'm Doctor fucking Mengele now! Right! Put your money where your mouth is! Throw you dad out on the side of the road! Give the whole fucking lot, lock, stock, and barrel, to Joseph's folks . . . you know the family well, the Omaras of Uganda! That's what you're saying! Take from your own and give it to them! Go on! Release Omara and give me your dad! That's it in black and white!

LEO. I've come home to tell my dad I saw the man I didn't believe in. He was burnt to death for the second time while I watched in Berlin. Can you explain that in black and white, Pillar?

PILLAR. You need a long rest, Leo. Now I've got a job to do. Any interference and I'm charging you with obstructing in the course of duty.

JOSEPH. Did he call my name, Leo?

LEO. No. But he whispered something else.

JOSEPH. What else did he whisper, Leo?

LEO. The red choo-choo and the blue choo-choo.

JOSEPH. Was he laughing?

LEO. He was smiling.

PILLAR. (*To Joseph, holding up handcuffs.*) Come on! Hands!

LEO. Joseph, you can go. (*Pause.*)

PILLAR. Over my dead body!

LEO. I'm ordering you to let this man walk out of here free. (*Pause.*)

PILLAR. I'd need that in writing from HQ, Leo. *Bill enters . . .*
stands in door.

BILL. Joseph, come on! Here's your bag.

PILLAR. I'm on duty here, Bill!

JOSEPH. My father is resting, Bill. Leo brought me the news.

BILL. Walk out the door, Joseph! Quickly!

PILLAR. (*Eyes on Leo.*) Move a muscle Joseph and you're dead
meat.

BILL. Leo's told you you're free. He's the boss. Come on! Out
the front!

PILLAR. I tried to spare you this disturbance, Bill.

BILL. Joseph, much as I've enjoyed your company, I'l be glad
to put up with the consequences of your next bold move! Go!
Huma!

JOSEPH. Burrulum!

BILL. Huma!

PILLAR. There's a squad of front-row heavies sitting in a car
fifty yards away. Step into the street and you're sandwich meat,
Joseph.

LEO. Run, Joseph!

JOSEPH. Run!? Where am I supposed to run to?

LEO. Disappear into the city. Like you said you could.

JOSEPH. Disappear!? (*Mary enters, stands in doorway.*)

MARY. Termonfeckin. Ballymote. Come on!

PILLAR. I'll write this off as a practical joke. Leo, ring the
Chief! Say you've been sick for a couple of days! Give it a shot!
Hang on to the job! Now take your dad upstairs while I finish
this!

MARY. Through the forest, Joseph!

BILL. Through the ravines!

JOSEPH. Burrulum!

BILL. Huma! Huma! (*Joseph runs for the door. He and Mary*
disappear.)

BILL. (*Blocking doorway.*) Did I ever tell you about the bombing of the North Strand, Pillar?

PILLAR. Leo! Leo!

LEO. Don't Pillar! He's sick. (*Pillar reaches for his mobile.*)

BILL. Mammy brought us all in under the stairs. Laughing and
giggling we were.

David Herlihy, Jane Brennan, Conor MacDermottroe, and Dave
Fishley in *Asylum! Asylum!*, by Donal O'Kelly.
Courtesy Amelia Stein.

PILLAR. (*Into mobile.*) They're out! Move it! Use force!

BILL. The bombers came down from Marino and Ballybough.
Then the windows shook.

PILLAR. Leo! Tell him to move!

BILL. Then the bombs! Pig-ignorant bombs, Pillar! Falling on
the sleeping people! Shocking what they did!

PILLAR. Tell him Leo! He's obstructing! (*Pillar grabs Bill and
throws him into Leo's arms. Pillar exits.*)

BILL. Where's your walky-talky!? Countermand his order!

LEO. I can't, Dad. I've blown it.

BILL. You've blown it sky fucking high, Leo! And thanks be to God for that! (*Blackout.*)

Lights up on Mary in Santry Garda Station. Nighttime. Bill visits.

BILL. Pillar rang from the airport just as I left the house. (*Pause.*)

MARY. What did he want?

BILL. He wanted to know was I going to go bail for you.

MARY. What did you say?

BILL. I didn't come down in the last shower, Mary. (*Pause.*) He was stuttering. Never heard him stuttering before.

MARY. He's terrified! Good! First taste, Pillar.

BILL. You'll be kept in Mountjoy tonight . . .

MARY. I know. Court case tomorrow morning.

BILL. You're going to defend yourself.

MARY. Yes.

BILL. You're determined?

MARY. Yes.

BILL. So is Leo.

MARY. What's he doing?

BILL. He's resigned. He's making up a statement for the papers. (*Pause.*) None of this is going to bring Joseph back.

MARY. There were crayons on the floor.

BILL. Where, Mary?

MARY. Here. This is the room where I first met him. He talked about his father carrying him to bed. They carried him today. Pillar carried him. Jesus!

BILL. Did they hurt him?

MARY. They caught us outside the shop on the corner. They pulled him onto the kerb. One of them sat on his head. There was a choc-ice stuck to his hair. A little girl had dropped it. She was watching. She was crying. He tried to pick the choc-ice out of his hair. They wouldn't let him move. Pillar came then. He cut Joseph's nose with the bodybelt. I bit him. I bit him in the face. Joseph screamed about *Kandooya*. He screamed in his village language, I think. He was gone delirious. The little girl screamed. Pillar put the gaffer tape on Joseph's mouth. Joseph tried to kick. They tied his legs together with the tape. They picked him up like a rolled-up carpet that buckled and bent. He struggled. He tried to scream. He made a funny long cartoony noise while they shoved him in the car. Two of them sat on him in the back. Then he went still. I was trying to shove his shoe back on. Stupid. His feet went limp. Jesus! His foot just flopped. Pillar tore the gaffer tape off. He gave him mouth-to-mouth. Huff and puff. He was squatting on him in the back of the car. Joseph's feet were sticking out under Pillar's arse. Pillar huffed and puffed. Then he hit him. He thumped him on the chest. Joseph cried. Pillar ordered one of them to call a doctor to the airport. He shoved me away. I knocked down the little girl who dropped the choc-ice. It was still on the side of Joseph's face. A bit of spit ran from his mouth and stuck to the stick. Pillar pulled the door and they drove away.

BILL. He's gone. Leo says he's in Stansted. Waiting for a connection. Maybe in transit by now. (*Pillar enters. He has a bandage dressing on the side of his face.*)

PILLAR. (*To Mary.*) Out!

MARY. Don't address me in that tone of voice!

PILLAR. You're free to go.

MARY. Out on bail!? Who paid!?

PILLAR. No need for bail. Charges dropped. Take it as a favour. (*Pause Bill and Mary communicate silently.*)

PILLAR. And Mary!? No need to apologise for the assault. I can understand how upset you must have been. (*Pause.*) If there's a sudden attack of media interest in our . . . incident, I'll have to explain who inflicted the wound. You couldn't expect me to lie! (*Pause.*) I didn't enjoy doing what I had to do today. I did the best I could in the circumstances. In your heart of hearts you know that, Mary. (*Pause.*) Now! Look after your dad! He's had a very full day. (*Pillar exits. Bill and Mary stay sitting. Mary starts to smile.*)

MARY. I'm not leaving.

BILL. Neither am I. (*Fade to blackout.*)

END OF PLAY

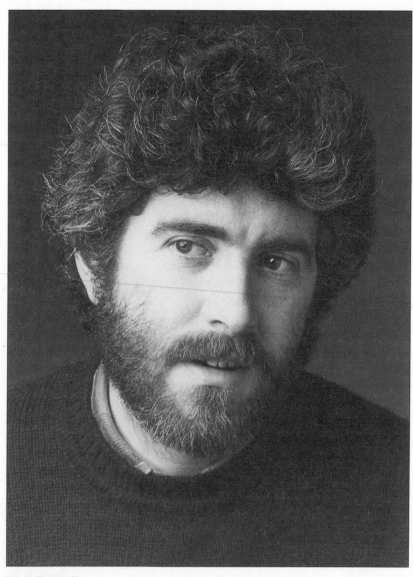

Neil Donnelly.

The Duty Master

NEIL DONNELLY

1995

Characters

PATRICK O'ROURKE, English master, in his forties
SARAH O'ROURKE, art lecturer, in her forties
PIPPA O'ROURKE, schoolgirl, twelve
MICHAEL O'ROURKE, farmer, in his forties
BREDA MAHON, student, twenty-two
ESTELLE HILTON, school secretary, in her thirties
BOB SMEDLEY, housemaster, in his fifties
MARK BAKER, sixth-form student, eighteen
GARY WILLIAMS, sixth-form student, eighteen
MICHAEL ANTHONY BRACE, sixth-form student, eighteen
FIONA CHESTERMAN-BOYD, sixth-form student, eighteen
ANNABEL BRIDGER, assistant gallery curator, twenty
SUZI ZOLLINGER, newspaper reporter, twenty
WAITERS/WAITRESSES

Scenes

ACT I
1. *Cricket field, a late afternoon in June*
2. *Sitting room, later that evening*
3. *Courtyard, following morning*
4. *School secretary's office, the same morning*
5. *Art gallery/café, early evening*
6. *Sitting room, later that night*

ACT II
1. *Sitting room, continuing that night*
2. *Courtyard, following morning*

176

3. *School secretary's office, the same morning*
4. *Sitting room, mid-morning*
5. *Housemaster's study, late morning*
6. *Art gallery/café, lunchtime*
7. *School secretary's office, late afternoon*
8. *Sitting room, later that night*

The action of the play takes place in and around a public school for boys in Leicestershire, England.

'At back' *is the rear where all slow motion tableau occur.*

ACT I

Cricket field. At back, three youths in cricket whites in a slow motion tableau cricket scene, while in front Patrick O'Rourke, in his forties, in cricket whites, sits on a bench shining a ball. Bach choral music in distance, off. Bob Smedley, in his fifties, enters. He wears casual slacks, sports jacket, etc. The three youths exit, at back.

PATRICK. Ah, Bob, good afternoon.

BOB. Patrick. (*Bob is listening to the music and singing along quietly.*)

PATRICK. Are you going to watch our cricket match?

BOB. It is a blessed relief that I no longer have to participate in these bloodlettings.

PATRICK. If I should declare myself unfit, then you could be drafted in as my replacement.

BOB. Oh, no, I have a prior commitment to my Bach rehearsal. Music is so therapeutic, and after the news I've just had I certainly need my rehearsal.

PATRICK. Oh, bad news then?

BOB. I'm in the doldrums.

PATRICK. Bob, what is it?

BOB. My most recent conversation with the Headmaster.

PATRICK. What has he said to you now.

BOB. He summoned me to his office for what he politely called a powwow. Froggy wants to move my geography department from the front of the school building around to the back, down beside the lockup garages.

PATRICK. But why?

BOB. He wants to turn my present classroom into a new gymnasium.

PATRICK. Throw a few of your famous leg breaks.

BOB. Froggy contends that a new gymnasium would present a more positive image to prospective parents. But also, with me being positioned at the back of the school, I won't be available to take the parents round. And the most shocking part of all is that Froggy wishes to conduct this tour himself.

PATRICK. That would be commercial suicide.

BOB. I could not express my disbelief and horror at this news.

PATRICK. His conducted tour would be dull and drab. He doesn't have any of your personality, Bob.

BOB. Many of the parents told me in later years that it was my introductory talk as I showed them round the school that decided it for them.

PATRICK. Froggy will soon learn the error of his ways.

BOB. Perhaps you're right.

PATRICK. Come on, Bob, I'm getting a cold waiting for you to bowl. (*Bob is ready to bowl but stops as a female voice sings off.*)

BOB. Isn't her voice magnificent!

PATRICK. Who is she?

BOB. She's the new musical director behind this year's Bach Festival. Her name is Melanie Warnock-Cooke. She doesn't wear a wedding ring. Though I doubt a woman like her wouldn't have a man tucked away in a cottage somewhere. I sing very nervously in her presence.

PATRICK. Why aren't you in the chapel rehearsing with the others?

BOB. She's rehearsing sopranos and tenors first, then later she will have us baritones. (*Two youths in cricket whites enter. They are Gary Williams and Mark Baker. Williams has pads on, Baker has an umpire's white coat.*)

WILLIAMS. Mr Smedley, will you be our umpire?

BOB. I thought Mr Brown was doing it.

BAKER. He was, sir, but he had to take his wife to hospital, she's having a baby.

BOB. I'd love to help, but I'm due to attend a rehearsal in a matter of moments.

WILLIAMS. (*Mimicking.*) "In a matter of moments".

BOB. Be careful, Williams, mocking can be catching. (*Williams laughs, signals to Baker, who slips the white coat on Bob.*)

WILLIAMS. Thank you, sir, we knew you'd say yes.

BOB. I did not say yes.

WILLIAMS. He could be mistaken for Dickie Bird, couldn't he Mr O'Rourke?

PATRICK. He looks the perfect umpire.

BOB. I am unavailable for umprie. (*He removes the white coat and throws it on the ground.*) I am awaiting my call to rehearsal.

WILLIAMS. You're always rehearsing, sir.

BOB. Anything wrong with that?

WILLIAMS. Nothing, sir, but when's the performance?

BOB. Williams, don't become too clever, it's unbecoming for you. (*Williams laughs, scoops the ball up, bowls it towards Patrick, and grabs the white coat from the ground and tosses it to Baker.*)

WILLIAMS. Howsattttt!

BOB. I have it on good authority, Williams, that you are frequenting a bookmakers again.

WILLIAMS. Only to bet on this cricket match, sir. And all winnings will go towards food and refreshments for our post debate social with Oakwood sixth-form girls tomorrow evening, sir. (*Baker slips the coat on Bob once more.*)

BOB. I told you.

BAKER. Sir, be a sport.

BOB. My rehearsal.

WILLIAMS. Our beloved Housemaster will never let us down. (*Bob stops struggling.*)

BOB. Alright, alright, who's batting first?

WILLIAMS. Perform the toss, sir. (*Bob tosses.*)

BOB. Call!

WILLIAMS. Wait! (*Bob catches, closes his hand on the coin.*)

BOB. Wait for what?

WILLIAMS. Show me.

BOB. I beg your pardon?

WILLIAMS. Show me the coin.

PATRICK. Williams, you calling or not?

WILLIAMS. Just wait. (*To Bob.*) Show me the coin please. (*Bob does so.*)

WILLIAMS. Just as I suspected.

PATRICK. You suspected what? (*Williams takes coin.*)

WILLIAMS. This side up. (*He tosses.*) One, two, three . . . (*Catches.*) The Queen.

PATRICK. What are you insinuating?

WILLIAMS. Fairplay and good sportsmanship are mottos of the school, are they not, Mr. Smedley?

BOB. What the devil are you up to?

WILLIAMS. I'm not saying that your toss would automatically favour the staff, but there would always be the suspicion, and like Caesar's wife. (*Patrick snatches the coin and tosses it.*)

PATRICK. Williams, call!

WILLIAMS. The Queen. (*Patrick catches the coin and extends it to Bob to read.*)

PATRICK. Mr Smedley.

BOB. The Queen.

PATRICK. The Queen?

BOB. I'm afraid, the Queen.

WILLIAMS. How about that?

BOB. Dear dear.

WILLIAMS. We're putting you in to bat. (*Williams begins to remove his pads.*)

BOB. Good Lord and you're not going to the wicket for some quick runs.

WILLIAMS. No, sir. With the sun pouring directly into the batman's eyes, we'll play with you as the cat does with the mouse before killing it. We'll totally annihilate you.

BOB. Oh, dear dear.

WILLIAMS. Baker, we're almost ready. Tell Bruiser Brace to warm up. (*Baker exits.*)

BAKER. With pleasure.

WILLIAMS. Unfortunately, this year it's going to be a massacre.

BOB. Dear, oh dear, oh dear.

BAKER. (*Exiting.*) Bruiser!

PATRICK. Williams, before we start, perhaps you might explain to your Housemaster, as to why, five weeks overdue, I am still awaiting your essay.

WILLIAMS. Mr O'Rourke, come on, this is a sporting occasion, not a tutorial.

PATRICK. Housemaster.

BOB. Williams, what's this about an essay?

WILLIAMS. Mr Smedley, is this sport or is it not?

BOB. Mr O'Rourke says it is five weeks overdue.

WILLIAMS. My typing hand was injured by a bouncer.

BOB. A night club bouncer?

WILLIAMS. Cricket practice, sir.

BOB. Williams, sometimes you're insufferable.

WILLIAMS. Yes, sir, but other times I even help old ladies across the road.

BOB. Upon completion of this cricketing event, upstairs to your study and complete your essay forthwith.

WILLIAMS. Sir, this isn't the appropriate time.

BOB. As your Housemaster I declare it *is* an appropriate time.

WILLIAMS. Yes, sir, but it isn't cricket. (*As Williams goes to exit, Estelle Hilton, enters. She is in her early thirties, attractive, wears a cotton dress. Williams attempts to go one way, they almost bump, he attempts to go another. They laugh.*)

WILLIAMS. Miss Hilton, you coming to watch us play?

ESTELLE. I've just finished work. I have to collect my racket in town, it's being restrung.

WILLIAMS. Strung or sprung! (*He blocks her.*)

ESTELLE. Gary.

WILLIAMS. Estelle!

ESTELLE. Move! (*He steps aside, bows, then exits.*)

ESTELLE. Cheeky devil. (*Estelle sits on the bench.*) Isn't the singing lovely?

BOB. Our new singing teacher, oh I forgot to tell you that I'm unable to join you and the other staff members for the meal in the Hog's Inn on Friday evening. My Housecaptain is reaching his majority this week, and we are cutting his cake.

ESTELLE. Oh, that's a pity.

BOB. Next month, most defintely.

BAKER. (*Off.*) Mr Smedley, you should be inspecting the wicket now.

BOB. Oh, dear, dear, no rest for the wicket. (*Bob exits.*)

PATRICK. He has probably arranged a rendezvous with Melanie

Warnock-Cooke for next Friday. (*Patrick sits with Estelle on the bench.*)

ESTELLE. It's the worst-kept secret in the whole school. Have you seen her, she's quite a big-shouldered lady.

PATRICK. He's very smitten.

ESTELLE. He's a slow operator.

PATRICK. It's better to travel than to arrive.

ESTELLE. That's one of your calendar quotations.

PATRICK. My calendar, no.

ESTELLE. You do look sexy in your whites.

PATRICK. Is there something between you and Williams?

ESTELLE. Between Williams and me, you're joking.

PATRICK. I'm not.

ESTELLE. I don't go in for cradle snatching, don't be ridiculous. Look, I won't be free until well after ten o'clock tonight.

PATRICK. Why not?

ESTELLE. I have a tennis league match.

PATRICK. When did this come up?

ESTELLE. It's been scheduled since last week.

PATRICK. Postpone it.

ESTELLE. No way.

PATRICK. Please, postpone it.

ESTELLE. I'm running into form just now, I've got a good chance of winning tonight. I can't postpone it.

PATRICK. If you are running into form you will be able to win any night.

ESTELLE. I'll see you after ten, okay?

PATRICK. But I cannot get away *after* ten.

ESTELLE. That is just too bad.

PATRICK. Please, Estelle?

ESTELLE. I've cancelled my own life too many times already in this relationship, but from now on I'm putting myself first. You get that? Tonight, I'm playing tennis, tomorrow night we can meet. I need to talk to you, Patrick.

PATRICK. What, what is it?

ESTELLE. Not now, it will have to wait.

PATRICK. You're not pregnant, are you?

ESTELLE. Do me a favour. Hey, I wish you good luck in the cricket. Wish me good luck in my match tonight.

PATRICK. Yes.

ESTELLE. Huh, such generosity of spirit.

PATRICK. I said good luck.

ESTELLE. But did you mean it?

PATRICK. What's going on with you?

BOB. (*Off.*) Mr. O'Rourke, we're waiting for you!

PATRICK. Coming now! Yes, yes. (*Patrick begins to pad up.*)

ESTELLE. See you tomorrow.

PATRICK. Yes. (*Estelle exits. At back, three youths return. Patrick bends to tie a pad. Michael O'Rourke, in his forties, wearing a mustard jacket and jeans, dark hair, and facial stubble enters with Breda Mahon, twenty-two, in denim jeans and shirt. She has a pair of binoculars draped over her neck. They stand motionless waiting for Patrick to notice them.*)

WILLIAMS. (*Off.*) Come on, sir, everyone's waiting!

PATRICK. Coming, coming!

MICHAEL. (*Smiling.*) Jezz, Pat, it's far from cricket you were reared. (*Patrick turns.*)

PATRICK. . . .Michael?

MICHAEL. The very same.

PATRICK. Michael, what are you doing here?

MICHAEL. I'm over here with some greyhounds. I'm runnin' them down in London at the weekend. Thought I'd just drop in and say hello on me way past.

PATRICK. You've caught me at an awkward moment.

MICHAEL. Well, if it's not convenient then.

PATRICK. You could have given me some prior notice.

MICHAEL. Didn't want to be puttin' ya to any trouble.

PATRICK. Have you been at the house?

MICHAEL. Yea, no one there. I asked one of the students where ya might be, and they told me about the cricket match and here I am.

PATRICK. You could have given me some forewarning.

MICHAEL. I could have.

PATRICK. You could have telephoned.

MICHAEL. I could have telephoned and I could have written but I didn't. I didn't phone and I didn't write, but here I am.

PATRICK. Yes.

MICHAEL. Ah, jezz, Pat, I haven't seen you for over three years

Dermot Crowley in *The Duty Master*, by Neil Donnelly.
Courtesy Amelia Stein.

and instead of bein' glad to see me you're givin' out because I didn't let ya know I was coming'. Jezz H. Christ. (*To Breda.*) Come on, I knew it'd be a mistake, let's hit the road. It's clear we're not wanted. Shouldn't have bothered me arse. (*At back; the three youths stare as Michael walks on past Breda, who remains.*)

PATRICK. Michael, please.

MICHAEL. Forget it, Breda, come on.

BREDA. Michael, wait. (*Michael stops.*)

MICHAEL. Breda, come on.

BREDA. Michael.

MICHAEL. No.

BREDA. Michael, wait.

MICHAEL. Wait for what.

PATRICK. Please.

BOB. (*Off.*) Mr O'Rourke, we're waiting!

PATRICK. I'm busy right this moment, but if you can wait until I'm finished.

BREDA. We'll wait.

MICHAEL. We'll see.

BREDA. We'll wait.

BOB. (*Off.*) Mr O'Rourke, for the last time!

PATRICK. I'm on my way!

BOB. (*Off.*) Quickly!

PATRICK. See you both later. (*Patrick checks the bat, pads, etc., in his hands as he is about the leave.*)

MICHAEL. Knock 'em for six, or whatever it's called.

PATRICK. Thank you.

MICHAEL. Hey, Pat, Up Meath! (*Michael and Breda sit on the bench.*)

Scene 2

Sitting room later that evening, Pippa O'Rourke, with her homework.

PIPPA. 'A volcano is a mountain with a large crater through which lava and smoke are discharged. It can lie sleeping for a long time and suddenly erupt. Volcanos are active for short periods. A few months, or at most one year at a time'. (*Sarah, in her forties, enters. She stands with her back to Pippa, combing her hair. She's dressed well and is obviously ready to go out.*)

SARAH. Don't forget you have a piano lesson tomorrow.

PIPPA. I'm doing my school project.

SARAH. I bet you haven't practiced your piano once since your last lesson.

PIPPA. I have.

SARAH. When?

PIPPA. I practice when you're not here.

SARAH. How convenient.

PIPPA. I don't like anyone listening to me when I practice.

SARAH. A good excuse but not good enough.

PIPPA. But, but, Sarah.

SARAH. Your piano, please.

PIPA. Later.

SARAH. Now. (*Slight pause. Telephone rings. Sarah answers it.*) Hello? . . . . . Oh, hello, just a moment. (*Sarah covers the mouthpiece.*) Pippa, your piano, immediately!

PIPPA. I hate you!

SARAH. Of course you do.

PIPPA. I do. (*Pippa exits. We hear the piano faintly come in during the next speech. It is a clunking Brahms piece.*)

SARAH. Reuben. You still there? Good . . . it's just Pippa, she's being a proper little vixen these days . . . . Yes, I'm a bundle of nerves about this bloody exhibition . . . . I'm hoping someone from the gallery will phone to say the entire thing has been abandoned . . . . Of course I mean it . . . . Yes, I do . . . . It's more than mere nerves at this stage . . . . I tried a little deep breathing, yoga, no good . . . eventually I took refuge in the packet of ciggies I have hidden upstairs for such emergencies . . . . Oh, Reuben, you flatter me . . . you're a tonic . . . what have I done to deserve you . . . alright, yes I do too, when? (*Patrick enters carrying his cricket things. Sarah turns away. Change of tone.*) Look, that is great news. Yes, I'll talk to you soon. Yes, oh yes . . . and you. Good-bye. (*She puts down the phone and looks at Patrick, who is waiting for her.*)

PATRICK. We have visitors.

SARAH. What visitors?

PATRICK. It's Michael, my brother Michael.

SARAH. Michael is here?

PATRICK. He's just parachuted in.

SARAH. Where is he now?

PATRICK. He's in the courtyard outside, parking his van.

SARAH. When did he arrive?

PATRICK. At the beginning of our cricket match, it was very embarrassing.

SARAH. How was it embarrassing?

PATRICK. His whole behaviour was embarrassing, deeply embarrassing. Standby for the failed vocation jokes. (*Slight pause.*)

SARAH. So, Michael is here. Gosh. Is he staying overnight or what are his plans?

PATRICK. I didn't ask him.

SARAH. You didn't.

PATRICK. His arrival was so unexpected, and I was so preoccupied. Oh, and he has this young person with him.

SARAH. A young 'person', what do you mean?

PATRICK. A young girl.

SARAH. A girl friend?

PATRICK. I don't know. He's probably brought her along to flaunt her. To show me that even though he's fat and greasy he can still pull the young girls.

SARAH. I cannot entertain them, I'm leaving in a few minutes.

PATRICK. What!

SARAH. I have my private view.

PATRICK. I cannot entertain them either, I'm totally exhausted.

SARAH. Somebody will have to.

PATRICK. If we do nothing, then they'll go away again.

SARAH. You cannot just do nothing, after all he is your brother.

PATRICK. He hasn't bothered to contact me for three or four years, and now that he has materialised out of thin air, I'm supposed to jump up and down with wild excitement.

SARAH. The least you can do is give them a cut of tea. Be friendly and polite and I'm certain they will soon be on their way.

PATRICK. But I've nothing to say to him. I don't know what to do.

SARAH. You never know what to do, thus you never actually do anything.

PATRICK. What should I do?

SARAH. Patrick, do whatever you like.

PATRICK. But what?

MICHAEL. (*Enters.*) Hello there, can we come in?

SARAH. Michael, this is a great surprise.

MICHAEL. I hope you don't mind me droppin' in like this.

SARAH. Of course not, it's lovely to see you.

MICHAEL. You're lookin' a million dollars.

SARAH. Thank you.

MICHAEL. Sorry about not givin' ye a proper warnin' an' that, but I didn't decide to come in this way until the very last minute.

SARAH. Don't apologise, as I've said already it's lovely to see you.

MICHAEL. Oh, this here is Breda.

SARAH. Hello, Breda, how do you do?

BREDA. Pleased to meet you. (*Sarah and Breda shake hands.*)

MICHAEL. Breda's a student in Dublin. She's travellin' over with me. She's goin' down to London to work for the summer.

BREDA. Yes, I'm looking forward to it.

SARAH. Good for you . . . . Sit down, just shove everything up. (*Michael and Breda sit on the settee.*) Patrick, will you make some tea?

PATRICK. Of course. (*Patrick hauls himself with his cricket things from the chair and exits.*)

SARAH. Have you eaten?

MICHAEL. We're not hungry, shur we're not?

BREDA. We had a meal before we came off the motorway.

MICHAEL. That's right, a big slap-up feed in one a them service stations.

SARAH. In one of those ghastly places?

MICHAEL. Ah, it was grand.

BREDA. Yea, it wasn't too bad.

SARAH. Are you sure?

MICHAEL. Honest, Sarah, we're fine. (*Sarah puts in earrings.*)

SARAH. And you watched the cricket match?

MICHAEL. Oh, yea, the students were like grease lightnin', so fit and fast compared to the teachers.

SARAH. I can imagine.

MICHAEL. Some of the older pot-bellied ones could just about stagger from the . . . Breda, what do they call it again?

BREDA. The crease.

MICHAEL. Yea, the crease, terrible names.

BREDA. Outside the off stump.

MICHAEL. Leg over the wicket.

BREDA. Silly mid-off.

MICHAEL. Silly mid-off, Sarah, what does that one mean?

SARAH. Thankfully, I have no idea. (*Slight pause.*)

MICHAEL. By the way, where's little Pippa?

SARAH. That's her murdering the piano outside.

MICHAEL. (*To Breda.*) She's not that bad, is she?

BREDA. She's very good.

SARAH. I'll call her in before I leave.

MICHAEL. You're goin' out?

SARAH. I have my exhibition opening tomorrow, tonight's the 'private view'.

MICHAEL. So you've been doin' the odd bit a painting.

SARAH. I have an exhibition opening tomorrow which must count for something. (*Breda indicates two small paintings.*)

BREDA. These are some of your paintings?

SARAH. Oh those, they are a legacy of my student days. (*Breda goes and looks at them.*)

BREDA. They're very good.

SARAH. I'm glad you appear to like them.

BREDA. Oh, but I do like them, I really do like them. The style in that one there reminds me of that American painter, what's this his name is, you know, the one who did that famous painting, the one with the girl in the foreground looking at the house in the distance.

SARAH. *Christina's World* by Andrew Wyeth.

BREDA. That's the one. I imagine you like Georgia O'Keeffe?

SARAH. I love Georgia O'Keeffe.

BREDA. Isn't she incredible!

SARAH. She's marvellous.

BREDA. Her work is just so powerful. (*Patrick enters with a tray on which are cups and saucers.*) But yours is too, especially that one.

SARAH. My more recent work is what I'm most proud of. I'm doing very large canvases now. (*Patrick places the tray on the coffee table and exits again.*)

BREDA. I'd love to see them.

SARAH. Well I'm having my 'private view', perhaps you might like to come along.

BREDA. Try and stop me.

SARAH. Right. Michael, have you anything planned for tonight?

MICHAEL. I didn't fix anything. I just came off the motorway on a whim and before I knew it I was drivin' in the school gates, I was just takin' a chance that ye might be in, that's all.

SHARA. We've a spare bed here.

MICHAEL. Are you sure it's no trouble?

SARAH. None at all.

MICHAEL. Great so. (*Patrick enters with the teapot.*)

SARAH. (*To Patrick.*) Michael and Breda will be staying tonight.

PATRICK. Right.

SARAH. And Breda's coming with me to the 'private view'.

PATRICK. Terrific.

MICHAEL. What's this 'private view' thing?

SARAH. It's a private showing for prospective buyers and critics before the official opening.

MICHAEL. A sneak preview?

PATRICK. More or less. (*Patrick stands with the teapot.*)

MICHAEL. Go on, Pat, you be Mammy. (*Patrick pours.*)

PATRICK. You can milk and sugar it yourselves.

SARAH. You didn't bring anything for them to eat.

PATRICK. There's nothing out there.

SARAH. Pippa's probably eaten all the biscuits again.

MICHAEL. It's probably Pat. When we were kids he was a terrible man for demolishin' all the biscuits in the place. Terrible man for the Kimberleys.

PATICK. I was?

MICHAEL. Ya used to swipe that big box of them we'd have at Christmas.

PATRICK. I did not.

MICHAEL. And you'd hide it under your bed.

BREDA. Probably to keep it away from you, Michael.

MICHAEL. Probably. (*They laugh.*) Look Sarah, I have two greyhounds in the back of the van outside. I was wonderin' if there was some place I could house them for the night?

SARAH. Our own garage is free. We don't put the car indoors this weather.

MICHAEL. You wouldn't mind then?

SARAH. Of course not. Have you any champions with you this time?

MICHAEL. A potential champion 'Up the Swanee'.

SARAH. You always have at least one outstanding dog.

BREDA. 'Up the Swanee' is the best, isn't she?

MICHAEL. She's easily the better of the two. I'm runnin' her at Haringey at the weekend. 'Up the Swanee', remember that name now.

SARAH. 'Up the Swanee'.

MICHAEL. Powerful bitch. The other fella's a bit of a donkey. If she makes it, we're talkin' about another Master McGrath; if she doesn't, we'll not hear a sausage about her ever again, will we Breda?

BREDA. I don't know, I've no interest in greyhounds at all.

MICHAEL. Haven't ya, I thought ya had.

BREDA. I'm totally against coursing and all blood sports.

MICHAEL. But we run after a mechanical hare.

BREDA. But it still reminds me of the dog terrorising a fightened little creature.

MICHAEL. Ah, it doesn't, does it?

BREDA. It does. (*Slight pause.*)

MICHAEL. Well, there ya are, just be a minute, I'll go and put them in the garage and have done with it. Is there a key?

SARAH. It's on the hall table as you go out.

MICHAEL. Thanks, Sarah, back in a minute. (*Michael exits.*)

SARAH. I'd better inform Pippa. She'll get a big surprise. (*Sarah exits.*)

PATRICK. Michael said that you are a student?

BREDA. That's right.

PATRICK. What are you studying?

BREDA. Life.

PATRICK. Of course.

BREDA. No, I'm being smart. Arts, U.C.D.

PATRICK. And what do you intend to do after university?

BREDA. I don't know. I'll have a degree, but that gives a body a zero to nil chance of getting a job. I don't know. Maths was my strong subject in school, though I always thought I'd like to be a photographer.

PATRICK. A phoatographer?

BREDA. When I was in school, but now. You see, I'm a blank when it comes to making a decision. Many interests, no direction, that's me.

PATRICK. All things being equal, what would you prefer?

BREDA. As I say, I don't know. I'm a 'road less travelled' person.

PATRICK. That's Thoreau, isn't it?

BREDA. Robert Frost, actually.

PATRICK. Oh, yes.

BREDA. Although I think Thoreau did say something similar.

PATRICK. What's this he said?

BREDA. 'If a man does not keep pace with his companions, perhaps he hears a different drummer. Let him step'.

PATRICK AND BREDA. 'To the music he hears however measured or far away'.

BREDA. It has a sort of religious flavour to it.

PATRICK. Yes, indeed it has. (*Breda is at the window looking out.*)

BREDA. Do you find it a bit claustrophobic, having to live so close to the school?

PATRICK. One gets used to it.

BREDA. I don't think I ever could.

PATRICK. You enjoy your privacy.

BREDA. I do and I don't. I love to be in the thick of things in a big city, all that hustle and bustle. But then I love the stillness of being in the middle of a big forest as well. I love just standing there, listening, drinking in the silence. (*Breda sits on the settee.*) It's one of my slight misgivings about London. The restaurant I'm supposed to be working in is in the middle of Covent Garden, right in the centre of pressure and noise. But I'm sure I'll be able to get days off and I'll jump on a train and head into the country.

PATRICK. You can get day excursions.

BREDA. That's what I'll do.

PATRICK. Breda, would you ask Michael to address me as Patrick.

BREDA. Oh.

PATRICK. At least in front of other people.

BREDA. Sure.

PATRICK. In the formal situation of the school.

BREDA. Oh, right. (*Slight pause.*) Actually, I was going to ask you how many years you've been here.

PATRICK. At the school, twelve.

BREDA. I meant in England.

PATRICK. England. Almost twenty-two. In fact, I've lived longer in England than I lived in Ireland. (*Breda laughs.*)

PATRICK. Why are you laughing?

BREDA. It's just one of Michael's jokes, that you're more English than the English themselves.

PATRICK. A variation on the famous theme. Where are you from?

BREDA. I'm from Macroom, but I'm living in Dublin. Sandyford.

PATRICK. Sandyford, the cinema?

BREDA. What cinema?

PATRICK. The Sandyford Cinema in Ranelagh.

BREDA. There's no Sandyford Cinema in Ranelagh. In fact there's no cinema at all in Ranelagh.

PATRICK. There is.

BREDA. I know Ranelagh, and there defintely isn't a cinema there.

PATRICK. There was once. There was, I know there was because I was is in it. The *Sandf*ord! That's what it was called, the Sandford Cinema.

BREDA. You're sure?

PATRICK. Yes, I am. Because what happened to me in the Sandford Cinema definitely changed the entire course of my life. (*Michael enters carrying a large round tin.*)

MICHAEL. A present from the mother.

PATRICK. Oh, a present?

MICHAEL. (*Handing him the tin.*) Don't eat it all at one go. (*Telephone rings. Patrick doesn't move to answer it.*)

SARAH. (*Off.*) Patrick, answer that, will you!

PATRICK. Hello? . . . oh, hello, Vicki, yes Sarah's still here. She'll be leaving for the gallery in a few minutes. I will get her for you . . . (*Patrick goes to leave.*) It's Vicki calling from Devon to wish you good luck. (*Patrick exits. A pause.*)

MICHAEL. Breda, what's goin' on here at all?

BREDA. Yea, I know.

MICHAEL. They're wired to the moon.

BREDA. Only a little.

MICHAEL. Jezz no, more than a little I'd say.

BREDA. Michael, your brother doesn't like being called Pat in front of people.

MICHAEL. Who said that?

BREDA. Patrick did, he prefers Patrick.

MICHAEL. What did I tell ya, seriously wired to the moon. He can go and hump himself, so he can. (*Pippa enters.*)

PIPPA. Hello, Uncle Michael.

MICHAEL. (*Pretending.*) Who's this?

PIPPA. Uncle Michael, it's me, Pippa.

MICHAEL. Pippa, Pippa who?

PIPPA. Pippa O'Rourke.

MICHAEL. Naw, couldn't be.

PIPPA. It is.

MICHAEL. Naw, Pippa O'Rourke is a tiny wee sprig of a thing, but this person here is almost a fully grown up young lady.

PIPPA. I was little the last time.

MICHAEL. Your mother will have to put salt on your tail to stop ya sproutin' up so fast. (*Michael shakes her hand warmly.*)

MICHAEL. I used to get a crick in me neck from havin' to look down at ya, but soon I'll have a crick from havin' to look up.

PIPPA. You're exaggerating.

MICHAEL. I am, but only a little bit. (*They laugh.*) Ya have your Granny's eyes and the same rounded forehead.

PIPPA. Have I?

MICHAEL. As ya get older you're gettin' to look more like our side of the family. This girl here is Breda.

PIPPA. Hello, Breda.

BREDA. Hello. (*They shake hands.*) I heard you playing the piano.

PIPPA. I'm not very good.

BREDA. It sounded lovely.

PIPPA. It did?

BREDA. It did, didn't it, Michael?

MICHAEL. Brilliant stuff altogether.

BREDA. What was the piece?

PIPPA. Something from Brahms. (*Indicates the binoculars.*)

BREDA. Where did you get these?

BREDA. My dad brought them back as a present from Singapore. (*Breda and Pippa go to the window. Michael reads a newspaper.*)

BREDA. I'll show you how to adjust it.

PIPPA. The sun's getting smaller, then bigger, then smaller again, hey!

MICHAEL. Oh, be careful of your eyes, don't look at the sun.

BREDA. Red sky at night, sailor's delight. Red sky at morn.

MICHAEL. Sailor bewarn. (*Sarah enters followed by Patrick.*)

SARAH. Ready Breda, I'm about to go.

BREDA. Am I dressed alright?

SARAH. You're perfect. Pippa, make sure you have a bath before going to bed.

PIPPA. Yes, of course, Sarah.

BREDA. (*To Michael.*) Will you be alright?

MICHAEL. Oh, go on . . .

BREDA. Patrick, you're not coming to the 'private view'?

PATRICK. I'll be along later in the week.

SARAH. When the crowds have died down.

PATRICK. See you both later.

BREDA. See ye's later. (*Sarah and Breda exit.*)

MICHAEL. Pat, fancy a pint later on?

PATRICK. I'm exhausted after that cricket match, first big match, not quite fit enough.

MICHAEL. I suppose you need your beauty sleep, proper order. (*Patrick indicates Pippa looking through the binoculars*) and ya'd have to stay in because of her ladyship. (*Patrick nods.*) It's gas though, all the same.

PATRICK. What is?

MICHAEL. Pippa calls ye both by ye're Christian names? Jezz, if either you or me had called the aul wan or the aul fella by their Christian names, we'd have got a belt round the ear for our troubles and told to watch our gobs.

PATRICK. Yes. . . . Ah, Pippa, give Uncle Michael the binoculars and go and have a bath. (*She hands the binoculars back to Michael.*)

PIPPA. Tell Breda, thank you.

MICHAEL. I will. See ya in the morning. (*Michael kisses her on the forehead and she comes away past Patrick.*)

PIPPA. Goodnight, Patrick.

PATRICK. Goodnight. (*She exits.*)

PATRICK. How are they, the parents?

MICHAEL. Bionic. Holdin' out for the President's telegram. The aul fella's gone quite gagga. Givin' away cattle, turnin' them out on the road. He has to be watched all the time now. Bad arthritis too, yet he can still shift when he wants to. She's still runnin' about like a headless chicken. It'll take a touch of the humane killer to put a stop to her gallop. She has the best health of all of us.

PATRICK. Still sparing with the electricity, are they?

MICHAEL. Oh, still at it. Ya go into a room and it's dark, ya turn on the light. What do ya see, there's the two of them sitting there; they've been sitting there since light faded. Then they eat the head off ya for runnin' up huge electricity bills. It never changes.

PATRICK. How old is he now?

MICHAEL. Eighty-five next birthday.

PATRICK. Eighty-five.

MICHAEL. She's ten years younger.

PATRICK. A great age.

MICHAEL. They're wearin' down though, every year they're stoopin' that little bit closer to the grave.

PATRICK. Close to it, but not yet in it.

MICHAEL. Don't be too hard on them.

PATRICK. It's a joke.

MICHAEL. You haven't opened your present.

PATRICK. Not yet.

MICHAEL. I saw her bakin' it herself. She wouldn't do that for me, I can tell ya. But then I'm not her privileged eldest son.

PATRICK. Some privilege.

MICHAEL. Some eldest son. (*Pause.*)

PATRICK. Breda's very attractive.

MICHAEL. She is, isn't she?

PATRICK. Are you lovers?

MICHAEL. Ah Jezz, Pat, for God's sake. An uncle a hers, a fella I know through the greyhounds, heard I was comin' to London and because she's a penniless student asked me if I'd give her a lift. (*Slight pause.*) There ya have it. And another thing, the mother asked me to ask ya, and all I'm doin is passin on a message, right. She asked me to ask ya, when you were thinkin' of comin' home.

PATRICK. Coming home?

MICHAEL. Comin' home for a visit, visit your homeland.

PATRICK. This is my home.

MICHAEL. This is England.

PATRICK. This is where my home is.

MICHAEL. Okay, alright, this is where your home is, Stop makin' this so hard for me. They haven't seen ya in what, five years. Your holidays this summer.

PATRICK. We're in France. Sarah tutors in an art summer school. It's a fixed event.

MICHAEL. Why not bring her to Ireland, a flying visit?

PATRICK. She hates the place.

MICHAEL. Pippa, then, the mother would love to see her.

PATRICK. I'll talk to Sarah about it.

MICHAEL. Do that. I've delivered the message, right?

PATRICK. You've delivered the message.

MICHAEL. So how are you keeping yourself?

PATRICK. I'm fine.

MICHAEL. Do you know what I'm going to tell you, the white suits you better than the black.

PATRICK. Does it really?

MICHAEL. I must go check on my greyhounds, at least I'll get some satisfaction outa talkin' to them. (*Michael exits. Patrick picks up the tin and opens it. He puts an envelope on the table as he looks inside. Pippa enters in her socks and drinking a glass of milk.*)

PIPPA. What is that, Patrick?

PATRICK. It's a cake from Granny O'Rourke.

PIPPA. (*Reading letter from envelope.*) 'Hope all is well, hope to see Sarah, Pippa and yourself soon, Love Mam'.

PATRICK. Thank you. (*He takes back the letter. She exits. At back, Estelle in tennis gear as she ralllies from the baseline with superb forearm and backhand as she volleys.*)

Scene 3

Courtyard. The School Assembly choir can be heard singing 'Morning Has Broken', off. Baker enters, hurrying, followed by Williams. They wear blazers.

WILLIAMS. Baker, stop!

BAKER. I'm late for Assembly. (*Williams catches up with Baker and stops him.*)

WILLIAMS. Skip Assembly, go to the computer room and finish the essay.

BAKER. I don't have the key to open the door.

WILLIAMS. Ask Miss Hilton for it.

BAKER. She wouldn't give it while Assembly is still on.

WILLIAMS. I'll get the key. I have to get O'Rourke and Smedley off my back. I must have this essay today.

BAKER. Why don't you finish it yourself?

WILLIAMS. I can't, I'm too busy with other stuff, including organising the party for after our debate. Don't forget I have already lined you up with one of Oakwood's ripest babes.

BAKER. So you say, but how do I believe you?

WILLIAMS. I stake my reputation on it.

BAKER. No way.

WILLIAMS. I give you my guarantee.

BAKER. Which is what?

WILLIAMS. A deed for a deed. You do the essay, I'll get you laid.

BAKER. I need a written guarantee.

WILLIAMS. Baker, do you want to lose it or not?

BAKER. Shhh, keep your voice. (*Williams starts to write on a piece of paper.*)

WILLIAMS. (*As he writes.*) I give a written guarantee that Fiona Chesterman-Boyd will box the compass with one Mark Baker. (*He hands it to Baker.*)

BAKER. What will I say to her, I can hardly hand her this.

WILLIAMS. She will know what to do.

BAKER. She will?

WILLLIAMS. I had her last year, so she's already well broken in.

BAKER. If you had her last year, why don't you want her now?

WILLIAM. I'm seriously into older women now, that's why I'm able to pass her over to you.

BAKER. But she might not like me.

WILLIAMS. The minute she sees you, she'll want you. Baker, she'll love you. Now, Mark, will you finish the essay and stop giving me all this grief? (*Bob enters.*)

BOB. Two sixth form boys absent from Assembly again.

WILLIAMS. We were on our way, sir, but Baker wanted to discuss the food arrangements for tonight.

BOB. What food arrangements?

WILLIAMS. I reckon the Oakwood Girls are mostly vegetarian, sir.

BOB. And what if they are?

WILLIAMS. I bet the Domestic Bursar hasn't thought of this, sir. I bet she'll just prepare the usual steak-and-kidney pie and chips. What a reflection on our school's eating habits, sir.

BOB. It is an interesting speculation, Williams, but I think you should allow the Domestic Bursar to make her own arrangements.

WILLIAMS. I'd hate those creamy complexions of the Oakwood Girls to come out in spots because of our school's greasy-spoon food.

BOB. Now, you are being facetious.

WILLIAMS. No, sir, I'm not.

BOB. This is just another diversionary tactic. What are you up to?

WILLIAMS. You always question my motives, sir.

BOB. Assembly at once, before I carpet the pair of you.

WILLIAMS. I have almost finished my essay for Mr. O'Rourke, sir.

BOB. You have?

WILLIAMS. Yes, Mr. Smedley.

BOB. Excellent news, now run along to Assembly, Williams.

WILLIAMS. Yes, sir. (*Williams smiles and exits quickly with Baker. Bob watches them a moment, then turns away.*)

Scene 4

School secretary's office. 'Morning Has Broken', off. Estelle working. Bob enters.

BOB. Morning has broken, indeed.

ESTELLE. I wish Kenny Butterfield would get the choir to sing something different for a change.

BOB. Speaking of change, I notice Headmaster's wife has taken delivery of her new car.

ESTELLE. Did you see! Shocking pink. To match the colour of her spectacles.

BOB. Poor Froggy, they say he was a brilliant student at Cambridge, but when it came to experience of the opposite gender, he had none whatsoever. When he required a wife, he went to the Lost Property Office where the future Mrs Froggy was the attendant.

ESTELLE. Don't be nasty.

BOB. He settled for a few weeks carnal bliss and now spends the rest of his life being daily reminded of his folly as Mrs Froggy sits across the breakfast table making even more outrageous demands.

ESTELLE. Is that why you've never married, Bob?

BOB. I'm not married because I've never met the right person. Until now, that is.

ESTELLE. My goodness.

BOB. This is the strictest of confidence, Estelle.

ESTELLE. Of course.

BOB. Completely confidential.

ESTELLE. Bob, you know I never would.

BOB. You know the music lady who's preparing us for the Bach Festival.

ESTELLE. O yes, Melanie Warnock-Cooke.

BOB. Yes. I need your assistance, actually. (*Patrick enters. He wears a dark suit.*)

BOB. Good morning, Patrick. I notice the van is still in the courtyard. I take it that that colourful brother of yours and your niece are still with us.

PATRICK. He's having trouble with his van.

BOB. Troublesome things, vans.

PATRICK. They are.

BOB. You'll both have to excuse me. Omnibus Incutiens Blandum per Pectora amoreni.

ESTELLE. Yes, Bob. (*Bob exits.*) You never told me you had a brother.

PATRICK. He's a brother in name only. How did your tennis match go?

ESTELLE. I take it that you don't like him.

PATRICK. We're total opposites.

ESTELLE. My tennis match was a disaster. My opponent had her supporters there. Even her husband turned up.

PATRICK. One seriously henpecked husband turns up, and you lose because of that.

ESTELLE. I lost because of lack of support.

PATRICK. I'm sorry I'm not better henpecking material.

ESTELLE. I wouldn't have anything to do with a man who was.

I'd never want that. I'd rather have a dog. (*He gently touches her face.*)

PATRICK. A little Pekinese? (*She playfully moves his hand away.*)

ESTELLE. Preferably a wolfhound or an alsatian. (*Patrick laughs.*)

PATRICK. What did Bob want?

ESTELLE. Oh, just some more female advice for his campaign to horizontally challenge the upright Melanie Warnock-Cooke.

PATRICK. You're in sparkling form.

ESTELLE. Yes, I'm glad you dropped in. I want to talk about the future.

PATRICK. The future!

ESTELLE. That which isn't the present and isn't the past.

PATRICK. I cannot talk about that now, I have a class in a moment.

ESTELLE. There you go again, evasion straight away.

PATRICK. My brother's unexpected arrival has thrown everything into utter confusion.

ESTELLE. Any thing else that you can dredge up as an excuse?

PATRICK. Estelle, please.

ESTELLE. What have you done about that job in Norwich that was advertised in *The Times* ed. two weeks ago?

PATRICK. You were to update my C.V. and type my application letter.

ESTELLE. It's been in your pigeonhole since last week. (*She hands him an envelope with a newspaper cutting clipped on.*)

PATRICK. It's not really a promotion.

ESTELLE. I thought the object of the exercise was to get away from here.

PATRICK. It is.

ESTELLE. And for us to be together.

PATRICK. That also.

ESTELLE. Patrick, why don't you admit that you don't really want to go through with any of it.

PATRICK. That's not true.

ESTELLE. Patrick, actions, not works, okay? (*Williams enters. Estelle turns back to work.*)

WILLIAMS. Excuse me, Miss Hilton, may I have the key to the computer room?

ESTELLE. What for?

WILLIAMS. So I can complete my essay for Mr O'Rourke.

PATRICK. So, you are working on it then?

WILLIAMS. Oh, yes, straight after the cricket match last night I was in my study making my final notes. All I have to do now is just go and type it all in. You'll be suitably impressed, sir.

PATRICK. It better be good.

WILLIAMS. Sir, it will be better than good, it will be brilliant. (*Estelle hands him a small bunch of keys.*)

ESTELLE. Be careful with that, I want it back here as soon as you've finished.

WILLIAMS. Yes, Miss Hilton, just to remind you of your chairman duties tonight.

ESTELLE. Excuse me?

WILLIAMS. Sorry, chairperson, your chairperson duties in our debate with Oakwood tonight.

ESTELLE. I have already been fully briefed by Mr Smedley.

WILLIAMS. Alright then, then everything is in order.

ESTELLE. Everything is in order.

WILLIAMS. It's going to be a memorable night.

ESTELLE. Just get those keys back to me straight away.

WILLIAMS. (*To Patrick.*) Have that essay in your hand within the hour. (*Williams exits.*)

PATRICK. You're far too friendly with him.

ESTELLE. Oh, Patrick is jealous.

PATRICK. Of Williams?

ESTELLE. You are.

PATRICK. Of him?

ESTELLE. Aren't you?

PATRICK. Don't be absurd.

ESTELLE. Go away and check that application. (*Slight pause.*)

PATRICK. Sarah may be reluctant to give me an immediate divorce.

ESTELLE. Some people might say she'd be only too glad to get rid of you.

PATRICK. She would be thinking of Pippa.

ESTELLE. Pippa is between you and Sarah. Besides, I'm in no hurry to get you remarried.

PATRICK. A breathing space would be welcome.

ESTELLE. Oh, I'm not hunting you for marriage.

Left to right: Dawn Bradfield, Susan Fitzgerald, and Jennifer O'Dea in *The Duty Master,* by Neil Donnelly.
Courtesy Amelia Stein.

PATRICK. Respectability then.

ESTELLE. All I want, Patrick, is just a little commitment, a little commitment, that's my respectability.

PATRICK. I will give you that.

ESTELLE. You'd better hurry up. I'm not having much fun these days. I want something in my life better than this. It's shape up or ship out time for all of us.

PATRICK. You'll get it. I will see you later. (*Estelle ignores him as she works furiously. Patrick exits.*)

Scene 5

Art gallery/café. Sarah, Breda and Suzi seated at a table.

BREDA. I didn't recognise anybody from last night in the gallery.

SARAH. Last night was private, tonight is the official opening.

BREDA. The world premier.

SARAH. If you like.

SUZI. Okay Sarah, just to wind up the interview. After the great anticipated success of this exhibition, you'll still continue to lecture at the college?

SARAH. Most certainly, I enjoy my students. (*Annabel enters carrying a bouquet of flowers.*)

ANNABEL. Sarah, sorry to interrupt, but these are for you. Barclay's Bank have just bought a painting.

SARAH. Oh, great.

BREDA. Oh, Sarah, that's seven now.

SARAH. Gosh. Which one did he buy?

ANNABEL. *Thunderstorm over Avignon.*

SARAH. Oh, really?

ANNABEL. They said they loved all that blood imagery in the sky.

SARAH. Yes, yes, yes!

ANNABEL. Oh, Suzi, tell Sarah about Waldemar.

SUZI. Right. (*Annabel exits.*)

SARAH. What's this about Waldemar?

SUZI. You know Roger.

SARAH. Roger?

SUZI. Salt-and-pepper beard.

SARAH. Oh, yes.

SUZI. Roger's friend Penny is coming up from London for the weekend.

SARAH. Yes?

SUZI. It seems that Penny lives near Waldemar, Waldemar Januszczak.

SARAH. What's the connection with Roger and Penny?

SUZI. Annabel's going to ask Roger to ask Penny to invite Waldemar to come up and review your work.

SARAH. Gosh!

SUZI. Anything stronger you could say as a response to that news?

SARAH. If he comes up and gives me a good review in *The Sunday Times,* well who knows?

SUZI. The exhibition could travel to London.

SARAH. Anything is possible.

SUZI. You might even get your own series on Channel 4.

BREDA. You might become the new Sister Wendy.

SUZI. Why not? (*They laugh.*) We'll have to wind this up, I have to get a taxi to Market Harborough. There's a gig there. Lots of A and R men up from London. There's a local band making waves, the big record companies are falling over themselves to sign them up.

SARAH. I hear they're brilliant. They're called, 'Sons of Nefetari'.

SUZI. 'Sons of Nefetari', that's what they're called. You know them?

SARAH. Pete, the bass player is an ex-student of mine.

SUZI. That's excellent. I can do a link between you and the band. Anything you can tell me about Pete?

SARAH. He did lovely lino cuts.

SUZI. That's perfect. (*She gets up and is packing away her things.*) The piece will be in the *Mercury* on Saturday. Thanks a bunch. (*Suzi exits. Sarah reads the card with the flowers.*)

BREDA. From an admirer?

ANNABEL. (*Off.*) Sarah, can we have you for a photograph please.

SARAH. Excuse me. (*Sarah exits. Baker is alongside Breda.*)

BAKER. Mr O'Rourke's niece?

BREDA. Oh, you're one of the students.

BAKER. In my last term. My name is Mark. (*He extends his hand. Breda shakes it.*)

BREDA. You like the exhibition?

BAKER. I'm still formulating my response.

BREDA. I just love it, I think it's wonderful.

BAKER. It's quite overpowering in some instances.

BREDA. It's not really your cup of tea.

BAKER. I'm not a visual person, I'm a wordsmith.

BREDA. You're a writer?

BAKER. I'm an actor.

BREDA. Oh.

BAKER. I'm applying to a number of our leading drama schools, and I'm in the midst of preparing my audition pieces. (*He produces a copy of Hamlet.*) I don't believe they ever consummated.

BREDA. I beg your pardon?

BAKER. Hamlet and Ophelia.

BREDA. You think not?

BAKER. My theory is that they are part of the same cosmology but separate strata within it. They remain separate because Ophelia is a lesbian and Hamlet is gay.

BREDA. But they could still consummate.

BAKER. Technically, yes, spiritually and sexually, no. (*Williams enters. He comes straight to them.*)

WILLIAMS. Miss O'Rourke, am I correct?

BREDA. Incorrect, I'm not an O'Rourke.

WILLIAMS. Aren't you lucky.

BREDA. I wouldn't say that now.

WILLIAMS. I like her accent Baker, don't you?

BAKER. You're interrupting a conversation.

WILLIAMS. I'm not interrupting, I'm joining in. What were you talking about?

BREDA. Mark was explaining his theory of *Hamlet.*

WILLIAMS. Oh, yes, Ophelia is a dyke and Hamlet is a fruit. The first time you hear it, it's plausible enough, but every night he goes on and on about all these gender benders.

BREDA. He has some original ideas.

WILLIAMS. So have I.

BREDA. Is that so? (*To Baker.*) Nice to have met you, Mark.

BAKER. See you around (*Breda exits into the gallery.*)

WILLIAMS. You fancy her.

BAKER. Male and female relationships are not all governed by the base instinct but by the intellectual and spiritual dynamics which constitute human . . .

WILLIAMS. Spare me the pseudo rationalisation.

BAKER. Did you give the essay to O'Rourke?

WILLIAMS. Not directly. I gave it to Smedley to give to him.

BAKER. I fear I didn't alter my style sufficiently, tender unfamiliar arguments.

WILLIAMS. Whatever happens, you'll never admit it.

BAKER. How can I, I have been so well bought off.

WILLIAMS. I fancy a crack at Pegeen Mike.

BAKER. Her name is Breda. I thought you're into older women now.

WILLIAMS. Life is full of new challenges. (*Williams exits.*)

PATRICK. Baker, what are you doing here?

BAKER. Mr Brown said we should visit all exhibitions, sir, keep our ideas fresh.

PATRICK. Mr Brown's not here, is he?

BAKER. No, sir, I presume he's with his wife and new baby. Sir. This passage here, I don't quite understand. (*Patrick looks about furtively.*)

PATRICK. Read it out.

BAKER. (*Reads.*) 'It will be shortly known to him from England what is the issue of the business there. It will be short. The interim is mine; and aman's life no more than to say "One".'

PATRICK. 'One' is a term used in fencing, when the fencer strikes, 'One'!

BAKER. It's not that, sir, but might it not also mean that though our lives are brief, we must always be ready for whatever befalls?

PATRICK. Yes, perhaps that even though our lives are brief we can still achieve moments of great insight and clarity which can determine us towards real and decisive action.

BAKER. The complete person. I was a child, I grew up, I then became an adult, and later I shall grow old. I am all of these stages and yet I am this one person, this one unit, this 'One', 'One'.

PATRICK. Really, Baker, it might mean any number of things.

BAKER. The circle. A person starts their life journey at a particular point and place in time; then they go outward into the orbital world, and as they grow older they come round on the inside rim of the arc and the circle of life is complete. (*At back, Williams is moving through the gallery following Breda.*)

PATRICK. Baker, would you go in and ask my wife how many paintings have been sold to date.

BAKER. The number of paintings sold. Yes, Mr O'Rourke. (*Baker exits. Breda enters.*)

PATRICK. You're back to see the paintings *again?*

BREDA. I wasn't doing anything else this evening, and besides I wanted to come along to lend my support.

PATRICK. What have you been doing today?

BREDA. When Michael finally got the van going, we went as far as Castle Ashby. He wanted to see this new dog track at Northampton. The castle is magnificent, isn't it?

PATRICK. Where is Michael at the moment?

BREDA. He's gone for a run with the dogs on the common. Listen!

PATRICK. What?

BREDA. It sounds like the sea.

PATRICK. The sea?

BREDA. Doesn't it?

PATRICK. It's traffic on the M.1.

BREDA. It's not, is it?

PATRICK. Because there is no breeze, the sound is carried uninterrupted over the fields.

BREDA. In my mind's eye it's the sea.

PATRICK. I have so little poetry left in me.

BREDA. I have too much . . . go on, give us a verse.

PATRICK. Of what?

BREDA. Whatever you like.

PATRICK. Whatever I can remember. (*Slight pause.*)
> The sea is calm tonight
> the tide is full, the moon lies fair
> upon the straits.
>
> Listen, you hear the grating roar
> of pebbles which the waves draw back, and fling
> at their return, up the high strand,
> begin, and cease, then again begin,
> with tremulous cadence slow, and bring the eternal
>   note of sadness in.

BREDA. That's beautiful.

PATRICK. 'Dover Beach'. Matthew Arnold.

BREDA. I don't know it.

PATRICK. Said to be written about his honeymoon, when he was particularly happy.

BREDA. I suppose everybody's blissfully happy at least once in their lives. (*Williams enters.*)

WILLIAMS. Your wife is a very good artist, sir.

PATRICK. So everybody keeps telling me.

WILLIAMS. You don't believe them, sir?

PATRICK. Thank you, Williams, and good-bye. (*Williams sits.*)

WILLIAMS. I detect a big Egon Schiele influence in her work. An Egon Schiele-like preoccupation with thin female breasts, skinny thighs, and great mounds of black pubic hair. Sir, I would say that the female genital area is one of your wife's major themes.

PATRICK. Would you now?

WILLIAMS. An unusual theme for a married woman. One would expect the female artist to be more interested in the male form.

PATRICK. Would one?

WILLIAMS. One would.

BREDA. That's not completely true you know.

WILLIAMS. Isn't it?

BREDA. No.

WILLIAMS. Name one male artist with the corresponding interest?

BREDA. David Hockney, Lucien Freud, Michaelangelo. Do you want me to go on? (*Estelle enters.*)

WILLIAMS. You're just in time for a brilliant exhibition.

ESTELLE. Yes, it's wonderful. You must be very proud of your wife, Mr O'Rourke.

PATRICK. This is Breda, she's travelling to London with my brother.

ESTELLE. Hello, Breda. I'm Estelle, nice to meet you.

BREDA. You're here to support Sarah.

ESTELLE. I'm only here for a quick spin around the gallery. I'm glad I came. It's given me great insight. Would you excuse me? (*Estelle exits. Baker enters.*)

BAKER. Nine, sir, nine paintings already sold.

PATRICK. Oh, thank you, Baker. (*Bob enters.*)

BOB. Williams and Baker, come along you two, the hall must be prepared and got ready for our big debate. Baker, into the gallery and fetch Brace and the others.

BAKER. I've just come from the gallery, sir.

BOB. Go back into it. Time is of the essence. The Oakwood girls bus was arriving as I left the school. They must be sitting down to their supper right at this moment.

BAKER. Yes, sir. (*Baker exits fast into the gallery. Bob produces Williams's essay.*)

BOB. Williams, is this your essay?

WILLIAMS. Yes, sir.

BOB. Perhaps you should hand it personally to Mr O'Rourke. After all it is the essay that has been outstanding for such a long time. (*Williams takes the essay and hands it to Patrick.*)

WILLIAMS. And now it is one outstanding essay. Breda, you're welcome to come along to our little debate also, there's a party afterwards.

BREDA. Thank you for inviting me.

WILLIAMS. You're welcome. You'll come?

BREDA. I'll try to.

WILLIAMS. See you later. (*Williams exits.*)

PATRICK. He has a bloody cheek.

BOB. Indeed. Oh, Patrick, don't forget that you are Duty Master tomorrow.

PATRICK. Am I? (*Patrick consults a small diary.*)

BREDA. What is 'Duty Master'?

BOB. The Duty Master's function is to monitor the timetable.

PATRICK. Thank you for reminding me, Bob. I must read the schedules for tomorrow. And I also must read Williams's essay.

BREDA. I'll read it for you.

PATRICK. I couldn't do that, that would be unprofessional of me.

BREDA. I know, I was only joking. (*Sarah enters.*)

SARAH. Look who's here.

PATRICK. I had intended to come later in the week.

SARAH. But the security guards couldn't keep you out.

PATRICK. I fought my way past them. Has Headmaster and his wife been yet?

SARAH. They were here when Sir Huntley did the honours. They each had a mineral water and apologised for leaving so soon, they had another engagement. She kept up this joke about cubism being a style of painting associated with Fidel Castro. She was quite funny actually.

BREDA. Did they buy a painting?

SARAH. She said she would love to buy one but she wouldn't know where to hang it in the house seeing as her Scots Presbyterian mother is liable to drop in at any time.

BREDA. Patrick, are you going to buy one?

PATRICK. Am I?

BREDA. Why not?

SARAH. Excellent idea, Breda.

BREDA. You should support the arts, and you should support your wife.

PATRICK. I support the arts and I support my wife, but should I have to buy one of her paintings?

SARAH. Oh, come on, Patrick.

PATRICK. I have never understood the licence which artists seem to think they have which permits them to display their nakedness.

BREDA. It's the true innocence of human beings.

PATRICK. True innocence does not always necessitate a graphic public display.

BREDA. It's in the eye of the perceiver. (*Slight pause.*)

BREDA. I think I'll head off for a walk.

SARAH. Go along by the river, it's beautiful there.

BREDA. Thanks. See you both later. (*Breda exits.*)

PATRICK. She's the president of your fan club.

SARAH. She gave you a run for your money.

PATRICK. I was outnumbered.

SARAH. I'm glad it's all over. The entire event has been so intimidating.

PATRICK. Intimidating. I'm sure the balloon under your ego is capable of absorbing a great deal more.

SARAH. No matter how carried away I become, you will always be there to cut me down to size. Would you excuse me, there are people in there I have to say good-bye to.

PATRICK. I won't be staying long.

SARAH. Fine. I may be somewhat late. (*Sarah exits into the gallery. Patrick stands listening to the traffic on the M.1.*)

Scene 6

Sitting room. Night. Pippa, in her dressing gown. On the floor is a newspaper with different pairs of shoes and polishing things. 'Poncho and Lefty', sung by Willie Nelson, plays on Michael's portable cassette player. Patrick enters.

PIPPA. Uncle Michael gave me some of his tapes to play. It's the music he plays in his van. (*Slight pause.*)

PIPPA. There are a lot of messages for Sarah on the answer machine.

PATRICK. Any for me?

PIPPA. None for you. Take off your shoes and I'll clean them for you.

PATRICK. They're fine.

PIPPA. I'll make them look better.

PATRICK. If it makes you happy. (*He removes his shoes.*)

PIPPA. Why is it that I don't see my grandad and granny in Ireland?

PATRICK. You saw them a few years ago.

PIPPA. Five years ago.

PATRICK. But you remember them.

PIPPA. I remember the pony.

PATRICK. And in the house next to the field where the pony was, live your grandparents.

PIPPA. I'd like to see them again.

PATRICK. You will.

PIPPA. When?

PATRICK. Soon, very soon.

PIPPA. In a few weeks?

PATRICK. Next year sometime.

PIPPA. We always go and see Sarah's grandad.

PATRICK. Sarah's father, you mean.

PIPPA. We always see him.

PATRICK. Because he's very ill.

PIPPA. The note that was with Granny's cake said she hoped she saw us soon. 'Hope all are well, hope to see you soon. Love, Mam'. (*Michael enters, cleaning his greasy hands on a cloth rag.*) Uncle Michael, give me your shoes and I'll polish them.

MICHAEL. Sure, this is better than the Hilton Hotel.

PIPPA. Uncle Michael, I really like that tape.

MICHAEL. Ya like it, great.

PATRICK. It's cowboy music.

MICHAEL. It's not Mr Mozart right enough, but I remember you once had a Hank Williams record, remember that, I bet ya don't, but ya did. I remember ya used to play 'I'm So Lonesome I Could Cry' all the time.

PATRICK. I don't remember.

MICHAEL. I remember that alright. (*Breda enters with a tray on which are cups, etc., plus a sliced section of the cake.*)

BREDA. I've taken the liberty of cutting the cake, I couldn't find anything else to eat.

PATRICK. Oh . . . right. (*Breda pours.*)

MICHAEL. She's dead handy to have about the place.

BREDA. Don't give me any trouble you or you won't even get a slice.

MICHAEL. Jezz, Pat, these young ones today. (*Breda serves Patrick first, then herself, it's playful.*)

BREDA. You get your own. (*To Patrick.*) I went to the public library this evening. I was looking for 'Dover Beach' but it wasn't in the anthology they had.

MICHAEL. (*As they all settle to tea and cake.*) That cake'll be full of health and vitality. Plenty of fresh milk and butter. Sure didn't I milk the cows myself. (*On the tape Willie Nelson is singing.*)

> Maybe I didn't love you
> half as much as I could have
> little things I could have said
> and done but I just didn't take the time

(*Michael sings along*)

> but you were always on my mind
> you were always on my mind

Now for ya, that's what I call poetry.

PATRICK. (*To Breda.*) I'll get 'Dover Beach' for you, I have all Arnold's work upstairs.

BREDA. Oh, no hurry.

PATRICK. I'll get it for you as soon as I have my shoes back.

MICHAEL. (Laughs). The poor fella hasn't had his shoes done yet.

PIPPA. Sorry, Patrick, but visitors come first.

MICHAEL. Oh, proper order. (*Pippa hands Michael his shoes.*)

PIPPA. There you are, Uncle Michael.

MICHAEL. Fantastic job, done in double quick time. (*Michael takes money from his pocket.*) Buy yourself somethin' nice.

PIPPA. I won't take any money, I do it because I want to.

MICHAEL. Ya sure?

PIPPA. Certain.

MICHAEL. Well. (*Breda exits. Patrick removes Williams's essay and begins to read it.*)

MICHAEL. Liam Conway and Fergus Pike were askin' for you.

PATRICK. Were they really? I vaguely remember them from National School.

MICHAEL. They were askin' for ya the other day anyway.

PATRICK. They were just making polite conversation.

MICHAEL. I suppose they wonder why ya never show your face. They probably think you're in jail or that you've turned homo or somethin'. (*Slight pause.*) But I'm always coverin' up for your lack of interest, I usually say 'Oh, he was on the phone last night and he was askin' for everybody. He was here a few weekends ago for a flyin' visit. Came Saturday, left Sunday, didn't have time to see anyone else except the family'. I'm always coverin' up for ya.

PATRICK. But all these cover ups are your problem.

MICHAEL. I'm thinkin' of other people beside myself.

PATRICK. I rescued myself. (*Pause, Pippa hands Patrick his shoes.*)

PIPPA. Here you are Patrick.

PATRICK. Thank you. (*Patrick puts on the shoes. Pippa collects up the paper, shoes, polish, etc.*)

PIPPA. Good night a gra. (*Michael kisses her on the forehead and slips the money in among the polish things in her hand, unseen by Patrick.*)

PATRICK. Wash your hands thoroughly.

PIPPA. I always do.

PATRICK. Sleep well.

PIPPA. Good night. (*Pippa exits.*)

MICHAEL. Pat, I'm still havin' trouble with the van, I'll need to take it in to a garage in the mornin', is there any you'd recommend?

PATRICK. Central Garage.

MICHAEL. I know it, it's just before the roundabout.

PATRICK. That's it.

MICHAEL. Great stuff. Oh and by the by, would someone please tell me what is that great big metal yoke that's goin' up in the middle of the roundabout.

BREDA. It's a sculpture.

MICHAEL. That! It looks like a lorry corkscrewed round a lamp post.

BREDA. It's a work in progress.

MICHAEL. Jezz, if that's a work in progress I'd hate to see it when it's finished. (*Sarah enters.*)

SARAH. Ah, good, you're all being looked after.

MICHAEL. We're having a ball.

BREDA. Would you like some tea, Sarah?

SARAH. No, I've had more than enough to drink tonight. There's great fun and games going on at the front of the school. Someone has let all the air out of the tyres of the Oakwood girls bus. The driver's gone to the pub. Half the girls are missing. Bob Smedley's lost among the semiquavers. There's a group of boys and girls out on the cricket field, and they're not playing cricket.

MICHAEL. Could I join in?

SARAH. You might be just a little too old, Michael.

BREDA. He's young in spirit.

MICHAEL. And in limb.

PATRICK. I'm off to bed. I have to be up early in the morning, I'm Duty Master tomorrow.

MICHAEL. I'll be hittin' the hay myself.

BREDA. I'll be off too.

SARAH. Have you had enough to eat?

MICHAEL. We've been well fed and watered and we're grand.

BREDA. We'll just say good night. We'll see you both in the morning. (*Michael and Breda are about to leave.*)

SARAH. Good night.

PATRICK. Breda, before you go.

BREDA. Yes.

PATRICK. I think, Sarah, that you should make up the settee bed in this room for Breda.

SARAH. Why can't Breda sleep where she slept last night?

PATRICK. Excuse me, but my understanding of Breda's presence here is that Michael is giving her a lift to London.

SARAH. Patrick.

PATRICK. Am I correct?

SARAH. Patrick, look.

PATRICK. You *look,* we have a young daughter. I don't want her to grow up with the belief that people of casual acquaintance automatically end up in bed together.

BREDA. It's no problem . . .

SARAH. Breda, you don't need to explain anything.

BREDA. I know I don't, but all the same I think it would be easier if I did use the sofa bed tonight.

MICHAEL. I don't believe I'm hearin' this.

PATRICK. I am Pippa's father and, as such, am responsible for her moral welfare.

SARAH. Really, Patrick.

MICHAEL. Listen, I've had it, I'm off to bed. (*Michael exits.*)

BREDA. I'll go and get my things. (*Breda exits.*)

SARAH. That really is the limit!

PATRICK. I'm putting a stop to all the humiliation.

SARAH. The only humiliation here is your own self-humiliation and the laughing stock you're making of Pippa and me.

PATRICK. He's making the laughing stock of us, that's why I'm putting a stop to this charade. I'm sick of him.

SARAH. And I'm sick of you, I have nothing left for you but utter contempt. (*Breda enters.*)

BREDA. Excuse me.

PATRICK. Come right in, Sarah will fix the bed for you.

BREDA. Thanks. (*Patrick picks up the tray.*)

PATRICK. See you in the morning.

BREDA. Good night. (*Patrick exits with the tray.*)

SARAH. Ridiculous behaviour. I must apologise.

BREDA. I suppose he does have a point.

SARAH. No, he does not.

BREDA. It's much easier if I stay down here.

SARAH. It's absurd, totally absurd. (*Sarah opens up the sofa bed, sheets are already on it, etc.*) He's past the point of absurdity. I still think you should ignore him.

BREDA. It's all settled now. (*Sarah finishes off the bed with pillows, duvet, etc. We hear Bob Smedley singing off.*)

SARAH. Bob Smedley, still rehearsing at this hour.

BREDA. I can throw my shoe out of the window at him.

SARAH. Ask him to leave the stage. (*Sarah dials. Breda combs her hair*). Bob! . . . yes, alright. (*Sarah finishes.*) He knows.

BREDA. He's always rehearsing.

SARAH. His life is one continual rehearsal.

BREDA. Sarah, thank you for everything.

SARAH. A pleasure, sleep well. (*Sarah exits. Breda removes her shoes, jeans. Pippa enters.*)

BREDA. Pippa, what are you doing here?

PIPPA. They were arguing.

BREDA. Are you alright?

PIPPA. Are you frightened? (*Breda pats the bed.*)

BREDA. Here. (*Pippa comes across.*) You're a lost, lonesome little thing, aren't you?

PIPPA. Only sometimes.

BREDA. You wish you had brothers and sisters?

PIPPA. I don't know. What about you?

BREDA. I'm the youngest, the rest are all grown up. I get away with murder. (*They laugh.*)

PIPPA. Will you help me with my project tomorrow?

BREDA. Pippa, I'd love to. (*Breda takes up the binoculars.*) It's a very clear night. You can see all sorts of different constellations, Saturn, Neptune, Venus.

PIPPA. The Plough and the Milky Way?

BREDA. All of them.

PIPPA. Thank you, Breda.

BREDA. Any time.

PIPPA. Good night. (*Breda watches Pippa exit. She turns off the light. Silence. At back, Pippa stands looking through the binoculars at the stars.*)

END OF ACT I

ACT II

Scene 1

Sitting room. Breda asleep in darkness on the sofa bed. A figure enters the room. It is Patrick in his dressing gown.

PATRICK. Breda? (*Pause.*) Breda?

BREDA. Who's that?

PATRICK. Patrick. I'm sorry if I startled you.

BREDA. No, it's alright.

PATRICK. I've been awake reading Matthew Arnold, not just his poetry but also his prose and particularly his great essay 'Culture and Anarchy'.

BREDA. What?

PATRICK. 'Culture and Anarchy'.

BREDA. Oh.

PATRICK. Listen to this, 'what the majority of people tell us, that the world wants fire and strength more than sweetness and light, and that things are for the most part to be settled first and understood afterwards. We have seen how much of our present perplexities and confusion this untrue notion of the majority of people amongst us have caused, and tends to perpetuate.'

BREDA. I'm very sleepy.

PATRICK. And listen to this, here we are, 'Culture however shows its single minded love of perfection'. Therefore the true business of the friends of Culture now is, to dissipate this false notion. (*At back, Fiona unbuttoning Baker's shirt.*)

FIONA. What type of career do you plan for yourself?

BAKER. Oh, a career where I'm respected for the integrity of the projects I undertake.

FIONA. Which means?

BAKER. I'll take risks. I'll be known in the business as a risk taker.

FIONA. I see.

BAKER. I'll work with people like Quentin Tarantino. Robert de Niro and Harvey Keitel would be my role models.

FIONA. Of course.

BAKER. As an actor I'll specialise in characters with an edge, psychopaths, sexual deviants, and anal retentives.

FIONA. I bet. (*She finishes unbuttoning his shirt—she waits for him to do something.*) Were you a forceps delivery?

BAKER. Eh?

FIONA. Nothing.

BAKER. Are you a nymphomaniac or what?

FIONA. Oh, get on with it. (*They exit.*)

PATRICK. (*Resumes.*) 'So that, for the sake of the present but far more for the sake of the future the lovers of culture are unswervingly and with good conscience the opposers of anarchy.' (*Patrick stops, looks at Breda.*) Breda, you have the most beautiful hair.

BREDA. Sarah has nice hair.

PATRICK. Her hair is nice, but it's not beautiful.

BREDA. How long have you and Sarah been married?

PATRICK. Oh, we might never have married if it hadn't been for us getting stuck with a pregnancy so early in the relationship.

BREDA. But Pippa is a lovely child.

PATRICK. I would run away, if only I knew where to run to. (*At back, Williams and Estelle.*)

ESTELLE. You've no idea, have you?

WILLIAMS. About what?

ESTELLE. Your whole life has already been carefully plotted. In a matter of weeks you'll be done from here to start your privileged life and brilliant career.

WILLIAMS. Yes, but I'll come back to visit.

ESTELLE. Oh, no, you're not visiting me.

WILLIAMS. You'd prefer it if we remained ships in the night then?

ESTELLE. Boats in a pond, more likely.

WILLIAMS. Let's go to the jeep, I'll take you home.

ESTELLE. You wouldn't dare. (*Williams produces some keys on a ring.*)

WILLIAMS. Wouldn't I? (*They exit.*)

PATRICK. Breda, there's something I must tell you, something that makes your visit here all the more extraordinary.

BREDA. Yes?

PATRICK. I had met this girl, and this is why I asked you about the Sandford Cinema. I first met her in that cinema. I just went in there to get out of the rain. The film was well in progress. About halfway through, I felt a tap on my shoulder from behind. I turned and heard the voice of a girl offering me a sweet. I took one and thanked her. All through the rest of the film my mind was on the girl, and when it was over and the lights came on I saw that she had a sad face but beautiful hair. She suggested we go for a coffee, and I agreed. This type of thing had never happened to me before. I'd been too preoccupied with study for the priesthood. We talked. Rather, she talked and I listened. She had lost her job in a factory. Her parents were always fighting. I left the seminary on account of her. I never told them at home. I knew they'd never understand. Even though her life was pitiful, she knew about love; she knew about love because she had none, and she picked me, who had even less. Because of that it couldn't last. But we had met at a time when both needed rescuing, and we had rescued each other. (*Slight pause. Michael sits up on the other side of Breda.*)

MICHAEL. I never heard such a load of old tripe. (*He gets out of bed and comes around to the angry Patrick.*) The same old tricks.

PATRICK. Stay where you are.

MICHAEL. Still tryin' to curry favour.

PATRICK. Get back.

MICHAEL. Stop all this lookin' for sympathy an' try earnin' respect for a change.

PATRICK. Back. (*Patrick pushes Michael and they grapple and tumble in a heap on the bed.*)

BREDA. Michael, Patrick, stop it, stop it the pair of ye. (*The room lights go on. Sarah runs in in her dressing gown followed by Pippa.*)

SARAH. What on earth! What is going on?

PATRICK. What do you mean, what is going on, *nothing* is going on. (*Pippa laughs.*)

SARAH. Pippa, back upstairs.

PIPPA. But everyone else is down here.

SARAH. Pippa, *upstairs.* (*Pippa exits.*) Patrick, I don't know what's happening to you, neither do I very much care any more. (*Sarah exits.*)

BREDA. I'm sorry, it's all my fault.

MICHAEL. No, it's not, it's his.

BREDA. No.

MICHAEL. Come on, Pat, we all know where we all stand now, let's get some sleep. (*Slight pause.*)

PATRICK. Yes. (*Patrick exits.*)

BREDA. It's all my fault.

MICHAEL. Not at all, it was right in character for Pat, it's the guilt that turns them on. (*Michael sits on the edge of the bed.*) Thank God, we're out of here tomorrow. (*At back, Bob Smedley rehearsing as he walks on the now deserted cricket field. There is a loud crash of a vehicle hitting a tree. Bob stops, looks, then begins to run.*)

Scene 2

Courtyard. The School Assembly choir can be heard singing 'Morning Has Broken', off. Williams waiting; he has a large dressing on his forehead. Baker enters.

BAKER. Gary, your forehead! Why didn't you come back last night? What's happened?

WILLIAMS. I'm in deep shit, and I need you to help dig me out of it fast.

BAKER. Oh, oh, I'm not doing anything else for you.

WILLIAMS. This one last thing.

BAKER. I've already done too much.

WILLIAMS. And look what I did for *you* last night.

BAKER. What?

WILLIAMS. Fiona.

BAKER. That was personal.

WILLIAMS. *This* is personal.

BAKER. Unless I say no I'll always be in your pocket.

WILLIAMS. Unless you help me, I'll be thrown out of school, I won't be able to do my exams; my father will disinherit me.

BAKER. Gary, I cannot help you any more.

WILLIAMS. Just one, this one last favour.

BAKER. You still haven't told me what's happened.

WILLIAMS. I was driving Estelle back to her flat in town, and I crashed the school jeep.

BAKER. You crashed the Land Rover?

WILLIAMS. This is what I want you to say, right?

BAKER. Oh, no.

WILLIAMS. I want you to say that you overheard her asking me to drive her home.

BAKER. I heard nothing.

WILLIAMS. I was asked to drive her home because she was intoxicated.

BAKER. No, I'm not getting involved in this.

WILLIAMS. You overheard her ask me, and then you *saw* her going towards her office, which you will say assumes she was going to get the keys for me.

BAKER. I heard nothing, I saw nothing, and I assume nothing. (*Bob enters.*)

BOB. Williams, you are in the most serious trouble!

WILLIAMS. It may appear that way on the surface, sir.

BOB. Your insolence is becoming insufferable.

WILLIAMS. I do apologise for my inexpert driving.

BOB. And, without insurance, and without permission to remove school property from the premises.

WILLIAMS. I'm sorry, but I have to correct you about the permission, sir, the permission I did have.

BOB. From whom?

WILLIAMS. There was a request from a member of staff, Miss

Hilton, who had honoured us by chairing our debate. She was very tired, and had rather too much to drink, and she didn't wish to be seen in this condition by a taxi driver taking her from the school. Thus she implored me to assist her to leave the premises discreetly.

BOB. A request does not constitute permission Williams.

WILLIAMS. From a member of staff, sir?

BOB. Williams, there is going to be an enquiry and all the facts will be uncovered.

WILLIAMS. I welcome a full enquiry, sir. In the interim I sincerely regret acceding to her request, all I wanted was to be a good sport. Baker will confirm overhearing Miss Hilton make her request and will corroborate the facts.

BOB. I'm sure he will. Run along now Williams to what remains of Assembly, you'll still be in time to make a grand entrance.

WILLIAMS. Yes, sir. (*Williams exits.*)

BOB. Baker, why didn't you intervene to prevent this?

BAKER. It all happened so fast, sir.

BOB. He galloped off on a charger like Sir Galahad.

BAKER. Yes, sir, there was nothing I could do.

BOB. Nothing at all?

BAKER. No, sir.

BOB. I see. Get along to Assembly.

Scene 3

School secretary's office. Estelle at the window, her back to us. Bob enters.

BOB. Good morning, Estelle, has Duty Master been in yet?

ESTELLE. He's on his way. (*She turns. She has two black eyes.*)

BOB. How are you?

ESTELLE. On the road to recovery.

BOB. Dear, oh dear.

ESTELLE. But earlier this morning you should have seen me, a frozen packet of peas in this eye and a packet of mixed veg. in the other; not a pretty sight. (*Patrick enters.*)

BOB. Duty Master.

PATRICK. Good morning.

BOB. You've been informed of the accident.

PATRICK. Indeed. Estelle, what happened?

ESTELLE. As you know I was chair at the debate last night and afterwards I drank a little too much; it was late and Gary Williams offered to drive me home and stupidly I accepted.

BOB. Dear, oh dear.

PATRICK. The headmaster wants a formal report as soon as possible. (*Patrick sits at his desk and writes.*) Could you repeat what you've just told us?

ESTELLE. As I said, it was extremely late, after midnight, I was very . . .

BOB. Tired.

ESTELLE. Tired. And Gary Williams offered to drive me home. He led me to believe that he had received Mr Smedley's permission to drive the jeep. This information provided to be

BOB. Erroneous.

ESTELLE. Erroneous, thank you Bob. I'm very embarrassed by the entire episode, and I will make financial restitution in respect of the damage done to school property.

BOB. The Headmaster will gladly accept that, won't he? (*Patrick stops writing.*)

PATRICK. There is the probability that the police will bring criminal proceedings against Williams.

BOB. Surely not, Patrick, dear oh dear.

PATRICK. There is the strongest probability, and this prospect is what is greatly alarming Headmaster.

ESTELLE. If the school wishes to avoid embarrassment and the resultant negative publicity, then it will endeavour to get the charges against Williams dropped, yes!

PATRICK. The school cannot interfere with a police investigation.

ESTELLE. It will have to.

PATRICK. It cannot.

BOB. Dear dear.

PATRICK. Bob, will you please stop saying that.

BOB. What?

PATRICK. Stop it!

BOB. Would you both excuse me, I'll leave you to your depositions, I have a classroom of unruly boys waiting for me. (*Bob exits.*)

PATRICK. Have you seen a doctor?

ESTELLE. And you can get out too.

PATRICK. Don't take your anger out against me, I wasn't the one who crashed the jeep.

ESTELLE. You sanctimonious hypocrite.

PATRICK. This is all to disguise the fact that you and Williams . . .

ESTELLE. Yes yes yes yes yes, we did it in the jeep.

PATRICK. What?

ESTELLE. Yes.

PATRICK. I knew you were flirting.

ESTELLE. I was fed up, I was pissed off, I was drunk.

PATRICK. But, with Williams.

ESTELLE. It's no big deal, he's just a premature, ejaculating, arrogant little prat. I know that, I know all that, I was just getting my own back at you.

PATRICK. Estelle.

ESTELLE. Don't. Don't say another word, don't. For whatever you say I've already said it to myself. (*Pause.*)

PATRICK. We can still take that post at Norwich.

ESTELLE. In a really twisted way this fiasco with Williams last night has opened my eyes to all my stupidity. If it had not happened, I might still have gone on giving you the benefit of the doubt, excusing you by telling myself, oh Patrick's a withholding man and therefore needs a lot of prodding before his true qualities can be revealed and in the end with sufficient patience he would come good. But what you really are Patrick is a careful but furtive muddler through life. You're okay in many respects, you're not a terrible person, you have many qualities. But, you've never known what you want in life and you never will.

PATRICK. I still love you.

ESTELLE. You don't even love yourself.

PATRICK. I'll change.

ESTELLE. Hey, you've forgotten to take off that record, it's still playing and no one is listening any more.

PATRICK. I still have that application letter.

ESTELLE. And you still haven't given it to me to post. See what I mean?

PATRICK. I'll get it.

ESTELLE. Patrick, when you were the one going through the motions and I was the one who cared, I kept giving you chance after chance; but now I *don't* care. So, I don't have to give you any more chances, see.

PATRICK. I'll get that letter. (*Estelle laughs; Patrick exits fast.*)

Scene 4

Sitting Room. Breda and Pippa working the 'Volcano'. Michael on the phone.

MICHAEL. (*On phone.*) I'm just checkin' on the weigh in time . . . 'Up the Swanee' and she's entered for the Oaks at a quarter to eight . . . . Is that Rory? . . . It's not. . . . Jezz, ya sound dead like him. Oh right, weigh in is between two and three o'clock . . . lookit here before ya go, I have this other fella that I half promised if the aul ligiment healed in time and it seems as though it has . . . yes.

BREDA. Ah, Michael you're forcing poor old 'Caribee Sunset' to run in a race, are you?

MICHAEL. (*To Breda.*) Shhh (*Into phone.*) If there was a withdrawal in any of the early races.

BREDA. If you try to run 'Caribee Sunset,' he'll die of a heart attack.

MICHAEL. Shhh . . . . Lookit, we'll sort it all out when we see ya at two o'clock . . . . Tell Rory, Mike O'Rourke was askin' for him. (*Michael finishes.*)

BREDA. I'm not letting you enter poor 'Caribee Sunset'.

MICHAEL. Jezz, Breda, you're soundin' like a bit of a fish wife.

BREDA. I can't imagine any woman ever marrin' you.

MICHAEL. The woman who'd marry me hasn't been invented, has she Pippa?

PIPPA. (*Bemused.*) I don't know.

BREDA. Don't forget to ring the garage to find out what time the van can be collected.

MICHAEL. Give us a chance, I'm going down in a minute. Jezz, Breda, God help the man that gets you.

BREDA. Well, it won't be you anyway.

MICHAEL. I soon won't get a word in edgeways. (*Michael exits.*)

BREDA. What we really need now are some photographs to show your project to its best advantage.

PIPPA. I have a camera.

BREDA. Is there a film in it?

PIPPA. There is.

BREDA. Then we're in business. (*Patrick enters, he wears his gown.*)

PIPPA. Look what Breda and Uncle Michael have helped me make.

PATRICK. It's very impressive.

PIPPA. It's a real life volcano and I'll have great photographs to go with it. I'll get my camera. (*Pippa exits. Patrick is searching for Williams's essay.*)

BREDA. I hope Sarah doesn't mind us using up all her tomato puree.

PATRICK. Oh course not.

BREDA. Patrick, Michael and I are inviting Sarah, Pippa, and yourself for a meal in town tonight.

PATRICK. A meal, oh, unfortunately I'm Duty Master until nine o'clock.

BREDA. We checked on that, that's why we've booked for nine-thirty.

PATRICK. I see.

BREDA. We want to do it as a thank you to Sarah and yourself for putting us up. And also to try to make up for any misunderstandings that might have happened.

PATRICK. But I don't think Sarah is free.

BREDA. She is, I've already invited her, and she's looking forward to it.

PATRICK. Oh, well, then.

BREDA. It would mean a lot to me personally if we were all to have this meal.

PATRICK. Look, Breda, I'm not here to make or break restaurant arrangements, I'm looking for Williams's essay. (*Pippa returns with her camera, and she and Breda go to the 'Volcano'.*)

PIPPA. Lift! (Breda and Pippa lift the tray with the Volcano.)

BREDA. There it is, it was under the volcano all the time. (*Patrick takes up the essay from the coffee table. Breda and Pippa exit with the Volcano, Michael enters.*)

MICHAEL. That Volcano is beginnin' to look like somethin' out of *Close Encounters*.

PATRICK. Yes, indeed.

MICHAEL. I've booked a bit of a slap-up for everyone before we hit the road tonight, okay?

PATRICK. Breda's just told me.

MICHAEL. I don't want to get on that motorway tonight with things still not settled between us; when I leave here I want the slate wiped clean. I'm sorry about the cock ups. I'm not talkin' about just last night and what happened here. Ah no, aren't we all liable to try it on and shur who could blame ya.

PATRICK. I wasn't trying it on.

MICHAEL. We now, Pat, you weren't goin' to hear her confession.

PATRICK. I wasn't trying to seduce her.

MICHAEL. After the skirmish, Breda an' myself talked, an' it seemed as how I'd sabotaged all my good intentions in comin' here in the first place. I came here to bury the hatchet, not in the back of your neck mind, no I came to bury the hatchet for once and for all and to apologise for the other time. That time back home when everything went wrong for you. I admit I did keep a low profile when maybe I should have defended ya more. In fact I didn't defend ya at all. I could have invented stuff about 'crisis of conscience' and 'lack of belief in a vocation' an' that, but I didn't; I did the ostrich on it. In fact I gloated. You'd always been given priority, and now you were the fallen idol.

PATRICK. I shouldn't have left without some attempt at explanation. But I didn't know how. You know how much it meant to her. I was just so ashamed at letting them down. I was consumed with shame and guilt. I had given in to temptation.

MICHAEL. That's what temptation is there for, to be given in to.

PATRICK. I seem to give in to it more than most.

MICHAEL. You're a serial temptation-giver-in-to.

PATRICK. Yes, well, look I'm on duty, I've got to be getting back to school.

MICHAEL. I'm off out myself; Jezz, Pat, you're a bit like Batman in that rigout. (*Michael exits. Patrick sits on the settee. He searches the jacket pocket lying there. He finds the letter. The telephone rings. He answers the phone.*)

PATRICK. Hello . . . Sarah . . . Yes, we must talk . . . where? . . . gallery, four o'clock. . . . Alright, I'll see you there. (*He finishes. He seals the envelope. Breda enters, stops.*)

BREDA. We're off to school with the Volcano, I'm just here to get my jacket. (*She takes her jacket from the settee.*)

PATRICK. You could have told me.

BREDA. I tried to.

PATRICK. I shouldn't have come downstairs, but I only wanted to talk.

BREDA. Yes.

PATRICK. I feel such a fool about it.

BREDA. You shouldn't.

PATRICK. But I do.

BREDA. No.

PATRICK. So ashamed.

BREDA. Stop feeling all this shame and guilt, stop being so hard on yourself. Stop hanging on to the past.

PATRICK. You don't understand.

BREDA. I think Sarah and Pippa are two lovely people that you are not being fair to.

PATRICK. There are a lot of complicated things going on in my life right now.

BREDA. Uncomplicate them.

PATRICK. Wave a magic wand.

BREDA. Yes, I know I'm a bit simplistic; but sometimes the solution is right there staring us in the face, and because we're so stubborn we refuse to see it.

PATRICK. What is it I'm refusing to see?

BREDA. The truth.

PATRICK. The truth is always relative.

BREDA. I can't help you then. (*Telephone rings. Patrick answers it.*)

PATRICK. Yes Headmaster, I'm on my way! (*He finishes. At back, Michael exercising his greyhounds.*)

Scene 5

Housemaster's study. Williams sitting. Bob enters.

WILLIAMS. Sir, what did the Headmaster say?

BOB. What the Headmaster said is confidential. He will make a final decision when he studies the Duty Master's report.

WILLIAMS. Sir, you check his report. Mr O'Rourke always has a down on me.

BOB. Have you not always been troublesome, Williams?

WILLIAMS. No, sir. (*Baker enters, then sits.*)

BAKER. Sorry I'm late, sir. I had to take a call from my father.

BOB. From Sri Lanka. Good news, I hope.

BAKER. Extremely bad.

BOB. Oh dear, nothing wrong I hope. (*Baker sits.*)

BAKER. Sir, did you meet that woman who was with my father on Open Day.

BOB. A woman with a big floppy red hat?

BAKER. Yes, sir, wasn't she appalling?

BOB. I thought she was rather nice.

BAKER. Nice, she's appalling; and what is truly appalling is that I am going to be that woman's stepson.

BOB. Your father is getting married again?

BAKER. He is, sir, but I'm not going to their wedding. They can do their worst, but I'm not going to it.

BOB. Oh, come, Baker, weddings are *such* good fun. (*Patrick enters. He has Williams's essay with him.*)

BOB. Duty Master.

PATRICK. Housemaster. Now, you two. The Headmaster wants a complete report as soon as possible. He doesn't want the newspapers involved.

WILLIAMS. Neither do I, sir.

PATRICK. Good. What we're concerned with here is the removal of school property without permission. Namely, the jeep. Baker (*Baker stands*). Baker! I want you to tell me what happened. To your knowledge.

BAKER. To my knowledge, at the conclusion of the evening's events, I heard Miss Hilton ask Gary Williams to drive her home; and then I saw Miss Hilton go towards the office, which I assume was to get the keys of the jeep.

PATRICK. You assumed this, why?

BAKER. Because I had heard Miss Hilton ask Gary to drive her home, and to get the keys she would have to go to her office.

PATRICK. And did you hear Williams's reply?

BAKER. Sir?

PATRICK. To her request.

BAKER. No, sir.

PATRICK. Why not?

BAKER. I think he just nodded his head.

PATRICK. You saw him . . . nod his head?

BAKER. Eh . . . yes, sir.

PATRICK. And you therefore assumed that this meant that he was agreeing.

BAKER. Yes, sir.

PATRICK. And then?

BAKER. And then, sir?

PATRICK. When Miss Hilton came back from the office.

BAKER. I didn't see Miss Hilton come back from the office.

PATRICK. You didn't?

BAKER. I had gone away at this stage.

PATRICK. But you would assume she came out with the keys?

BAKER. I would assume that.

PATRICK. Would you?

BAKER. I would.

PATRICK. A lot of assuming, Baker.

BAKER. Yes, sir.

PATRICK. Now you knew as you stood there listening to Miss Hilton request Williams to drive her home, that if Williams did so, he would be breaking school rules and the laws of the land. And also, Baker, as you are considered somewhat more intelligent and more responsible than Williams, it is reasonable to expect that you would have intervened to dissuade him. And yet you stood idly by and did nothing. (*Baker glances at Williams.*)

BAKER. I know, sir.

PATRICK. Why?

BAKER. I cannot explain, sir. (*Slight pause.*)

PATRICK. Williams! (*Williams stands.*)

PATRICK. Williams, I have your essay here. Or rather what passes for your essay.

WILLIAMS. You don't think it's any good, sir?

PATRICK. On the contrary I think it is *very* good, but should I award that compliment to you? (*Patrick looks from Williams to Baker.*)

WILLIAMS. I did discuss it with Baker; after all he is considered more intelligent and more responsible than me, so it's not surprising that some of his thinking would find its way into my final draft.

PATRICK. Not alone his thinking, but also his writing style. Though he has made attempts to disguise this.

BAKER. Sir?

PATRICK. Baker, your tortuous moral disgressions from the text are legendary. (*Patrick flips open Williams's essay.*)

PATRICK. Shakespeare putting violence into his plays to attract the general public into the theatre we know to be one of your pet theories . . . though the next bit is what I would indeed expect from Williams's fertile mind, drawing parallels between Shakespeare's violence and the violence in the films of Sylvester Stallone and Arnold Schwarzenegger.

WILLIAMS. But that is what I do believe, sir. The news items that really grab our attention are those scenes of football hooligans wrecking a bar in Germany or Holland. It's a basic human instinct, sir. Take, for example, your own country, Ireland. Ireland has had a recent history of bloodshed and violence, has it not?

PATRICK. You mean Northern Ireland?

WILLIAMS. Yes.

PATRICK. Northern Ireland is part of the United Kingdom, is it not Mr Smedley?

BOB. It is.

PATRICK. Thank you.

WILLIAMS. Playing with words, sir, won't alter the facts. Sir, that's a cheap shot. You're throwing up a smokescreen to demolish my argument because your own is full of vapour.

PATRICK. I'm giving Baker back this essay because I still have not received yours. (*Patrick pushes the essay into Baker's hands.*)

WILLIAMS. Mr Smedley, it is mine.

BOB. Baker, did you write it for him?

BAKER. No, sir.

PATRICK. They're both lying.

BAKER. I'm not, sir.

BOB. Baker, don't incriminate yourself further. (*Slight pause.*)

PATRICK. Alright, Baker, you're dismissed for the moment. (*Baker departs with Williams's essay.*)

PATRICK. Williams, last night's episode is easily the most

reckless and outrageous in your time here at the school. You removed property without permission, property which was not insured to be in your possession, property which you later damaged. You endangered the life of your passenger, Miss Hilton. Miss Hilton luckily escaped with minor scratching and bruising, but her injuries were entirely unnecessary, as indeed was the entire expedition. Furthermore, you placed members of the general public in great risk. And now your desperate and pathetic attempts to wriggle out of responsibility for all of this by getting Baker to concoct an alibi. Miss Hilton did *not* cajole you into driving her home, and Mr Smedley did *not* grant permission. Neither did you write this essay.

WILLIAMS. But Baker has vouched for the fact that Miss Hilton had made a request.

PATRICK. The veracity or otherwise of Baker's statement is not the principal consideration at this moment.

WILLIAMS. But, sir.

PATRICK. What we're addressing is your flagrant breach of the school rules and for this you must receive the appropriate punishment.

WILLIAMS. Yes, sir.

PATRICK. Housemaster.

BOB. When we're finished here, I'm taking you to the computer room. There I'm standing over you while you write your essay.

WILLIAMS. Yes, sir. (*Bob opens a large book and extends a pen to Patrick.*)

BOB. Duty Master, please sign. (*Patrick writes in the book.*) Now Williams, do you understand this punishment?

WILLIAMS. Yes, Mr Smedley.

BOB. Are you padded.

WILLIAMS. No, sir.

BOB. Shake hands with your Housemaster. (*Williams shakes hands with Bob.*) And with Duty Master. (*Williams and Patrick shake briefly.*) Now, bend over. (*Williams leans over the back of a chair and grabs the seat for support. Bob produces a long cane, which he hands to Patrick.*) Duty Master, six of the best.

PATRICK. Yes, Housemaster. (*Patrick swings hard and connects with Williams's bottom.*)

BOB. One! (*Patrick swings again, but this time the blow is milder and hits the spine.)* Two! (*Patrick swings again and catches Williams halfway up his back.)* Three! (*Patrick swings again but doesn't bring the cane down. Instead he throws it on the floor.)*

BOB. Duty Master?

PATRICK. I'm unwell.

BOB. Oh, Williams, you're dismissed. (*Williams straightens up. Patrick stands rooted staring at him.)* To your study, get on with the essay. I'll be there presently.

WILLIAMS. Yes, sir. (*To Patrick.)* Mr O'Rourke, hope you get better soon. (*Williams exits.)*

PATRICK. I lost complete concentration.

BOB. But you were doing ever so well with the enquiry.

PATRICK. I lost all sense of purpose.

BOB. Why don't you rest.

PATRICK. Would it be too much to ask you to take over my duties.

BOB. Certainly. Are you sure you're alright? Shall I fetch Matron?

PATRICK. No, Bob.

BOB. I'll see you at lunch then? (*Patrick doesn't reply; Bob exits.)*

PATRICK. There are so many lies. (*At back, Breda and Pippa carrying the 'Volcano'.)*

Scene 6

Art gallery/café. The end of lunchtime. Music. Baker and Fiona are drinking white wine at one table. Sarah, Breda, and Pippa are at another assembling a small kite. A waitress is busy wiping down a table, left.

BAKER. To acquiesce in a deception, to be a party to wilful criminal behaviour; or to lose one's friend in an exercise of moral correctness, that is the question.

FIONA. Is the waitress looking?

BAKER. No, why?

FIONA. I love these glasses. (*Fiona scoops her empty glass into the bag on her lap.)*

BAKER. What are you doing?

FIONA. Drink up fast, I want yours too. (*Fiona reaches across and takes Baker's glass, it is half full. She drinks it fast and puts the glass in her bag also.)*

BAKER. Hey, here I go again, I am an accomplice in another morally compromising situation. (*Fiona is closing the bag on her lap.*)

FIONA. What's up with you?

BAKER. You're a kleptomaniac.

FIONA. Last night you called me a nymphomaniac.

BAKER. I think I prefer what I called you last night.

FIONA. I always do this.

BAKER. Every time or just once a month?

FIONA. Once every few months.

BAKER. Last year you went with Williams, right?

FIONA. Did I?

BAKER. Didn't you?

FIONA. He tried it on. He fancies himself a bit. He's too flash for me.

BAKER. Oh.

FIONA. I prefer you. I prefer complete weirdos.

BAKER. I'm relieved you told me, now I can seriously consider falling in love with you. (*She stands.*)

FIONA. Don't bring love into it, just say that last night we had a superb exchange of bodily fluids, okay, are you coming? (*Fiona exits. Baker gets up to follow.*)

BAKER. You're still with us?

BREDA. We're leaving today.

BAKER. Have a good trip.

BREDA. Thank you. (*Breda indicates Baker's blazer on a chair. He goes back for it, Patrick enters.*)

BAKER. Oh, Mr O'Rourke, how are you?

PATRICK. How am I?

BAKER. I was told you were ill.

PATRICK. Do I look ill?

BAKER. You look pale, sir.

PATRICK. I may look pale to you, but my health has never been better. (*Fiona stands in the doorway.*) Your young lady awaits. (*Baker exits.*)

PIPPA. Look what Breda and Sarah have made with me.

PATRICK. It's excellent.

SARAH. A reward for her getting her project completed on time.

PIPPA. Miss Monserat will be very pleased. I just have to get the photos developed and hand them in.

BREDA. We can do them in one of those 'One Hour Photo' places.

SARAH. Perfect.

PIPPA. There, it's ready to fly. (*Pippa holds up the small kite.*) Sarah, did you know Miss Hilton she has two black eyes.

SARAH. She must have bumped into something.

BREDA. Michael said she had an accident with the school jeep.

SARAH. Was she in it or under it?

PATRICK. In it. Pippa, why don't you and Breda go and launch the kite.

SARAH. Equally exciting.

BREDA. Yes, let's do that (*Pippa and Breda get up. Pippa picks up her camera from the table and focuses on Patrick and Sarah.*) Last on the role of film. Move in closer. Patrick. Smile. (*Pippa takes a photograph and exits.*)

PATRICK. (*To waitress.*) May we have another mug.

WAITRESS. Certainly, sir. (*Waitress exits.*)

SARAH. Pippa's in great form.

PATRICK. Breda has brought her out of herself.

SARAH. Yes. And she has brought you out of yourself too.

PATRICK. She's just a doe-eyed undergraduate.

SARAH. Don't patronise her, she's nothing of the sort and you know it.

PATRICK. She has a very simplistic view of the world.

SARAH. As usual you've completely misunderstood what I'm saying.

PATRICK. What?

SARAH. It's irrelevant, it's a red herring.

PATRICK. What is?

SARAH. Oh for Christ's sake, Patrick, sometimes.

PATRICK. What? (*Slight pause.*)

SARAH. I don't want this to degenerate into a shouting match.

PATRICK. Nor do I.

SARAH. I came for a rational laying of cards on the table, if such a thing is possible.

PATRICK. It is possible, because it is exactly what I want too.

SARAH. Good.

PATRICK. Right.

SARAH. I was never one for lies or deceit.

PATRICK. Yes. I want to stop all the lies.

SARAH. Good.

PATRICK. It was never the intention to cause pain in the deception.

SARAH. Of course not.

PATRICK. If things had been well in the marriage then there might be some great mystery as to why one of the partners strayed.

SARAH. Precisely.

PATRICK. One must appreciate how these relationships develop. One works alongside someone one gets on with extremely well, and then this working relationship develops into a personal one, and then there is this extremely difficult situation of acknowledging this other relationship.

SARAH. I totally agree.

PATRICK. Of course it is understood that when the separation occurs there will naturally have to be a period of adjustment, a period of transition, a period in which the most important person in all this, Pippa, has to be the recipient of the most careful monitoring.

SARAH. Absolutely. But it's not going to be forever.

PATRICK. It's not.

SARAH. Of course not. I think we've agreed that that is what we both want.

PATRICK. Yes.

SARAH. Well?

PATRICK. Well what?

SARAH. Excuse me?

PATRICK. You were talking about . . .

SARAH. Sorry?

PATRICK. You're not talking about . . .

SARAH. What did you think I was talking about?

PATRICK. I thought . . . I don't know what I thought. Sarah, I honestly don't know how it began, don't ask me. I tried to force it away but it wouldn't go. Perhaps as you say a fine working relationship develops into something more. In the end I had to acknowledge it, it is important. (*Slight pause.*)

SARAH. From the way you were talking, it was clear that you already knew.

PATRICK. Yes, oh yes.

SARAH. I am sorry but . . .

PATRICK. Do I know him?

SARAH. No.

PATRICK. Have I met him?

SARAH. No.

PATRICK. The owner of the gallery here?

SARAH. God, this is like 20 questions. He lives at Lough-borough.

PATRICK. Not that Israeli sculptor, the one who did that piece on the roundabout outside town? Come on, you can't, what are you telling me?

SARAH. But nothing has actually happened yet.

PATRICK. But you said . . .

SARAH. I said I would never embark on a deceit.

PATRICK. Sarah, what are you talking about?

SARAH. The fact that nothing has happened is due to great restraint and control on our part, and I would hope that, if you were in a similar situation that you too would muster the appropriate restraint and self-discipline in the matter.

PATRICK. Yes.

SARAH. Exercise the honesty to tell the other person.

PATRICK. Yes.

SARAH. If I was fulfilled in this relationship, I wouldn't have given it a moment's consideration.

PATRICK. Oh, what you want is permission to have an affair.

SARAH. This is not a step I'm taking lightly.

PATRICK. You want permission to betray me, is that it?

SARAH. Surely after this conversation you cannot call it betrayal.

PATRICK. What do you call it, then?

SARAH. Look, he's only in England for a further few months, then he's returning to Israel for good. He has been tremendously supportive and helpful to me in the preparation of this exhibition. Being an artist himself, he understands the problems. He's a great encourager.

PATRICK. I used to encourage you.

SARAH. A long time ago.

PATRICK. Recently, too.

SARAH. For years you've ignored me and you know it. (*Slight pause.*) Now, about France.

PATRICK. You want to go with him?

SARAH. I will be tutoring in the summer school, and you've always hated being there. I would have thought that you not having to go there would be a great relief to you.

PATRICK. And Pippa?

SARAH. I could take Pippa with me.

PATRICK. And she will go with you and him as family? No, I will not allow that. Pippa stays here.

SARAH. Alright. (*Slight pause.*) Well, that would be better. Every other year you balked at the idea.

PATRICK. I could never get through to her.

SARAH. You had no interest.

PATRICK. In the future my relationship with her will be different.

SARAH. Good, you will have to get into practice, then, and you can start when she comes back by actually talking to her.

PATRICK. I'll talk to her.

SARAH. And when the time for going to France comes, if she doesn't want to stay with you, then she doesn't. It's up to you to make the effort. (*Slight pause.*)

PATRICK. And when France is over, what then?

SARAH. He'll be back in Israel and I'll be back here.

PATRICK. It won't be the same.

SARAH. No, it won't be the same, it might even be better.

PATRICK. It might be worse.

SARAH. It couldn't be. (*Pause.*) Sometime in the future, if you wish to take a break with someone, I'll take the necessary steps with regard to Pippa. (*Sarah exits. Slight pause. Pippa enters.*)

PIPPA. I'm going with Breda to fly the kite.

PATRICK. Yes. (*Pippa turns to exit.*)

PATRICK. Oh, Pippa. (*Pippa stops.*)

PATRICK. See you later then. (*Pippa exits puzzled.*) (*At back, Breda and Pippa walk with the kite held high ready to launch.*)

Scene 7

School secretary's office. Estelle working. Williams enters.

WILLIAMS. Hi.

ESTELLE. What do you want?

WILLIAMS. I came to see how you were.

ESTELLE. I'm very busy.

WILLIAMS. I'm very busy also. I'm back doing the bloody English essay again, can you believe it? I'm still not out of the woods with that dammed thing. O'Rourke's cracking up. He was to cane me but he funked it. Smedley's taken over as Duty Master.

ESTELLE. Gary, I don't really have the time.

WILLIAMS. Neither do I, I just came to say I really enjoyed last night.

ESTELLE. Hey buster, last night never happened, it was all a fantasy in your head, get it?

WILLIAMS. But you enjoyed it.

ESTELLE. I'm not enjoying today. Look, I was a wager you had with your chums. You can collect your winnings now. There's no further need for you to be in here.

WILLIAMS. Just because I crashed the jeep last night doesn't mean we can't have a relationship.

ESTELLE. A relationship with you, don't be ridiculous.

WILLIAMS. You have to say that now because you're hurt, but in a few days you'll view things differently.

ESTELLE. You've got some nerve.

WILLIAMS. Some girls say it's part of my charm.

ESTELLE. Some girls must be very silly.

WILLIAMS. Yes, but they are mere girls, not a mature woman like you.

ESTELLE. And this mature woman is calling time on this *event*. Now, will you leave my office. (*Patrick enters.*)

PATRICK. Williams, what are you doing here?

WILLIAMS. Apologising to Miss Hilton for my accident last night.

PATRICK. Yes, you've done that, now will you go. (*Williams remains where he is.*) I must talk to you alone. (*Estelle shows Williams the door. Patrick produces the letter from his inside pocket.*)

PATRICK. The job at Norwich. (*He hands it to her.*)

ESTELLE. The eleventh hour passed days ago.

PATRICK. Yes, but here it is.

ESTELLE. But it's too late. (*She goes to tear it up.*)

PATRICK. No! (*She hands it back to him.*) That's it?

ESTELLE. That's it. (*He tears up the letter.*)

PATRICK. I suddenly feel very old.

ESTELLE. Patrick, you are old. (*Bob enters with Baker followed by a sheepish Williams.*)

BOB. Miss Hilton, Mr O'Rourke. As acting Duty Master I have been informed by Baker that he had not fully disclosed all matters relevant to last night's accident. Baker.

BAKER. You know how I'm always wrestling with moral questions on the periphery of life, and how I prefer to be an observer rather than an active participant.

BOB. Get to the point.

BAKER. I wish to withdraw my previous account of events.

WILLIAMS. What are you doing?

BAKER. I did not overhear Miss Hilton ask you to drive her home, nor did I see her going towards her office to get the keys.

WILLIAMS. You did.

BAKER. Gary had a copy made of the keys and those keys are in his pocket.

WILLIAMS. What have they paid you to say this?

BOB. Williams, will you consent to a search?

WILLIAMS. It's a stitch up.

BOB. If you are found to be completely innocent, then you shall receive a full written apology.

PATRICK. I'll do the search.

BOB. Thank you, Mr O'Rourke. (*Patrick puts his hand into Williams's right pocket but withdraws it empty.*)

PATRICK. Nothing there.

BOB. The other one. (*Patrick puts his hand into Williams's left pocket and withdraws the ring with two keys on it.*)

BOB. These look like the keys? (*Bob takes them and hands them to Estelle.*)

ESTELLE. Yes.

BOB. Thank you, Baker, you may go.

BAKER. Sorry, Gary. (*Baker exits.*)

BOB. I'll speak with the Headmaster. (*Bob dials an extension number.*)

PATRICK. You really are a nasty little shit, Williams.

WILLIAMS. She doesn't want you any more. You're too old, Paddy. (*Patrick hits him an angry blow in the stomach. Williams doubles over.*)

ESTELLE. Patrick, stop! (*Estelle goes to the wounded Williams.*) Gary, you alright!

WILLIAMS. I'm getting him sacked from this school. (*Williams is upright again but holding his stomach.*)

BOB. Williams, out of here.

WILLIAMS. I'm going to the Board of Governors, and if I don't get satisfaction there, I'm going to the national newspapers.

BOB. Williams, out!

ESTELLE. I'll take him. (*She exits with Williams still feeling his stomach.*)

BOB. (*Ruefully.*) Dear, dear, Headmaster is going to love this. (*Bob exits.*)

PATRICK. Up Meath! (*At back, Estelle walks slowly away.*)

Scene 8

Sitting Room. Night. Patrick, Sarah, Michael, Breda, and Pippa, in her dressing gown, are looking at photographs. Michael and Breda's luggage is on the floor.

MICHAEL. The quality is very good, especially for one of them one-hour places.

PIPPA. This one really does look like a volcano.

MICHAEL. You'd swear it was Mount Etna.

BREDA. Or Vesuvius.

MICHAEL. Or Krakatoa, east of Java. (*Michael and Breda laugh.*)

PIPPA. Sarah, Uncle Michael is giving me a pony.

SARAH. Aren't you lucky.

PIPPA. He's brown and white colour, isn't he, Uncle Michael?

MICHAEL. There's three or four ya can choose from.

PIPPA. Isn't that great, but where will we keep him?

SARAH. We'll have to think about that.

PATRICK. Maybe we could use a stable at the back of the school.

SARAH. That's a good idea. Come on, Pippa, we'd better say goodnight, they have a long journey to London. (*Breda kisses her on the cheek and removes the binoculars from around her own neck and places them around Pippa's.*)

BREDA. And here's a present for you.

PIPPA. I can't take these. These are your Dad's.

BREDA. I want you to have them.

PIPPA. But, but.

BREDA. No buts, I want you to have them.

PIPPA. Thanks ever so much.

MICHAEL. Big kiss for me. (*He lifts her up and they hug.*)

PIPPA. Thank you for coming, too, Uncle Michael. Will you come again soon?

MICHAEL. Of course we will, but we'll be seein' you before then, when you come over to collect the pony.

PATRICK. Good night, Pippa. (*Pippa kisses Patrick on the cheek and exits.*) Thank you for the meal.

MICHAEL. It was very fillin'. You're usually half-starvin' when ya leave one of them Indian places, but I'm as full as a house.

PATRICK. Can I offer you a coffee?

MICHAEL. As soon as Sarah comes down, we'll be heading off.

BREDA. I'll go out and check the van.

MICHAEL. And make sure there's no young fellas tryin' to mess about with the greyhounds. (*Breda picks up the luggage and exits.*)

PATRICK. Alright, Michael, this is what I'm prepared to do. I'll send the tickets. They can fly over and I'll collect them.

MICHAEL. Pat, they're too old to be crammin' into a plane and comin' over. It's just not on. Not to mention the fact that there's not a Catholic church for miles. She'd be lost without bein' able to see the spire. (*Michael laughs.*)

PATRICK. You're right.

MICHAEL. Jezz, d'ya remember the Sundays we'd go into the front room to say mass? Us with the fancy coloured tea-towels pinned to our backs. You of course were always the priest.

PATRICK. Of course.

MICHAEL. And I was always the altar boy.

PATRICK. Yes . . . that is where it all started.

MICHAEL. And this is where I hope it all ends. (*Michael extends his hand. Patrick shakes it.*) It's been good to see you.

PATRICK. You, too. (*Breda returns.*)

BREDA. All set.

MICHAEL. Let's hit the road, Jack.

BREDA. Well, Patrick, it was nice meeting you.

PATRICK. And you, Breda, this is for you. Matthew Arnold— 'Dover Beach' is in there.

BREDA. I really appreciate this.

PATRICK. Enjoy your time in London.

BREDA. I intend to. (*Sarah enters with the painting that Breda first admired.*)

SARAH. I have something for you, I want you to have this.

BREDA. No, I couldn't.

SARAH. It's the one you liked the evening you arrived. It's yours.

BREDA. Don't you want it for yourself?

SARAH. I'm not sentimental or nostalgic.

BREDA. It was part of your blue period.

SARAH. My yellow period to be precise. Speaking of blue periods, some of Picasso's are in the Courtauld, that's worth checking out.

BREDA. Oh, right.

SARAH. It's where Patrick and I first met. I had all these canvasses and was weighed down, and he was just coming out from Birkbeck. He kindly offered to help . . . it was quite romantic in it's own way.

PATRICK. It was.

MICHAEL. Are we right?

SARAH. (*Kissing Breda.*) Bye, Breda, you've been a breath of fresh air.

BREDA. Thanks for everything.

MICHAEL. Sarah, you made us feel at home. (*They exchange a brief hug.*)

SARAH. Bye, Michael, and good luck with the greyhounds.

PATRICK. Michael, drive safely.

MICHAEL. Ah, sure you'd have to. (*Michael and Breda exit. Patrick looks through the photos, and Sarah sits on the settee alongside him.*)

SARAH. You all appear to have parted as friends. Pippa asked me to give you this photograph. She didn't keep it with the others. It's the one of us she took at the gallery. (*She gives him the photograph. He examines it.*)

PATRICK. She has your talent.

SARAH. She frames her shots very well.

PATRICK. Yes. (*He looks at the photograph.*) When I come upon you unexpectedly, see you walking on the other side of the street, I'm struck by how attractive you are and how I would like to be the man you are going to meet. (*Slight pause.*) And then I remember that I once was that man. (*He looks at the photograph. Pause. She kisses him briefly on the head.*)

SARAH. Goodnight, Patrick. (*Sarah exits, Pauses.*)

BOB. (*Off.*) Patrick.

PATRICK. Come in, Bob. (*Bob enters, he wears a different sports jacket.*)

BOB. Just a flying visit. The Headmaster wishes to see both of us in his office at 8.30 in the morning.

PATRICK. Oh, the Williams business.

BOB. And attendant matters. But I will back you to the hilt.

PATRICK. Thank you, Bob. Your usual nightcap?

BOB. I'd love one, but I cannot stay. As I was leaving this evening's rehearsal, I was aware of Melanie walking beside me and for some strange unexplained reason I was able to find the appropriate words. I invited her for a late sandwich supper at the Railway Hotel, and the darling girl accepted.

PATRICK. She did?

BOB. Isn't it remarkable?

PATRICK. Yes.

BOB. As one gets older one becomes more and more acutely aware of that awful silence between the picking up and putting down of that solitary cup on that solitary saucer. A curse on him who said bachelors like quiet in the morning.

PATRICK. Is that Tennyson?

BOB. No, it's Robert J. Smedley. (*He goes to leave.*)

PATRICK. Good luck in the Railway Hotel.

BOB. A posse ad esse. Let's hope so. (*Bob smiles, exits singing Bach. His voice fades. Patrick picks up the telephone and dials.*)

PATRICK. Hello? . . . Hello, Mam . . . apologies for calling so late . . . . No, it's not Michael, it's Pat . . . *Pat* . . . . I'm calling to thank you for the cake . . . the *cake*, Mother . . . yes . . . (*He continues talking as the lights dim.*)

END OF PLAY

Niall Williams.

A Little Like Paradise

NIALL WILLIAMS

1995

In memoriam, Michael O Neill, 1958–1992

Characters

JAY FENNEY, publican/undertaker/greengrocer/agent for Marty
KAY BREEN, a widow, his sister
CISSIE REIDY, a woman of sixty
MICK MAGUIRE, bachelor farmer, in his sixties
FATHER FRANCIS MCINERNEY, elderly parish priest
MARTY MCINERNEY, Senator, his brother, in his fifties
MARY MCINERNEY, Marty's new daughter-in-law, in her twenties

ACT I

Scene

Winter afternoon 1992, Caherconn, a rural village on the Atlantic in Clare, the light dying. There are two principal playing areas but they run together without walls, both with the same sandy and shifting quality. We are on the periphery of the island, and it is almost eroding as we watch.
Centre is the interior of Jay Feeney's, one of Caherconn's two small bar-come-grocery shops. Upstage behind the counter leads into the house/shop. Downstage, right, the street and entrance to the pub.
Extreme downstage left are the beach and the sea. These suggested, but some continuity established between shore, street, and interior, a place already going to the ghosts. It is the sandiness of everything, the blown and shifting quality that dominates.
Darkness. Then the rising seasounds as lights come up on late after-noon in Caherconn. At the counter sitting over empty stout glass is Mick

248

Maguire, farmer, in wellingtons, muddied and rough-looking coat. He is unshaven, sour, grim. Lifts his shoulders in some agitation, as if trying to shake off something. This continues for some moments.

MICK. (*Shouts upward over his shoulder.*) Christ! (*Turns back towards shop.*) Jay! Jay! (*Moving around on the stool as if something were at him.*) G'way you hoor! Go 'way! Go on! (*Turns back to empty glass.*) Jesus! (*Calls toward shop.*) Where the hell are ye? (*Quickly back to presence behind him.*) Keep off, Mick Maguire, you hear? (*He coughs heavily, bangs his hand on the counter.*) (*Turns quickly back.*) Go 'way! Jesus! I've some flamin' life left in me yet! (*Calls.*) Jay? Jay! (*A moment, nothing, then a breath with some difficulty as if something had stopped his air, he gasps and calls above him.*) G'way you hoor! (*Waves a hand.*)

From the shop comes Jay showing in Cissie, a roundish woman of sixty who holds her hands together in front of her locked onto her black bag. Jay wears a worn black suit. He is the undertaker as well as publican, shopkeeper, and the Senator's agent; he considers the pub/shop central intelligence for the village. He collects the parish troubles in a book beneath the counter which he keeps for Marty. He is by nature a mean and unsympathetic man, tight with everything, while at the same time acting caring to his customers. He has found that politics has been good for his business. Although he fixes a smile on his customers he is constantly on the watch for details which will prove useful. Considers himself a good amateur doctor.

MICK. (*As they enter.*) Well Jesus I though ye were dead! . . .

JAY. (*Entering, to Cissie.*) He'll take care of that for you alright Cissie. I have a few things in the book already. I'll just slip your form in here and he'll take a look over it when he comes in . . .

MICK. Nearly was myself. Did ye not hear me calling?

CISSIE. (*To Jay.*) I don't like to be asking only . . .

JAY. (*Draws portable p.c. from beneath counter.*) I know. But. Yes. All the same . . .

MICK. (*Looks behind him, presence gone.*) I'm dry . . .

JAY. I'm expecting him shortly . . .

CISSIE. Is that right? . . .

JAY. (*Looks at the form.*) Deadline, next Friday. Oh yes, you'll get the grant alright, Cissie (*Types.*)

MICK. Man could be dead . . .

JAY. (*To the notebook.*) No problem. (*Continues looking down the screen on the p.c.*) Yes. Yes. No (*pause while he reads*) problem. (*Looks at her, whispers.*) We'll take care of it for you. Good as in the bank.

CISSIE. Thanks very much.

MICK. (*Moving coins on counter.*) A bit short always . . .

JAY. (*Closes computer, to Cissie.*) Look after the people . . .

MICK. Amn't I dying here in front of you?

JAY. Personal motto . . .

CISSIE. I know.

JAY. Now, I'll just gather up your bits and pieces inside, Cissie, settle yourself there now. (*Pours her short whiskey in a large mug.*)

CISSIE. (*Fake objection.*) Oh . . .

JAY. To keep out the cold, Cissie . . .

CISSIE. Well for medicinal purposes.

JAY. Correct . . .

MICK. My prescription's run out. (*Pushes forward glass.*) One to keep body and soul together?

JAY. Mick, you're ready for road . . .

MICK. Measuring more like . . .

CISSIE. (*Throws eyes to heaven before drinking.*) Dear Tommy in heaven . . . (*Drinks.*)

MICK. (*Raises dregs of his glass.*) The Lord between us and 'ating turf. (*While Jay gets him a drink, towards Cissie.*) I pulled a calf into the world this morning wasn't inclined to come . . .

JAY. (*To Cissie*). God rest him . . .

CISSIE. (*To Jay.*) I never forget the lovely burial you gave him . . .

JAY. If you're going, go proper . . .

CISSIE. Lovely. (*Drinks.*) The blue suit you put on him with the brown tie. Handsomest day of his life . . .

MICK. Slimy devil . . .

JAY. Make a good first impression. I have a selection of ties there in the shop. Hardly sell one until I'd be laying out somebody and see they hadn't anything suitable. Begin the afterlife with a clean set of clothes. Correct . . .

CISSIE. He was always that bit peculiar, you know . . .

MICK. Oh, Christ yes . . .

CISSIE. About his certain things a certain way. Lemonade for ladies. That was Tommy Reidy.

MICK. It's you or me, I says to him, . . .

CISSIE. (*Drinks.*) Thats nice now.

MICK. Do you want to be born or not?

JAY. That's right, Mick, Major, Cissie?

CISSIE. (*Taking one from box, Jay makes note of it.*) Dear God.

MICK. (*Reaching for one.*) And His blessed Mother. (*Jay makes note.*) Caught between the two places, half of him in the world, half not out. Bastard of a thing stuck there hanging and me looking at him.

CISSIE. Sacred Heart . . .

MICK. 'Might as well join the rest of us', says I, stood back and had me fag, and didn't he decide to slide out like jelly in the end. Nice friesan bullock.

JAY. That right?

MICK. That's right, then. Just that (*Clicks fingers.*) Between living and dying.

JAY. You're alright there, Cissie? I don't know where that sister of mine's got to. (*Calls in back.*) Kay? Kay? (*No response.*) I'll just slip in, get your things together in a box. Bit of the gammon. (*Jay exists into shop with list.*)

MICK. Don't I know it myself. Just that.

CISSIE. (*Calls.*) Smoked. (*Vague direction of Mick.*) Himself never let me have the smoked.

MICK. Not that he's worth a damn.

CISSIE. I beg your pardon?

MICK. Fool's game now the small farming, but we know nothing else. (*Pause.*) Rain coming,

CISSIE. That's right.

Marty and Mary have appeared out on the beach. He is a handsome man of sixty in his good, worn suit. He is a senator and a widower. His good looks have roughened with age and he has an unkempt air about him. His suit pockets are filled with scraps of paper, notes, things he mustn't forget. Mary is his new daughter-in-law. She is in her twenties and newly arrived in the west.

MARY. (*Looking seaward.*) What time is it there?

MARTY. (*Inhales deeply.*) Ah, breathe deeply, Mary, the sea air.

MICK. Christ but d'you know we'll be glad of hell itself after all the rain.

CISSIE. Mr Maguire, I'm here taking a medicinal and sharing a few minutes wait for my bits and pieces but I'd rather you didn't use language. One thing my Tommy couldn't tolerate at all. Language.

MICK. No but, excusing your presence and his and that. Sorry, mam. I'm not that used to the ladies. Any chance I could borrow another nail for me coffin? (*After a beat.*) A cigarette?

CISSIE. (*Offering box.*) Let your last act be a charitable one, as Father Griffen used to say.

MICK. God rest the same man, wasn't he almost an apostle? Thanks now. (*Takes one, smokes.*) The glass is good for you but these are the boys that'll come against you.

CISSIE. I'm down to three a day . . .

MICK. Oh, yes . . .

CISSIE. On a Tuesday . . .

MICK. Take the wind out of you . . .

CISSIE. And a Thursday. Eight Friday and Saturday . . .

MICK. The deaf doctor himself said it to me and himself wheezing and sputtering like an old tractor. (*Loudly.*) 'Fags'll feck you, Maguire', he roars across to me, and of course he's right there . . .

CISSIE. Bingo . . .

MICK. They have me shittered . . .

CISSIE. That's Wednesday, fourteen, well depending on Mag and Sheila.

MICK. Like bursted old fertilizer bags.

CISSIE. What?

MICK. The lungs. With these flittering things. (*Inhales.*)

MARTY. Breathe, Mary. Rejuvenate.

MICK. Forty I'm on. Thirty years. Makes you feel numb cold too. Did y'ever stamp around in the wellies of a morning and not feel yourself? Toes smoked away. Gone to the divil in hell.

CISSIE. Well, Mr. Maguire . . .

MICK. Not able to feel a thing. Ah no you're only having the few. Don't mind me. Enjoy your pleasures, as the man says. Thanks very much. (*Smokes.*) Give me soul for a pack of Majors some days. Whatever way the divil has me d'you know I can't give 'em up.

CISSIE. I know.

MICK. But they'll come against me yet. I know that sure. I feel him coming up on me . . .

CISSIE. Who?

MICK. Death, sure.

CISSIE. (*Smokes.*) Dear God.

MARY. What do you think he's doing out there, right now?

MICK. Any bit of a hill now and there he is, hands on me shoulders pulling me back. (*A pause then low threat to behind him.*) Get off me! Get back! (*Turns, some contentment.*) Either Death or the Divil, one of 'em anyways.

CISSIE. Merciful . . .

MICK. Cold bloody fingers he has too. Inside me clothes . . .

CISSIE. Hour . . .

MICK. (*Choking cough.*) You wouldn't mind maybe if I had another?

CISSIE. Well, Mr Maguire maybe you . . .

MICK. Aren't we living only one step ahead of the afterlife, as Paddy Dick says. (*Laughs. Takes one.*) Same man more tar in him than any road in west Clare. No, you have to shout the bastard down. Go 'way!

Kay enters from the house. She is a handsome widow of fifty, sharpened by life. She comes to the counter, finds a kettle, fills it.

CISSIE. (*With relief.*) Morning, Matron.

MICK. Mam.

KAY. (*At the bar sink.*) There's no matron here, Cissie.

CISSIE. Well not right . . .

KAY. Unless you mean of the parking lot?

CISSIE. Well no, no, but you were before and you will be again, please God.

KAY. It would want to please more than Him.

CISSIE. We'll have our own little hospital so we will and be all the better for it. Aren't we only waiting on the letter. And do you know ever since Mr McInerney and your brother inside said about approaching the lottery for funds I've been buying two tickets every Wednesday and Saturday.

KAY. Very charitable, Cissie.

CISSIE. Isn't it a good cause? Our own hospital. Tommy always maintained the nearer you are to a hospital the less you get sick.

KAY. We won't need any doctors so. Just the building and a matron.

CISSIE. St. Senan's.

KAY. What?

CISSIE. Has a lovely ring to it, I was thinking. Senan's. Very solid kind of. And welcoming. I have to go in to Senan's with my kidneys. Reassuring, that's what you need in a hospital.

KAY. Of course it is.

CISSIE. If . . .

KAY. Your Tommy . . .

CISSIE. Well, yes . . .

KAY. A building and a solid saint and we'll all be fine.

CISSIE. (*Drinks.*) I suppose it'll be Saint Martin's for Senator McInerney. Patron Saint of . . .

KAY. Three cleared fields and twenty-five lorry loads of gravel.

CISSIE. The Lord comes to those who wait.

KAY. He'll never make it beyond the pothole at Conways.

CISSIE. His ways are not our ways. We'll understand all the mysteries on the last day, please God. (*Finishes her glass with relish, then guiltily.*) I'm just waiting for your brother to get me my few things. Only he told me to wait here I'd be gone . . .

KAY. Have another . . .

CISSIE. Well now I . . .

KAY. Live dangerous . . .

CISSIE. Don't know that I should. Tommy never . . .

KAY. And what can he say about it now?

CISSIE. Well, Matron, I like to think of him as always being with me, just right there (*Gestures to the air.*) when I need him . . .

KAY. That's a handyman alright.

CISSIE. I'm sure your Donal, God rest him, is there too if you ever need him, Matron . . .

KAY. Oh, he is, like . . .

CISSIE. (*Takes up second glass.*) Only Tommy's probably round the village looking for me at the minute. He never liked the ladies in the public house. (*Drinks.*)

KAY. I see. Well, I must go over to St. Senan's, Cissie, if I see Tommy I won't let on. (*Moves to leave.*)

JAY. (*Calls from inside.*) That you, Kay? Would you come here a min? . . .

KAY. I'm going out . . .

JAY. (*Off.*) Hold on, will you give me a . . . (*Kay exits.*)

JAY. (*Appearing out at the door as Kay goes outside.*) Jesus. Sorry, Cissie, right with you. (*Returns to shop.*)

CISSIE. Most peculiar. Wasn't that most peculiar? Did you notice that? Dear Sacred Heart look down on her in divine mercy.

MICK. Amen.

CISSIE. (*Whispers.*) Of course the whole family's that bit peculiar (*pause*) the brother inside . . .

MICK. (*Imitating.*) 'I'll take care of that for you.' . . .

CISSIE. (*Nods.*) Oh, yes, there's stories there I'm telling you . . .

MICK. Taking care of me the other way before long too . . .

CISSIE. . . . Wanted her to move in after her husband died, encouraged her to sell the house, and then she with no place of her own. Thought he was getting a free servant he did. That's right. Most peculiar, that pair of them. Himself's as tight of course, and she the other way. Only he has the papers and handles the few things for Senator McInerney and picks me up in the car to bring me down pension day. I'd go down the street to Micky Ryan's. Then again you can't be going against them either, can you? Peculiar and all as they are.

JAY. (*From shop.*) The low fat, Cissie?

CISSIE. What? Oh, certainly, yes. Thank you. (*Holds pause, then to Mick, who has put down his head.*) God Almighty did he hear me? (*No reaction from Mick.*) Mr Maguire? Mr Maguire? (*Pause, she drinks, low voice.*) Very civil. Well, not another word. Cissie Reidy keep your mouth shut and your mind on heaven. (*Down the beach move Marty with Mary. As they come forward Marty pauses to catch his breath. Mary is gone a step ahead of him.*)

MARY. Why is he never there when I phone? It just rings and rings. And he hasn't written either. Not even . . .

MARTY. (*Panting a little.*) No, no, correct and affirmative negative as the fella says, he . . .

MARY. He promised me. He said, all the time, 'I'll write all the time, Mary' . . .

MARTY. Stop! (*Chest expanded.*) Oxygenation of lungs, Mary, blood brain and other etceteras not to be underestimated.

MARY. What?

MARTY. Breathe before action.

MARY. Right. (*Deep inhaling.*) But what'll I do? I mean you're his father, can't you . . .

MARTY. Whist! (*Inhales, holds breath. Cissie in the bar has a coughing fit, helps herself to a little drink.*) Not to be underestimated.

A paper on the same theory. Japanese breathe more than any one else. Proven fact. Make the drawing of breath . . . (*Draws breath, looks about*) . . . daily habit.

MARY. (*Huge inhale.*) Yes, but Mr McInerney . . .

MARTY. Oh, now desist that. Marty. Marty?

MARY. Marty.

MARTY. That's it. You're one of us now, remember, and when you married the McInerneys you married Caherconn. Forget the Pale. Marty it is. Now breathe. With Francie away you could do worse than peramble the shore profile on a daily basis until he returns . . .

MARY. Returns? Well . . .

MARTY. I'll tell you something too, familiarity with the locality, a key. Look at that will you? Look at the beauty of it.

MARY. Francie loved it down here, it's where we . . .

MARTY. Soul of the place. Fourteen million pounds to interrupt the erosion, worth every penny if we can convince HQ.

MARY. I bet he misses it. I bet he . . .

MARTY. I missed it all week myself, but the exigencies of office, the price of power, Mary. So be it. Whenever and wherever McInerney has had to go he had to go . . .

MARY. (*Closes eyes, calls softly.*) Francie? . . .

MARTY. With Caherconn and this beach in his pocket . . .

MARY. Francie?

MARTY. A lifetime carrying it, Mary, to Dublin and beyond, sand in pocket, and approaching short-legged Belgians and hard-nosed Germans who don't donate a flying canary or figarie, as the man says, for our three-eighths of an inch of the map. (*Draws exasperated breath.*) The sorry state of it, Mary, our oxygen, H_2O, winds, sands, soil, and other etceteras are not that (*clicks fingers.*) to anyone east of Nolan's cross, lest we convince them otherwise. Ah! Draw breath! The sea air. (*They breathe.*)

MARY. Do you think he really misses me?

MARTY. It's a certain fact. He does. (*A moment, his voice drops.*) He does even when he hasn't said so.

MARY. But he should.

MARTY. (*Slightly flustered.*) What? Yes. Affirmative, he should and he will. He will, Mary.

MARY. But . . .

MARTY. (*Drawing her quickly away from the continuing of the conversation.*) Yes, yes come on, to the rocks and back! (*They go off down the shore briskly. Jay comes back into the pub with boxed groceries.*)

JAY. Now I think I have everything there. No smoked bacon until tomorrow, Cissie. But I've thrown in some of that new pudding, the Bonina. You'll like that. And a bag of the soft caramels came in in the van this morning.

CISSIE. I was just saying my few prayers . . .

JAY. No charge, Cissie. (*Crossing to Mick.*) Mick? Mick, home now! Come on.

CISSIE. He dozed off there a little while ago, right when I was talking to him. Not very civil.

JAY. Mick? (*Shakes him.*) Mick, wake up. (*Mick slumps over, dead.*)

JAY. Mick, Jesus!

CISSIE. Mary and Joseph!

JAY. Mick?

CISSIE. Padre Pio pray for us!

JAY. Stay there and I'll go call Dr O Neill.

CISSIE. I won't.

JAY. What?

CISSIE. I'm not staying here with him. What if somebody came in? What would I look like? God help me, I should never have had that second drink. Oh, God help me and I gave him the cigarettes too and he after telling me as much as he was dying from them. Oh, dear Sacred Heart!

JAY. (*Checks Mick for heartbeat.*) Cissie!

CISSIE. What?

JAY. He's dead.

CISSIE. Oh, sweet angel of mercy pray for us!

JAY. We'll never get O Neill either, he could be miles away. Listen, you go across the road for Father Mac, will you? I'll stay with him.

CISSIE. Right. Yes. I'll go for Father. Righto (*Stops suddenly.*) I can't feel my feet! Oh, merciful, my toes, I can't, it's how he started, his feet, and . . .

JAY. Jesus, Cissie will you go get Father Mac!

CISSIE. (*Shaken.*) Well there's no call for language! (*Starts to walk gingerly.*) I just can't feel my feet.

JAY. Jesus will you hurry? (*Cissie goes out, rosary beads in hands. Jay props Mick up, then lifts him with great difficulty onto the counter. He thumps Mick on the chest a few times, big windup but gentle thump in the end. Nothing.*)

JAY. Mick? Mick? (*Nothing.*) Nobody home. You're dead alright. Wherever you are. (*Pauses a moment, takes out p.c. and begins measuring him quickly, makes notes, as he continues, straightening the clothes on Mick, buttoning up, tidying him, taking off his wellies and standing them alongside.*) We'll put down mahogany and brass handles, brother Declan in England, isn't that right? Correct. Best of sendoffs for all customers J. Feeney. Put you down for the tie too. Hardly find one above there in Ballyrea. Not that I'm sure you ever voted for us. Still. (*Inspects the face.*) Shave and haircut. (*Notes it, goes in back comes out with socks and puts them on Mick.*) Socks, black. (*Notes it, pause.*) Won't get much for the house, then. (*Writes.*) Premises, outhouses, and . . . fifty two acres, ten turbery. You could have done better minding it. How many cattle? Ten? (*Writes.*) Maybe a dozen. Two cows, newborn bullock calf. (*Pause, erases.*) Buy him from you myself.

Cissie enters with Father Mac, the elderly parish priest. He is seriously ill, suffers severe pains in the chest which he disguises as best he can.

FATHER. God bless. (*walks over, makes sign of cross on Mick, begins Latin prayer.*)

JAY. Father . . .

CISSIE. (*Can't look at corpse, whispers.*) Oh, dear Sacred Heart . . . (*Father prays in Latin. Cissie stands alongside as does Jay, who then fills some whiskey into her mug and slips it onto the counter. At a pause in the prayers.*)

JAY. Brother in England, Father, I'll call him this evening.

FATHER. (*Distracted.*) em . . .

JAY. Father . . .

FATHER. Sorry, em, yes, right.

JAY. No others that I know of . . .

FATHER. No. I'm not sure em, yes. Certainly . . .

JAY. I'll handle the arrangements then so, Father?

FATHER. Good. Yes. Fine.

CISSIE. The poor man . . .

FATHER. I suppose he (*Sharp pain, he turns away.*)

CISSIE. (*To Jay.*) Next to me alive as yourself and then gone to heaven in the fiery chariot.

JAY. I suppose he was happy enough at that, Cissie.

CISSIE. Ours not to know the minute nor the hour, isn't that it, Father?

FATHER. A few prayers, I think.

CISSIE. I was only waiting on my few things, Father, I wasn't partaking at all, only a small problem for your brother the senator, mentionin' it here to Mr Feeney because I don't, Tommy never . . .

JAY. I'll just get a blanket or something. (*Exists.*)

CISSIE. It's a terrible feeling, Father. One minute living presence, and the next, just like a fly or a bee or something flown away. (*Pause.*) Is he there yet do you think Father?

FATHER. What?

CISSIE. Is he there? Paradise, Father?

FATHER. (*Hesitates.*) Well I . . .

CISSIE. (*Drinks.*) Oh, God almighty, sorry for putting you in the imposition, Father, begging your pardon. I shouldn't have asked. He wasn't in the state of grace? . . .

FATHER. I think I need a drink of water . . .

CISSIE. Blessed Jesus and His Angels to be caught unprepared like that . . .

FATHER. Cissie . . .

CISSIE. That's one consolation I had with my Tommy, Father, and he taken from me on his way home from church. It was like the Almighty's personal intercession I always maintained. Taking him with his soul newly confessed and everything. A beautiful thing, Father.

FATHER. (*Pain, distracted.*) What?

CISSIE. That's what I pray for, Father. To be taken like Tommy in that state of grace on the way from church. Tripped by the foot of God and on your way to the choirs of Angels, Alleluia.

FATHER. (*Turning away, beginning to pray.*) Sanctus i . . .

Father continues to pray and they stand there hands in prayer listening, Cissie flushed with drink. During the following, Father gets an attack of pain low in his stomach, pauses but carries on.

CISSIE. (*Whispers to Jay.*) The think of course is how the sacred soul gets there.

JAY. What?

CISSIE. How it gets out of the body. Mrs Considine has these notions of course, God forgive me for saying so, but He knows the whys and the wherefores. (*Pause.*) The personal orifices.

JAY. (*Whispers.*) Cissie.

CISSIE. That's what she ways. The personal orifices. Maintains the soul gets out through all the personal orifices at the same time.

JAY. I see.

CISSIE. Nose, ears, and not to mention. Sort of assembles above again. If it didn't, she says, how could you hear the hymns and smell the flowers on the graves?

JAY. A point there.

CISSIE. Everyone knows the soul goes out the mouth with the last expiring breath. (*Exhales almost onto collapse.*)

FATHER. Perhaps if you stopped talking Cissie and went home . . .

CISSIE. (*Whispers.*) No, no, Father MacInerney. Go ahead now. I'll be into confession Friday. (*Aside to Jay.*) He wasn't in the state of grace.

FATHER. (*Hesitant.*) Our Father . . . who art . . .

CISSIE AND JAY. In heaven . . . (*They continue to pray quietly, Cissie and Jay with easy quick rhythm, Father is obviously disturbed. On the shore Marty and Mary return from their walk. Marty is a few steps ahead of the possibility of conversation. Within moments Kay is seen before the pub.*)

MARY. (*Catching up to him.*) I forget you know that you miss him too . . .

MARTY. (*Sees Kay, stops abruptly.*) Yes . . . yes, certainly. Em, no problem, (*Automatic. Kay approaches.*)

MARY. What?

MARTY. Christmas. (*Turns towards Kay, quite jumpy.*) Ah, Mrs Breen, (*claps hands*) how are we, em, doing today?

KAY. Mary, Mr McInerney.

MARTY. I just landed, as the fella says, from Europe.

MARY. I thought this was Europe.

MARTY. What?

MARY. Aren't we in Europe?

MARTY. (*Looking at Kay as he jabbers on to Mary.*) What? Well, no, Caherconn never joined Europe as such, sense of the verb being active. No, no, furthest toe, submerged in sea of neglect on that score, a periphery on the extreme peripheral and conglommered . . .

KAY. Conglommered? . . .

MARTY. . . . Em, yes, with Highland huts and the man in the moon in the eyes of Brussels. A donkey at the horse fair, as the man says, hardly an asset mentionable.

KAY. Aren't you our asset?

MARTY. Well now, assets, as the fella says, are baby donkeys. (*Pause.*)

KAY. Well?

MARTY. Well . . .

KAY. Aren't you going to tell me?

MARTY. Well perhaps if . . .

KAY. Tell me.

MARTY. Well not so well.

KAY. Nothing?

MARY. What?

MARTY. Little of good import at the present moment.

KAY. You mean nothing.

MARY. What?

MARTY. But that's not the end of it yet . . .

KAY. Nothing means nothing.

MARTY. No, no private funds as such. At the present moment.

KAY. Shite.

MARTY. Everything has to go through the proper channels. With Brussels regulations . . .

KAY. There are no proper channels down here. There never were.

MARTY. I know, Kay . . .

KAY. Seventy-six beds in the County for ninety-three thousand people.

MARTY. Sure we're not done yet . . .

KAY. No maternity ward anywhere . . .

MARTY. I'll be going back, I'll . . .

KAY. Shite . . .

MARTY. With what we've collected to date in the parish fund and the National Lottery cheque when that comes . . .

KAY. If. . . .

MARTY. No, no. This is Marty McInerney here. Marty McInerney will get it yet, Kay, em, I'm going to get it for you, (*catches himself*) for for all of us, us all, for my own ailing brother, Father Mac, and for every man and woman in the parish and outlying townlands. Oh, no, not done yet, I'll be at them, they'll find me in their breakfasts, dinners, and teas; incubators, in all ambulances, first line of attack . . .

KAY. More luck to you. It'll never happen.

MARTY. Now Kay . . .

KAY. Do you know, Mary, how you close a hospital?

MARY. I think it's terrible . . .

KAY. Facts and figures . . .

MARTY. Nothing is final, it's . . .

KAY. Men in the women's ward, beds in the corridors, . . .

MARTY. Kay . . .

KAY. Turn down the heating Tuesdays and Thursdays. 'To make it economically viable'. Shite. Can't replace those windows that are falling out either. Not economically viable. Bingo, close the doors, away you go home now and find some relatives you can die on . . .

MARTY. (*Whispers.*) Please Kay . . .

KAY. Hospitals, roads, bus services, and post offices, facts and figures'll close them all. (*Kay has turned to walk away.*)

MARTY. Kay! (*To Mary.*) If you'll just excuse me a moment now, Mary, em, matters of state. Just partake of a sup of tea there in Feeney's and I'll be with you in a trice.

MARY. I'm alright, thanks . . .

MARTY. In a trice, in a trance, go on let you. Mary!

MARY. What? Oh, right, I'll just be inside then. (*Passing Kay.*) Mrs Breen.

KAY. Good-bye, Mary. (*Mary goes into the praying pub.*)

MARY. What's? Oh, my God!

JAY. Shush!

MARY. Is he? Right. Okay. Alright. God. Fine. Good. Okay. (*She joins the prayers a moment.*)

MARTY. Kay.

KAY. I'm sorry. (*Long sigh.*) Blowing up like an old bag.

MARTY. No, no, not at all now, I know exactly what you're feeling. Believe me.

KAY. I know you do. I don't know why it burst out of me like that. I must be getting simple.

MARTY. I'm endevouring to do everything I possibly can on all fronts, Kay . . .

KAY. What's the use? How many days, weeks did we spend planning it out, our own clinic in Caherconn, our own people's hospital, picking the colour paint for the walls! God Almighty. Simple! It's not going to happen, it was never going to happen . . .

MARTY. We have to think it will sure . . .

KAY. Didn't we go in droves to march in Dublin, singing in Garvey's bus, marking out placards? They just wait for us to get tired. And the facts and figures are still waiting to come and get us.

MARTY. Granted it's bleak, Kay, granted. The times we live in, the place as such, locale, end of the country, but we have to hold out hope, the National Lottery could . . .

KAY. If Donal was alive he'd be laughing at me. A clinic in Caherconn! If you're feeling sick, he'd say, the quickest way to get into hospital is to row out a mile in Ryan's little boat jump in the sea and be rescued by the Shannon helicopters.

MARTY. (*Losing his bluster, in half-belief himself.*) Faith is, em, paramount. Sure we can't give up just. . . . We must all believe . . .

KAY. Well I don't anymore, Marty. Christ I'm so tired of it all . . .

MARTY. I know, Kay. (*Pause, decides to go for it, tenderly.*) But that's why we need one another to (*embraces her*) . . . Kay . . .

KAY. Yes?

MARTY. (*Hesitates.*) In fact I've often said it. And honesty is the best policy, if you're going to vote, vote, as the fella says, and avoid the maliferous climate of the unspoken harbouring the undeclared will, isn't that it?

KAY. What?

MARTY. And, em, so, I've been thinking, on a more personal basis, about needing, well, stop me now if I'm, yes well it's that, of course, there's no requirement on your behalf, no need at all in fact if, well but to speak the mind do you see, to face the ball and get it right out down the park and, flappit to hell, say the thing out and out, clean breasts of it, and take the comeuppance from the tallymen of life, and if I've been wont to mislay myself in public affairs I'm still a private man, Kay, and as such and insomuch as the heart demands, and the etceteras of office setting aside for too long the personal McInerney I decided abroad, Kay, no more.

KAY. No more what?

MARTY. The thing is, I have something . . .

KAY. Oh, shite, Is it serious?

MARTY. What? No no, well, yes, of course it is, serious in the upper extremity and for too long neglected, Kay, something that I have that I want to (*Mary has backed out of the prayers and comes looking for Marty and Kay who must immediately disentangle.*)

KAY. Yes?

MARTY. Yes? Do you mean it?

KAY. What is the question? (*Mary arrives.*)

MARTY. And the elements are most clement for it, Mrs Breen.

MARY. Oh, God, I'm after having a terrible fright.

MARTY. I know.

KAY. What is it, Mary?

MARY. There's . . . There's, you know, well.

MARTY. What? . . .

KAY. There's a what, Mary?

MARY. A man . . .

MARTY. Yes?

KAY. Who?

MARTY. Looking for me?

MARY. No. He's . . . he's ghostly pale, he's you know, he's . . .

KAY. What?

MARY. Well. Oh, God. Deep breath. This is what my book says to do. In. Out. It's just a body, that's the thing to remember. We're all just bodies. Some are fat, some are thin, whatever, we're just in them for a short brief, in, (*holds breath, blows out*) time . . .

MARTY. Mary!

MARY. Like, like we're shirts, you know?

MARTY. Shirts?

MARY. Hanging on this line, just filled up with wind. (*Exhales.*) And then we're gone . . .

KAY. Mary, what are you talking about?

MARY. The thing to think of is (*breathing*) spirits.

KAY. Maybe you should sit down?

MARTY. That's it, sit down, over here.

MARY. No, no, I'm fine. (*Breathes.*) We're dust and worms . . .

MARTY. Of course we are . . .

MARY. That's all our bodies are . . .

MARTY. Now sit up here. (*Whispers to Kay.*) Later?

KAY. What?

MARY. Worms and dust. (*Lets fall a handful of sand.*) Like that. (*To Kay.*) I've never seen one before . . .

MARTY. (*Quick whisper to Kay.*) Here on the shore, later, an hour say, I'll wait by Killourey's sandhills.

MARY. Not dead. Cut, bleeding, broken, yes, but not . . .

KAY. (*To Mary.*) What?

MARTY. (*To Kay.*) Say yes.

MARY. You know? . . .

KAY. (*To Mary.*) Yes. Dead?

MARY. Yes.

KAY. (*Urgently to Mary.*) There's somebody dead? Where? In the bar? Is Jay? . . . (*Kay hurries towards bar, pursued by Marty then slowly Mary. They stop before the scene of the praying, the corpse under the blanket.*)

MARTY. (*A nod to his brother.*) Francis.

JAY. (*Underbreath.*) Mick Maguire, Marty.

MARTY. Don't I know him well.

JAY. He's dead.

MARTY. Out and out?

JAY. (*Underbreath report.*) Brother Declan in England. Funeral Friday, ten-thirty. Bit of business for Cissie Reidy, have it in the book for you.

MARTY. (*Stepping forward.*) God rest the man . . .

CISSIE. And may perpetual light shine upon him.

KAY. Amen. (*Mick stirs beneath the cover.*)

CISSIE. Aaaaahhhhh!

JAY. Christ!

CISSIE. Aaaahhhhh!

FATHER. Dear Lord!

KAY. Jesus!

CISSIE. Aaaahhhhh!

MARY. Oh, God!

KAY. (*To Cissie.*) Stoppit! Shush!

JAY. Shit!

KAY. Wait! (*Mick sits up, eyes closed. Long pause. Then he draws breath.*)

MARTY. Mick? (*Nothing.*) Mick? (*Mick slowly opens eyes.*)

MARY. (*Inhaling and exhaling urgently.*) Deep breath, deep breath, deep . . .

MARTY. Mick Maguire?

MICK. (*Long pause.*) Marty, how are you?

MARTY. How are you?

MICK. Christ, man, I've been worse. Oh, sorry, Father, didn't see you there.

JAY. You're not dead, Mick?

MICK. No.

JAY. But you were.

MARY. (*Inhales.*) In.

MICK. What?

JAY. You were dead.

MICK. (*Pause.*) I was I'd say. Dead out. I pulled a calf this morning and . . .

JAY. No. You were dead. I have you measured for the coffin. You're to be buried after mass Friday.

MICK. I'll hardly make it . . .

FATHER. Are you alright, Michael?

MICK. D'you know it's coming back to me now alright.

KAY. What?

MICK. Jesus. I was.

MARTY. What?

MICK. Dead. I remember it.

MARY. Ooooouuuuutttttt!

CISSIE. (*Takes out cigarette, smokes with great difficulty.*) Dear God above.

FATHER. What do you mean?

MICK. Well, d'you know, I remember, the cold feel of it down the back, the fingers of him alright, just stopping me like. You know? Like a tackle'd wind you, and him standin' over me and then he was gone I was sort of above looking down on myself, floatin . . .

MARY. (*Nodding, stepping forward.*) Floating.

JAY. Is that right?

CISSIE. Living saints preserve us . . .

FATHER. Where, Michael? Where were you?

MICK. I couldn't quite say now, Father. Just I suppose about (*points a little above him*) there.

CISSIE. Dear God and his flying angels.

MARTY. You were dreaming some class of hypno mumbo jumbo . . .

JAY. No, Marty, then, I know the dead. He was dead and gone, poor man.

MICK. I was.

KAY. What do you remember Mick?

MICK. Jesus where'd I get the socks? I don't remember them . . .

KAY. Mick?

MICK. I had a beautiful death. Just like I was stopped, d'you know, on the hill? And felt myself kind of peeling away from myself . . .

CISSIE. Lord save us . . .

MICK. Going out of myself . . .

MARY. Your soul.

MICK. I suppose . . .

MARY. That was your soul travelling. That's right, I've read about it, an out-of-body experience. That's what happened. You took off, went on a journey out of your body . . .

CISSIE. Most peculiar . . .

MARTY. Soul-travelling?

MARY. Yes.

JAY. I've heard of it alright.

CISSIE. Blessed Saint Lazarus.

MARTY. Rubbish . . .

FATHER. Marty . . .

MARTY. Took off? No stopover in Shannon, I suppose? Took some class of a flight up to Knock? No, no, no, tell them, Francis.

FATHER. Tell them what?

MARTY. A plain explanation. What our mother would have said to that: all in the mind. A decoration of fantasy as the fella says. It was all in your mind Mick.

MICK. No then, it wasn't. I was dead.

MARTY. You were not dead.

MICK. Well, I wasn't livin' . . .

MARTY. You were . . .

KAY. Marty!

CISSIE. (*To Kay.*) Ask him did he see anybody?

KAY. Did you see anybody?

CISSIE. Did he see my Tommy?

MARTY. Of course he didn't see anybody . . .

MICK. I did then, whole gangs of people . . .

MARY. Souls . . .

MICK. Throngs of 'em, d'you know, floating around without so much as a wave of a wing . . .

CISSIE. God protect us . . .

MICK. All floating up and down and in and out and through each other, I did, Christ yes, the air above this place is thronged with 'em, so it is . . .

CISSIE. Angels!

JAY. Jesus!

MICK. Thronged I'm telling ye. God, but it was powerful strange.

FATHER. Did you see Joe Melican? . . .

CISSIE. And he only buried a week . . .

MICK. No then, I didn't.

FATHER. Peadar Fitz, Tessie Brogan, did you see Haulie Clancy?

MICK. No. I couldn't say them now. Do you know but funny enough, Father, they were all kind of like children, you know?

FATHER. Children?

MICK. Floating without a bother on 'em and all in a kind of white whiteness d'you know?

FATHER. Did you see the Carthy's child?

KAY. God rest him . . . (*Pause.*)

MICK. Well, Father, I couldn't rightly say . . .

CISSIE. Why aren't they all gone to Heaven, in the name of God? . . .

FATHER. Well . . .

CISSIE. Oh, sweet Sacred Heart (*looking up at the ceiling as it if were a crowded window into heaven*) this could be heaven above here . . .

FATHER. Well now, em, wait a minute, Cissie. You saw a lot of them Michael?

MICK. There's a parish of 'em father.

FATHER. Like children?

MICK. I'd say that alright. Like kind of whiteness too. Just there now above our heads. D'you know, dancing.

CISSIE. (*Bursting forth.*) Did you see my Tommy Reidy?

MICK. Well now . . . no, Mam, I didn't.

CISSIE. Then it wasn't heaven. My Tommy's in heaven so he is. And if you were there he'd say hello, and come over for the chat. (*Speaks upwards.*) Isn't that right, Tommy pet? Isn't that right, love. (*Pause, they are looking at her.*) Of course he never comes into public houses. So. Cissie Reidy is going to take herself down to the church. (*She stands a moment, lost.*) Good-bye to ye now. (*She doesn't move, transfixed by the ceiling.*)

JAY. (*Leading her to door.*) Right, Cissie. Thanks very much. I'll pack your things and be down to collect you in a little while after your few prayers and that . . .

MARTY. Right then. Well you're alright Mick. We'd better get you home to your leaba.

MARY. I'll go with him.

MARTY. (*Helping Mick off the counter.*) Come down off that like a good man.

JAY. How do you feel, Mick?

MICK. (*Geting into his wellies.*) Do y'know, I feel great.

JAY. Of course you do. I'll put you down for those socks.

MICK. I though the bastard had me you know? But jayz he went off and left me, right there (*waves hand*) with the children . . .

FATHER. Would you like me to come along? I could . . .

MICK. Thanks, Father. There's no need. Sure won't this girl see me right?

MARY. I will, Father. I'm going up that way and (*to Mick*) maybe you'd tell me again? (*Mary and Mick exiting.*)

MICK. (*At the door.*) Well, one thing but it was really powerful strange. I'd sort of forgotten, you know, what it was like. Children playing, all flying around, floating and dancing goodo. (*Smiles, pause.*) My only disappointment was I missed seeing Himself. There was no sign a Him above.

MARY. Who?

MICK. Himself, God.

JAY. (*At the door.*) Maybe next time, Mick.

MICK. (*Exiting.*) God yes.

FATHER. Well now, I think I need a bit of air myself. (*To Marty.*) I'll see you later.

MARTY. I'm going up to the house myself . . .

FATHER. Yes, well, later, I, later yes. (*Father exits to the beach, Kay goes upstairs.*)

JAY. (*To Marty, as he opens the notebook and turns it for Marty to read.*) How'd you get on? Any news?

MARTY. Sweet fry all. Blue in the face talking us up, and Christ at the end of it, what, mistranslation, strudel, and caffe Mr Mac.

JAY. I hear An t'Uasal's making out there'll be no roads west of Shaughnessy's cross getting done for six months.

MARTY. That man'd be happy if we all went down a pothole and never came out of it again. Impossible to understand how a man like that gets elected.

JAY. I saw Small Tom talking to John Daly last night.

MARTY. Is that right?

JAY. Correct. Talking to him when I was coming up, and still talking to him when I was coming down. I wonder, is he putting the land up? Talk of him moving into Ennis.

MARTY. Maybe I'll have a word with him.

JAY. If he does itself, well maybe it'd be a nice spot for your Francie when he comes home from the States. Nice house there always.

MARTY. That's a fact. (*Makes a note.*) Make a few enquiries.

JAY. I will.

MARTY. Right so.

JAY. Yankee Maguane's rumoured to be thinking of it too.

MARTY. Is that right?

JAY. So I heard anyway.

MARTY. (*Pause.*) Jesus. We'll be left with nothing but empty houses with people's names on 'em.

JAY. My point.

MARTY. I'll talk to Maguane personally.

JAY. A few grant applications to look over. Form for Cissie, deadline Friday . . .

MARTY. (*Takes the form.*) Yes, yes, righto. Now I must. What's the time? Right. I'll be back later.

Marty exits. Jay makes a note in the book and then slips it away under the counter. From a peg he takes down his jacket and slips it on, goes into shop, takes box of groceries, comes out, calls up stairs.

JAY. Kay, are you there? (*Nothing.*) Kay? *Kay?* I'm taking Cissie home. If it won't be too much trouble to you, do you think you could mind the place? (*No response, he shrugs impatiently, underbreath.*) Don't put yourself out like, will you? (*No response, as he exits.*) Might as well be running a morgue.

Mary comes back to the pub, and enters as Father reappears on the beach. His walk has exhausted him. He is in pain and short of breath, given to racking coughing fits. As Mary comes in she moves with the sense of the spirits floating above her, and especially to the place where Mick 'died'. She brings with her a book she had been reading on out-of-body experiences.

MARY. (*To inside the shop.*) Hello? Anybody there?

FATHER. (*Sudden pain.*) Jesus! . . .

MARY. Hello? . . .

FATHER. Christ . . .

MARY. (*Upwards, quietly.*) Hello?

FATHER. (*Upwards, pain subsiding.*) Sorry.

MARY. It's me, Mary.

FATHER. Christ but you're killing me.

MARY. (*After a quick look around, takes out her book, deep breaths, reads.*) 'Divine masters and Universal spirits' (*stops, looks upward, closes eyes, breathes*) . . . and everyone else. I believe in . . . you, I really do, so please, please, please guide me out into the vastness of . . . whatever and help me to . . . float. . . . Amen.

FATHER. You there?

MARY. (*Opens eyes.*) Please.

FATHER. Forty-one years ordained and not a peep out of ye to me.

MARY. You see, I really miss him. And well, if I could be with him, well in spirit form, it would be . . . Oh, God! Well, so, thanks very much and. . . . Alright? (*Shuts eyes.*) Whenever you're ready. In. (*Deep breath.*)

FATHER. (*Grimaces, pain.*) Shaggit.

MARY. Out.

FATHER. (*Sits down.*) Do ye pick the cancer yourselves? Or what? Colon for your man there, intestines for her. Stomach for me. (*Pause, difficult breaths.*) Any time now I suppose?

MARY. Where are you, Francie? (*Breath.*) In.

FATHER. Now if you like. Go ahead. (*Pause, nothing.*)

MARY. (*Long blow.*) Out . . .

FATHER. (*Takes out small whiskey, drinks.*) I had a woman once told me she couldn't stand the suspense of it. Life.

MARY. Relax the arms . . .

FATHER. How it was going to turn out . . .

MARY. Relax the legs . . .

FATHER. Waiting for next week's enstallment afraid she was going to hear this was the last episode.

MARY. And in.

FATHER. 'What's the second channel going to be like, Father', she said. 'Like the first only less talk more music', I said.

MARY. Out.

FATHER. And that seemed to make her happy alright. 'I like the music', she said. The Bannerman maybe.

MARY. In.

FATHER. And then you had her run down in Dublin that Easter Monday.

MARY. Out.

FATHER. Hello, Mrs Donellen.

MARY. Hello, Francie?

FATHER. (*Drinks.*) Mick Donoghue of course tells me you're deaf and dumb.

MARY. Can you hear? . . .

FATHER. (*Loudly.*) You let his mother and two brothers die the same day . . .

MARY. Can you hear me?

FATHER. Do you hear me? (*Silence, sea sounds.*)

FATHER. You were never that great for replies, of course. (*Cough, pain, drink.*) Forty years telling you confessions on this bit of the beach and not a peep out of ye. No. Mysteries and puzzles. (*Looks up.*) Where's the Angel Gabriel? Will I hold my breath for him? (*Waits, holds breath, Mary holds hers. They both blow out together.*)

MARY. You're not relaxing . . .

FATHER. I suppose he isn't the cancer by any chance?

MARY. Come on, Mary, come on. Relax! I know you're up there. I know it.

FATHER. (*Drinks.*) The thing is now, well, I'm not sure you're there at all. Are you?

MARY. You know you can do this. Just let your soul float up. Now Relax!

FATHER. Sometimes I thought, well you know what I thought, nuisance of confession isn't it, the ridiculous monotony, the boredom of us for you . . .

MARY. (*Through gritted teeth.*) Don't forget to breath, Mary (*Sucks.*), breathe.

FATHER. Well anyway . . . ever since the Carthy's child was killed. There was no call for that, was there? No saviour for her. Youngest child in the parish, why? Why? I couldn't explain it. Were you in my church that day? Were you? Did you see the faces asking me? Why does someone kill a child? Christ! where were you?

MARY. Breathe . . .

FATHER. Where in the hell were you?

MARY. Breathe . . .

FATHER. (*Drinks.*) Nice bit of pain today. If that's a sign of anything. And then the Lazarus Maguire. (*Half laugh.*) Souls flying and floating above us? Is that it? No heaven at all? Full up is it?

MARY. (*Whispers.*) Francie?

FATHER. Or empty?

MARY. Francie?

FATHER. Christ! Talk to me now or kill me, whichever you like. (*Closes eyes, waits.*)

MARY. (*Opens eyes, lets out a cry of frustration.*) Aaaahhhh!!! (*Gets up.*) Okay. Alright. Sorry. I'm not relaxed. (*Stretches, shakes her arms about head, sits down.*) Okay. Now. Here we go. Please? (*Eyes shut, blesses herself.*) Divine Masters. Please. (*Nods, blesses herself.*) Amen. In. Out. Go on.

FATHER. Go on. (*Pause. He lies slowly down on the sand, Kay emerges from inside the house, dressed to go out and meet Marty on the shore. Mary lets out another cry of frustration, startling Kay.*)

KAY. Mary?

MARY. Kay, hello, how are you? . . .

KAY. What are you . . .

MARY. It's no good I can't . . .

KAY. What?

MARY. Go . . .

KAY. Where?

MARY. (*Emotional.*) Oh, it's silly but no, no, never mind. Well,

KAY. What?

MARY. I know you won't laugh. But.

KAY. I won't. Mary what is it?

MARY. Ooooh!

KAY. Mary?

MARY. Did you ever sit down and think of all the things you thought about somebody and never said to them?

KAY. Well . . .

MARY. Never said you know I really admire the way you did this or that. There's something about the way you walk or talk or the way you say my name or . . .

KAY. Mary . . .

MARY. Silly things. I like your handwriting. I keep bits of it in my purse, envelopes, anything. Or I'm still buying the cornflakes you liked and you're not even here. I let the toothpaste be squeezed from the middle now and I'm sorry I ever made a fuss about it; of course you have to get dirt in the house getting turf in, ashes do go everywhere, and you always said, and I disagreed, God and I was stupid to keep bringing it up and I should have said so, and I should have said you know I love that red jumper on you and you're really great you know, you lighten up the place, oh hundreds and hundreds of other things, every day, and oh God I didn't and now I don't know . . .

KAY. Don't know what Mary?

MARY. Well he hasn't written or called me back.

KAY. Maybe a letter's on the way. And it won't be long anyway until he's coming home . . .

MARY. He's not coming home . . .

KAY. Of course he is, now you . . .

MARY. No, he's not. He told his father that he was, that he was only going out to make the money for the house and come home, because he couldn't bring himself to tell him. Not then anyway, not when he was going. You know what Mr McInerney's like. And well, Francie's supposed to just get things set up out there and then I'm coming out to him.

KAY. And Marty doesn't . . .

MARY. We're going to live in San Francisco. I have the visa got and everything, and now he hasn't written to me, and he's out there, you know, out there, and I'm thinking maybe he's changed his mind and met someone and doesn't . . . well maybe he's remembering the way I was on at him, they were stupid, stupid things—God, Mary, you're such an eejit, you are such an eejit—telling him how to fold his shirts and he packing, asking him how much, well how much do you love me, Francie, go on, tell me, and he all knotted up in himself with his father downstairs fuming and he firing the things in the case and enough Mary he says enough and I said, well fine, well fine for you Francie McInerney excuse me for asking but that's not enough for me. I charged out of the place and he didn't come after me like he always does, he didn't come after me at all. And then the next morning going to Shannon in the car he hardly said a word either, just sitting there watching us leaving Caherconn out by Shaughnessy's and the Heihir's old place where he told me he used to help with the baling, and all the time nothing, not a peep out of him up in the front next to his father, neither of them cracking a word between them, and me, oh I was lovely balling my eyes out like a right eejit at the bottom of the crying stairs. The last I saw of him. (*Pause.*) And then he was gone.

KAY. God love you . . .

MARY. Well so, anyway I have this book and it says, you know, you could do it, go out on your soul sort of, communicate in spirits, and so I was thinking maybe I could, like Mr Maguire, and maybe I know, I know it sounds crazy but I could sort of get on to Francie you know, sort of let him know and that I loved him. What do you think?

KAY. Well . . . I'm sure he knows you love him, Mary.

During the following we see Marty preparing to come out and meet Kay. He is doing his tie and rehearsing the speech that has been waiting a lifetime.

MARY. Oh, God, I don't know. I mean sometimes I think there's some kind of great map, you know, a plan for everyone, with who our special person is all marked out and just waiting there . . .

MARTY. Kay, dear Kay . . .

MARY. Because, God here I go again, but otherwise why, why Francie? Like when you read you know that in one flash of a moment he saw her across the room and his deep blue eyes met hers and with a flash set fire to her soul and he knew and she knew and . . . well it's like it was all planned that way. I mean it could be . . .

KAY. Just . . .

MARY. (*Closing her eyes.*) Their souls. Couldn't it? Touching. Couldn't it? Souls touching. I think that's lovely.

MARTY. (*Beginning again.*) My dear Kay, I . . .

MARY. (*Kay says nothing; Mary opens her eyes.*) Well, who am I telling? I mean you were married to Mr Breen for a long time, weren't you?

KAY. A very long time . . .

MARY. And he must have been a wonderful man . . .

KAY. He was, once.

MARY. Oh, I know . . .

KAY. The Master Breen . . .

MARY. I heard he was . . .

KAY. Mean as a boiled shite. Closed the book of himself when we couldn't have children. And I found out I'd married my father . . .

MARY. Oh, God, I'm sorry.

KAY. Not as much as I was. Frightened of him I was, watching him become the most self-centered, conceited, craitach that was ever reared in the parish.

MARY. Oh, God.

KAY. Feck you if you're listening, Donal!

MARY. I'm so sorry . . .

KAY. Oh, don't be. I gave him my life and he took it. Not a single man, woman, or child in Caherconn who he hadn't a cross word or a sour face for, some remark or other as to how so and so was doing this, that, or the other all wrong, why did they not ask his opinion, why was the government ignoring the obvious, couldn't the amadains see there could be no such thing as a common market for the likes of us, what did these poor fields have in common with anywhere, Kay, and how was it all of his pupils were gone to America or England or Australia and the place empty and him giving up sanding their names off the schooldesks in the summertime. (*Slowly, tenderness despite herself.*) Kay this. Kay that. Kay the other. That was Master Breen.

MARTY. I have waited a lifetime for this chance . . .

MARY. I didn't know . . .

KAY. And I loved him.

MARY. You did? Of course you did.

KAY. It was a lifetime ago.

MARY. And he took part of your soul.

KAY. What?

MARY. I know. That's what's so wonderful. I mean there couldn't be anyone for me like Francie, because . . .

KAY. (*Abruptly.*) Shite. What am I doing?

MARY. What?

KAY. (*Pouring herself a drink.*) I should have just said no to him.

MARY. But you had happy years, that's what you have to think of, and that in spirit he's there, just watching you and floating about and waiting . . .

KAY. I kissed him.

MARY. What? Of course you did, Matron you were married.

KAY. Not him.

MARY. Oh . . .

KAY. It was nothing. It was what ten years ago . . .

MARTY. I have a waited a lifetime since, and, Kay, I, Kay. (*Begins again.*) My dear Kay . . .

KAY. He came calling. Well, he sometimes had to come calling, and of course I knew, a woman knows, I knew when I was nineteen what way he was about me, and I visited him a bit when he broke the two legs, but any Christian would have done no less. There was nothing in any of that.

MARY. No . . .

KAY. Not at all. But well, the night he was elected, that night, ah, but what was it, a kiss.

MARY. A kiss . . .

KAY. Nothing . . .

MARY. (*Not agreeing but nodding.*) Nothing.

KAY. And what good would it have done to tell the next morning? A kiss, and of course I didn't. (*Pause, looks up.*) Oh shit!

MARY. God, I don't know what to say.

KAY. (*Snaps.*) Nothing. (*Catches herself.*) Sorry. Say nothing, Mary. I shouldn't have said anything . . .

MARY. No, no, that's just it, you see. You have to. We have to say things. I'm really glad. (*A moment.*) Matron, I'm going to say this and I know you don't want to but would you try with me for a minute?

KAY. What? . . .

MARY. Maybe there needs to be more here than just me . . .

KAY. Mary, I've go to . . .

MARY. And you could tell Francie . . .

KAY. Really, I don't . . .

MARY. You could tell him too how much I love him. Please, (*Kay hesitates*) just sit down and breathe first, here beside me. Please? Just for five minutes . . . (*Mary leads Kay into the snug and sits her down and begins her breathing.*)

MARY. A few deep breaths to start you off. Close your eyes. Now just think souls. And breathe.

Marty appears down the street in the gathering darkness for his appointment. He is dressed in his good suit, a red tie, black shoes, carries in the absence of roses a bunch of montbretia flowers. He is nervously rehearsing his opening speech.

MARTY. (*Sweeping down the street, must catch his breath.*) Kay, my dear Kay. My darling, no, no. Divinity! K, L, M, N, O, P! Jesus wept, (*Clicks fingers.*) Alphabet of love. No, no. Oh Christmas! (*Runs quickly down the street to the sea shore to gather himself.*)

MARY. Breathe . . .

MARTY. The sea air, oxygenation. Now, 'I have waited a lifetime for this moment, Kay. And, Kay, I love you.' Simple as that. Plain as an egg. 'Kay I love you. Kay I love you.' That's it. No problem. 'I Love you, Kay. You, Kay, I Love.' No, no. Christmas, rewind. 'I love you, Kay.'

FATHER. (*Sitting up behind him, watching.*) Will you marry me?

MARTY. (*Spinning around.*) God Almighty, you, you lunatic, what the blazes are you doing?

FATHER. (*Coming down, empty bottle.*) Hearing confession.

MARTY. You're gone completely bananas now, is that it?

FATHER. That's it.

MARTY. I see, well . . .

FATHER. Will you marry me, that's the next bit.

MARTY. I know that. Will you marry me! Go home to bed in the name of God.

FATHER. She will.

MARTY. What?

FATHER. You'll be married before Easter. But you'll wait until then in respect after my funeral.

MARTY. Now stop that, I don't want to hear that class of . . . ballsology, do you hear me, Francis, that class of thing is no use to anyone, going on about that and you in the pink of blossom . . .

FATHER. I'm dying, Martin.

MARTY. Aren't we all. Living and dying simultaneously, natural, par for the course and perfectly normal . . .

FATHER. Shut up, will you?

MARTY. What?

FATHER. Do you mind if I have the last word? If I'm going to drop dead at any minute I'd prefer to go in a bit of hush. (*Marty vexed somewhat, a pause between the brothers, sea gazers, sense of the gathering cold.*)

FATHER. Children.

MARTY. What?

FATHER. What the Lazarus Maguire said. Do you know what was funny about that?

MARTY. Everything was, you couldn't believe the gospel and he reading it.

FATHER. There's no children.

MARTY. Where?

FATHER. Here, in Caherconn. None. None for communion this year. Two for confirmation. The Master's school down to one teacher. We're dying out.

MARTY. We are not.

FATHER. You deny everything, Martin . . .

MARTY. Negative . . .

FATHER. So you do . . .

MARTY. I do not . . .

FATHER. That's what makes you so loveable. (*Pause.*)

MARTY. I won't deny it. (*Marty makes move to leave.*)

FATHER. Do you know Mick Devine says that when an old man or woman dies a child's born somewhere.

MARTY. Is that a fact, well . . .

FATHER. Yes. but where are they? (*Calls.*) Where are you?

MARTY. Now, Francis . . .

FATHER. Just the sea and people getting older. That's Caherconn. I was at fifteen funerals this year already, do you know that? So where are all the new (*Pain*), oh God!

MARTY. What? Francis are you . . .

FATHER. (*Recovering.*) Comes in waves. Like the sea. (*Pause.*) No, no new souls here.

MARTY. They're on their way.

FATHER. What?

MARTY. Haven't I been all week in Europe extolling our seawaters to the Germans, and while they didn't name names or date dates, one and one is two as the man says, and I can surmise. The Germans. They're the men for the big fish. There's hope there alright. Germans need hospitals, my point. We'll be walking down the street one day, Francis, look out and there'll be a fleet of 'em.

FATHER. A German colony?

MARTY. Sure isn't it a little like Paradise?

FATHER. Near enough. There were only two living in Paradise. And they left.

MARTY. Will you stop that now, that defeatist mentality'll . . .

FATHER. Year 2000, nobody at all. A few holiday homes. Interpretative centre maybe.

MARTY. Francis . . .

FATHER. Dolphins Siney Maguane says. He saw one. Flock of dolphins in Caherconn, sanctuary for whales and dolphins. (*Pause. Seasounds. Stargazing. A moment.*)

MARTY. (*Hand on Francis's shoulder, moving him along.*) Well, time for you to be . . .

FATHER. Last time they were here, he says, half a century ago. Was a place of children, time you were born. (*Stops.*) I remember that, you know? . . .

MARTY. Like . . .

FATHER. I do. I remember the great tantara upstairs and Peggy Devine coming and going with the water Dad brought from the well . . .

MARTY. Is that right?

FATHER. You could hear the rosaries humming on the ceiling above. I thought you were a seagull.

MARTY. What?

FATHER. When I heard the cry. I went to the window, thought is was a gull falling or dying or something. Then I heard it again and there you were. You were given to me in the kitchen on the brown setee, the little eyes of you squinting up at me and I thinking, I'll be gone from you, little man, I'll be away in some parish somewhere saving souls, you'll hardly know me. And your own soul laying there in my lap with a gleam on it like a hay-knife. I often thought of that.

MARTY. Of course you did.

FATHER. Especially when Dad died so soon after. Near twenty years between you and me and then him to die as soon as you were born. You don't remember this place then. Children on the sand, horses, Carthy's donkeys. Three butcher shops and five pubs. God's village. Gone. Where? (*Pause, stargazing.*) If there's any chance I'll try and tell you after I'm dead.

MARTY. (*Putting his arm around Father warmly.*) Will you stop dying in every second sentence. Now go home to your bed, go on, out in the middle of the night like some becapered eremite, as the man says, instead of in your bed. Go on now, good man. (*During this, Kay opens her eyes in snug, whispers.*)

KAY. Mary. (*No reaction, she gets slowly up.*) I shouldn't do this. I shouldn't. Of course I shouldn't. (*Stands, waits, decides.*) Oh, shite! (*Tiptoes, comes outside, heads down to the seashore, to Marty and Father.*)

FATHER. Well perhaps I should stay awhile longer . . .

MARTY. Awhile? Here? Well . . . Ka . . . Mrs Breen . . .

KAY. Mr McInerney, Father.

FATHER. I'll just walk down the shore. Don't worry yourself, I'll be fine. (*Father walks down the shore.*)

MARTY. (*Breathless suddenly.*) Well there you are.

KAY. Here I am.

MARTY. Exactly. Yourself.

KAY. Exactly.

MARTY. There you are. Yes. (*Handing over flowers.*) No. There you are.

KAY. From your own garden?

MARTY. The garden of Clare.

MICK. Will we root here or go down to the shore?

MARTY. (*Starting.*) Oh the shore, right, yes, certainly, come on, can I (*Offering his arm*) may I mind if I (*She takes it, he blows out*) that's, that's it, the shore. (*He doesn't move.*)

KAY. This way.

MARTY. Yes, certainly. Absolutely. (*They walk downstage to the edge, stand, Marty prepares to launch his question.*)

KAY. It's cold.

MARTY. Yes, yes . . .

KAY. Another winter . . .

MARTY. Kay.

KAY. Yes?

MARTY. Kay (*She looks at him.*) Kay, (*breath*) I wanted, I said earlier, that at my request you might, well you have, as the fella says, landed, and well, oh flappit to blazes . . .

KAY. I shouldn't have come.

MARTY. What?

KAY. I shouldn't, I'm not what you . . .

MARTY. No, Kay, listen, listen, stop now (*he steps away from her*) stop, now, (*deep breath*) look at me . . .

KAY. I know what you're going to say, Marty, and . . .

MARTY. No, no, you don't, and even if you did know part of it you don't know all of it. Just look, look at me a minute. (*Deep breath.*) I'm no oil painting, I'm a plain buscuit both sides. But I'm a man who thinks you the loveliest woman ever to walk the bounderies of his parish. (*She goes to interrupt.*) Shush, Kay, whist now a minute. A man who you refused outside the kitchen door after a dance in Batty Melican's house thirty-four years ago, a man who married his Brid only after you married your Donal, (*she goes to interrupt*) no listen, whose Brid died long before your Donal died, and who had to wait twenty-one years, three months, and seventeen days knowing that his youth was draining away from him like an ebb tide and his hair falling out and his teeth with it, losing everything bit by bit except that feeling, not that, Kay, and waiting a decent interval until now, here and now, to tell you again. And ask you, knowing that his best dream in the world will perish if you answer no. You're a beautiful beautiful woman . . .

KAY. And you're blind.

MARTY. To everything else. My soul's thumping, beating, crashing around inside the walls of myself . . .

KAY. That can be treated . . .

MARTY. Great crowds of feelings like a Fair Day pushing and shoving along every by-road and boreen of the heart and all saying Kay, tell Kay . . .

KAY. Marty . . .

MARTY. No, Kay . . .

KAY. No, Marty . . .

MARTY. Exactly. No, Kay, no, Marty, the very voice in my eardrum drumming like Clancy's bodhran . . .

KAY. Stop . . .

MARTY. I can't even breathe.

KAY. It's foolish.

MARTY. Isn't all of life? Isn't mad foolishness the name of our every endevour, our toing and froing in the vicissitudes?

KAY. (*Looks away.*) Oh, God . . .

MARTY. I haven't been possessor of a personal thought in years, Kay. Not for McInerney, not holusbolus for me fein, because I knew, I knew. Donal was there, you were married.

KAY. Don't say any more . . .

MARTY. I had dreams for companions. Dreams of you to make waking—not that I was sleeping—seem Christmas backwards. Everything gone when you oscail your eyes, and worse, everything gone when you close them again too, arise to cancel the thought, postpone pick up business of the parish and put aside one day she might say yes and she might say no, and what can you do because for twenty-two years and two hundred and twelve days and nights she has been moving in, occupying, the interior dimension, until I can't go on, because every jot and iota of Marty McInerney inside and out, upstairs and down, is alive with devotion and what-have-you, love, for you, Kay. (*He drops to one knee. Pause.*)

KAY. (*Reaches out her hand to him.*) Oh, God, Marty.

MARTY. (*breathless whisper.*) Yes?

KAY. You're a gorgeous idiot.

MARTY. (*Claps hands together.*) Dear God . . .

KAY. But . . .

MARTY. Kay, wait now . . .

KAY. No, Marty . . .

MARTY. This is our chance, Kay. Our own chance at happiness. Divinity knows I've shilly-shallied my way enough. Cobbled my etceteras into whatever could be done and can be done for Caherconn, the whole parish copper fastened onto me and into me every day and night. Haven't we been side by side for months on the campaign for the clinic sure, aren't we part of the same voice, the same person, the one vote, and still split apart in our own private loneliness and separation . . .

KAY. We're too old, Marty . . .

MARTY. For what? Haven't I this feeling stored in the cellars of myself this past twenty-two years. It's only now, Kay, that we're fit for it, only now that we're old enough. . . . Do you remember that kiss?

KAY. Yes.

MARTY. It's on my lips these past ten years.

KAY. Don't . . .

MARTY. He'd gone to bed.

KAY. I should have thrown you out.

MARTY. But you let me in. Reelected I told you, and after falling off the table in Feeney's in media reis. Poleaxed on the floor. 'Take me to the Matron', says I. And thirty of 'em beyond outside steaming in their cars waiting while you touched the old wound on my head. And kissed me, Kay. It's what gave me hope, to wait, to let it build up inside me, and I could be high or low in the fates, here, there in the whereabouts of mockery and begrudery, my habituals of office, and think of that, just think of it, Kay. (*Kneels.*) Please, marry me.

KAY. Get up, Marty.

MARTY. Please.

KAY. Oh, shite, You're an impossible man.

MARTY. I am.

KAY. Marty . . .

MARTY. Yes?

KAY. Marty, Marty, Marty . . .

MARTY. Sweet divinity if you're there in heaven!

KAY. I did love Donal once.

MARTY. Of course you did.

KAY. Then it just died. Just stopped one morning. Like that.

MARTY. It wasn't your fault, he . . .

KAY. And then you came that night . . .

MARTY. Ten years ago in September . . .

KAY. And . . . God forgive me. Little by little I wondered what if he died. And then little by little he did.

MARTY. Ten years. The hand of God, Kay, isn't he happy dead in heaven?

KAY. I pretended I loved him after I didn't.

MARTY. Of course you did. Isn't it normal? What else were you going to do.

KAY. Don't you see, Marty, I gave him my life. I can't start another one.

MARTY. No, Kay, listen . . .

KAY. I can't . . .

MARTY. It's our chance . . .

KAY. I can't be eighteen again, can't feel like that again . . .

MARTY. Of course you can. Amn't I eighteen this past twenty-two years? Isn't the heart and soul of me as young as a new bird with love for you, Kay? Let that life go, Kay. That man is gone, look here, look at this one standing before you and waiting a lifetime . . .

KAY. Oh, God . . .

MARTY. For your. Don't say . . .

KAY. Marty, stop please. No. (*Pause.*) I do love you in a . . .

MARTY. Yes! . . .

KAY. But I'm not a girl anymore. That part of me is dead, Marty, and I can't, no, no, I can't. I just can't . . .

Kay kisses his face and walks quickly off back to the pub as Marty sinks in the sand and Father walks up behind him watching. Throughout the above Mary has been slowly moving with eyes closed, opening her arms wide as if for an embrace, and then standing up in the place Mick 'died', her arms open to the air just above her as if to draw to her a spirit figure. She begins to climb up onto the stool, and is there by the time Kay arrives hurrying in. Her entrance startles Mary from the trance.

KAY. (*Entering in a torment.*) Oh, Christ! Why? Why this? Jesus! I can't, I . . .

MARY. (*Opening her eyes, long, long sigh, beatific, wonderful.*) Oh, . . . God. Kay! It's wonderful! He's there!

END OF ACT I

ACT II

It is late afternoon one week later. The light is dying. The bar is now spread with many flowers and wreaths, particularly around the area where Mick died. It has become the focal point of the village life. Cissie enters the bar. She is carrying a large bunch of flowers. She moves with reverence beneath the floating host of spirits. Has her rosary beads for protection and begins praying in a mumble as she moves over toward the bar where the Lazarus Mick died. It is as if she is surrounded by the presence of the spirits.

CISSIE. (*Very fast.*) Hail Mary full of grace the Lord is with thee blessed art thou amongst women and blessed is the fruit of thy womb, Jesus. (*Pause, looks up, whispers.*) I'll be there soon, Tommy love. (*Waits, nothing, whispers.*) Holy Mary, mother of God, pray for us sinners, now and at the hour of our . . . Amen. (*She steps forward and puts the flowers on the bar counter.*)

JAY. (*Entering from the shop door.*) Cissie.

CISSIE. (*Very cool.*) Afternoon.

JAY. Haven't seen you with a week . . .

CISSIE. (*Indicates her praying.*) Shush . . .

JAY. (*Waits until she finishes.*) You didn't take ill, or anything?

CISSIE. I did not, thank you very much.

JAY. No. Well that's good then. (*Pause.*) Only I've been having everyone else in the parish in and I missed you. Not that they're buying anything. How could you sell drink in heaven, says Mick, and of course that started them off. Don't care that it's killing me, of course. (*Pause, Cissie remaining cool.*) Maybe you haven't been out much? Have you a list for me and I'll start making it up? Maybe you'd like a . . . no . . .

CISSIE. (*Urgent whisper.*) No thank you, Mr Feeney . . .

JAY. How's that? Nothing at all? . . .

CISSIE. No, thank you, I'm just paying my respects until Father comes.

JAY. I see. (*Pause, Jay working the counter a moment.*) I didn't think you were going for this crack at all Cissie . . .

CISSIE. I beg your pardon? . . .

JAY. Thought you thought it was, you know, outside the teachings, my point, not legitimate. Dead souls floating above here in the pub. Not gospel.

CISSIE. Father says we should come and pray . . .

JAY. I wish he'd say it was alright have drink after. Well you're a small bit early for the others, give us over your list anyway and I can be . . .

CISSIE. (*Cooly.*) Just a carton of milk please.

JAY. A carton of milk?

CISSIE. Thank you.

JAY. That's it then?

CISSIE. That's it. I'll sit here and wait. Thank you.

JAY. A carton of milk?

CISSIE. A carton of milk, thank you very much.

JAY. I have the Bonina pudding in?

CISSIE. No, thank you.

JAY. (*Puzzled, about to go out.*) Tell me, did we get that little business taken care of?

CISSIE. (*Looking into the distance.*) He never called.

JAY. Didn't he?

CISSIE. No.

JAY. Jesus, you missed the deadline. Well listen, Cissie we'll get on . . .

CISSIE. It's taken care of now.

JAY. What?

CISSIE. It's fine, thank you very much. I got another form. And it was attended to.

JAY. Is that right?

CISSIE. Very promptly.

JAY. So I won't tell him to call up?

CISSIE. No, thank you.

JAY. I see. (*Pause.*) A carton of milk so.

CISSIE. Yes, please. (*She reaches for her purse.*)

JAY. No need, Cissie, I'll put it in the book, won't you be . . .

CISSIE. No, I'd prefer to pay now, thank you. There you are. (*Hands over the exact change.*)

JAY. Right.

CISSIE. I'd like to settle up for the month on Friday, if you could make it up for me please.

JAY. I see. Well, alright then, Cissie. (*Jay allows a cool pause to spread between them.*) You believe in it so, Cissie? The souls and that?

CISSIE. Ours not to know the whys or the wherefores.

JAY. Correct. But what do you think of yourself? I mean is it only in here? Is it only an affliction of J Feeney's? My point, are there crowds of 'em floating around in Ryans too only Maguire hasn't seen them and so old Larry can keep pulling pints?

CISSIE. I don't think you should be talking . . .

JAY. And what young Mary says now, this out-of-body crack, making out she did it herself here, was dancing with a child and sitting still all the time if you can credit it. God knows I can't and He can strike me deaf and dumb if He likes.

CISSIE. Dear God! (*Automatically goes for her cigarettes, but remembers where she is, the grotto in front of her, and doesn't light one.*)

JAY. Spirits, the Lazarus proclaims . . .

CISSIE. A sacred mystery . . .

JAY. Loads of 'em, packs of 'em above here? . . .

CISSIE. Shush . . .

JAY. (*Enjoying her nervousness.*) What if supposin' that they were lost . . .

CISSIE. Dear God . . .

JAY. That they had been out there somewhere and decided to travel outside of themselves like Mary there and sort of blew across the Atlantic or over from Norway or somewhere, got a small bit lost, can't get back into their bodies.

CISSIE. Merciful hour.

JAY. And were screeching, hollering, wailing the whole time only we couldn't hear 'em.

CISSIE. (*Looking up.*) Lord protect us . . .

JAY. Could be, you know?

CISSIE. Wouldn't it be awful?

JAY. My point, we can all kick a ball, but how many can catch it?

CISSIE. Blessed Oliver Plunkett.

JAY. But I'm not knocking the business either mind. I'm all for progress. And look at Maguire and he dead there a week ago and now, granted, the stated of him. To be seen to be believed. And the shine off him, pure gloss, that's something alright. And even Mary bit of a bloom on her since she's been having the go, that bit brighter isn't she? Correct. What time are ye off?

CISSIE. What?

JAY. I thought that was the plan, ye were all to meet here with the Lazarus and Mary and try to take off, make contact or something with them?

CISSIE. It's a prayer meeting.

JAY. Is that right?

CISSIE. Yes.

JAY. I see. And what are ye hoping for?

CISSIE. Well, (*a wave of anxiety*) I'm going to stay if Father doesn't come . . .

JAY. You're right there too, Cissie. Never know what might happen if you got out of yourself. Can't be good for a body either. Have you a St. Christopher? (*Opens bottle of whiskey.*)

CISSIE. What? (*Looks heavenward, underbreath.*) Mug.

JAY. What?

CISSIE. Mug. (*Jay slips away glass, puts up coffee mug.*) I wouldn't be here only for Father Mac mentioning it mightn't be any harm. Might be the site of a miracle as I said to May Clancy, remember Knock. How are we to know, and it could be, God and his blessed angels preserve and guide us and where would we be if we didn't at least come and pray.

JAY. At least . . .

CISSIE. We might be able to reach them . . .

JAY. Them? . . .

CISSIE. The blessed souls in heaven, could be the entrance to paradise right here above us and we wouldn't know it and as Mary says aren't there more Caherconn people in heaven than in Caherconn?

JAY. She has a point there.

CISSIE. We should at least come to pray.

JAY. Maybe ye could put in a word about what's keeping the Lottery money?

Marty hurries down and into the pub. He is a shattered man, unable to eat or sleep, on the wild edge of himself, near collapse.

JAY. Good day, Senator.

MARTY. Where is she?

JAY. Who now? Kay, is it?

MARTY. Is she in or out?

JAY. In and out all the bloody time.

MARTY. Christmas man, tell me! Is she here?

JAY. I wouldn't say so.

CISSIE. Shush, Mr McInerney.

MARTY. (*Turning sharply.*) What?

CISSIE. (*Indicating with her rosary beads.*) A little respect.

MARTY. Yes, yes, yes. (*Turns back.*) Did she make any mention of me to you? Did she say anything?

JAY. Well like what?

MARTY. Like what women say about men who have asked them to marry them . . . (*Cissie half-turns to hear.*) Twice in a lifetime, twenty odd years apart, did she say anything?

JAY. Well, no, I'm not sure.

MARTY. (*Loudly.*) Not sure!

CISSIE. Mr McInerney you really . . .

MARTY. Will you shut up shop, woman! Christmas, Jay . . .

CISSIE. Very nice . . .

MARTY. Do I look like I want not sure? I don't want not sure, I don't live with not sure. Sweet Lucifer will you think and throw out the facts: Did your sister say anything about me?

JAY. No.

MARTY. No?

JAY. Not that I recall. Now she might have and I might have forgotten . . .

MARTY. (*Thumps counter.*) Remember! . . .

CISSIE. Dear God!

JAY. Well . . . no, Marty. No. She might have said your name, . . .

MARTY. Yes!

JAY. Marty, but . . .

MARTY. And, and what, Marty, in what context Marty, Marty what, Marty dear, darling, doting, what kind of Marty? Tell me.

JAY. (*Thinks to be sure, very calm.*) I haven't see Marty for a few days. That's all. (*Marty bangs his forehead onto the counter.*)

CISSIE. Dear God! (*Stands up, lights up.*) I want you to know I think this is disgraceful, Mr McInerney. I can't even pray in peace . . .

JAY. Ah no, now Cissie . . .

CISSIE. Cissie Reidy knows when she's not wanted.

JAY. (*As she moves away to the ladies.*) There's no need . . .

CISSIE. My Tommy isn't standing idly by and letting me be insulted like that, I can tell you. No then. He is not. Are you, Tommy love? No. There's rewards in the hereafter . . . and punishments too. That's all we have to remember. (*She puts down her mug on a table and goes off to the ladies, prayerful, coming-back-from-communion face.*) I'll wait in here until he's gained his right mind.

JAY. Right, right, Cissie. (*Backing up to Marty, underbreath.*) Marty, what the blazes is happening to you? Are you alright? You never went up to Cissie with the grant form? (*Marty raises his head, no reply.*)

JAY. And the Nolans were on about the road. No sign of it being done yet. You weren't at Morans funeral either. And you were missed too. God, Marty are you alright? You're looking very shook. So you are. Get a grip a yourself. I'd swear Cissie's after dealing with An T'Uasal inside. Went in on that bus he's running to the supermarket too. Got on out at the cross so as I wouldn't see her, God blast her. Bad enough the bloody souls taking all my business, now I'll have to woo her back again now on top of everything. (*Pours glass of whiskey.*) Well anyways you can't miss out on ones like Cissie Reidy, Marty, bad and all as she is, she's a mouth on her broadcast you better than Clare FM if you do something for her at all.

MARTY. Were you ever in love?

JAY. What?

MARTY. Did you ever fall in love?

JAY. In love?

MARTY. In love.

JAY. What the hell? Listen Marty, with all respect, we're slipping. Feel it in the grassroots . . .

MARTY. You were never in love. Answer the question.

JAY. No. (*Pause.*) But I didn't miss it either. There's more serious business than . . .

MARTY. You were never in love.

JAY. Listen to yourself man. Jesus listen. As you often taught me Marty, examine the question before answering, you get me? Examine the language. Why 'fall'?

MARTY. What?

JAY. (*With growing bitterness.*) Why 'fall', like it was a pothole you'd fall into on the way to Kilkee, fall, falling in . . . you know. My point? You can only 'fall' downwards; and then, worse still, 'falling *out of* love', well, not 'climbing' out of love, or 'rising' out of it or even 'walking' out of it as if it was on the flat, no, always falling. Falling lower than the first fall, and after it all, leaving you where? The sewer of life. Jesus no, it never struck me as any great temptation. (*Slow and bitter.*) Thanks be to God. You and me Marty are here for higher matters . . .

MARTY. Higher matters? Higher matters? Jingle jangle, my whole flaming life burnt to my fingertips, blackened . . .

JAY. What are you . . .

MARTY. Bombed with failure, that's me, that's M McInerney. And for what? Christmas in Christ what? Tell me. Four lines is it, four lines. Thirty-seven words for a parish? . . .

JAY. What words? Marty . . .

MARTY. A cara. Lucifer no. Goodnight and saranoya says he to the future and what, what hole, what fallen man, amn't I fallen deeper than lost angels, the digging every minute deeper, the light? No light, hope, faith, love, and no coming out of it, failures past, present, and we're to have no future. Caherconn to the tide and McInerney with it, holusbolus gone, gone. Christ in heaven I have to talk to her! . . .

JAY. Might as well love a blackthorn bush as my sister, Marty.

MARTY. Would she have set out?

JAY. What . . .

MARTY. If she knew the end of the road? If you knew. Christmas if any of us knew. Would we? (*Shouts toward ceiling.*) Because I know now, you hear, I know, nature of life, mockeries and sport, games, throwing us like salt from a shaker and blowing us about. McInerney no more than a pinchworth tossed off heaven. Oh to hell with him! Here, let him pulse, beat, and near burst with love, draw nearer to it, edge him onto the brink, as the fella says, this McInerney man, and watch him there now, look! Plumasing the length and breadth of the Continent for a hospital, the best bouquet of flowers he wants to grasp in his hand and hand over and say there you are now and watch that bloom in his own place, . . .

JAY. I know, Marty but . . .

MARTY. Get his brother into it to rest and have love and life and the whole shebang running side by side in his own parish of paradise as the fella says. That's it, let him off with it, you say, throw him a few Germans and give him a sliver, give him a rind of hope, let him get this close, let him reach his laimh into within the very shadow of it all, and then slash him down into a heap, for the fun, the indefatigueable mockery of it, see if he can pop up again. Pop! Down, pop, pop up, McInerney.

JAY. Marty, whist man will you . . .

MARTY. Jesus Christ do you hear me? I've known failure, know the taste and the touch of it, the hard feel of it and I sleeping with it beside me the past twenty years, (*heavenwards*) you hear me? Do you? (*Looks away, drops voice.*) You can't be born to your father dying, see a woman you married fade away and an only son gone to America and not know, banging away at the other side of the country all your living days like an old bodhran beating the one note that's still not heard and not know the man upstairs was playing some class of lunatic willynilly ludo with M McInerney. (*Hush.*) I know.

JAY. Jesus listen, Marty, have a drink. Listen. We've trouble from An tUasal and his Clinics. Talk of a flaming blow-in candidate of the other shower in Ennis, God blast him, and now with Cissie . . .

MARTY. Laughter and mockery . . .

JAY. You're not listening to me . . .

MARTY. You think you're doing something all your life and you're doing nothing, you think you're remembered and you're forgotten. Not a personal though in twenty years and (*heavenwards*) Christ but I can hear them laughing at me now. (*Stands up, pulls letter from his pocket, balls it as he roars at soul-ceiling.*) Well damn it all to hell! (*He fires the balled letter at the ceiling.*) Christ, damn ye! (*He grabs a bunch of the flowers, and fires them wildly into the air, reaches for another and throws that. And another. Jay quickly comes out and tries to hold him.*)

JAY. Marty, stop, stop it. (*Jay wrestles Marty into quietness.*)

MARTY. (*Gets his breath within Jay's hold.*) Jesus. Jesus, what's to become of us? (*He rushes out.*)

Marty storms out as Cissie has returned from the ladies and seen him throwing the flowers at the ceiling. He exits down the street. Father walks into view stage left on the beach, he is in some pain, breathing with difficulty, sits down to rest.

CISSIE. Oh, Dear God and his blessed mother! I've never seen the like of it.

JAY. He's not well, Cissie . . .

CISSIE. There's no excuse. Dear God, no, that's not right at all. Poor man must have drink taken or something.

JAY. (*Unballing and opening the letter from the Lottery*) Oh Christ, the lottery!

CISSIE. Mr. Feeney!

JAY. What, no, sorry, Cissie, Jesus. Nothing.

CISSIE. What?

JAY. (*Goes and pours himself a drink*) No, no, em nothing, Cissie. Just. Nothing. God. (*Looks upward at ceiling.*) Nothing. (*Drinks, looks at letter, pause.*) I'll pick up the flowers now.

CISSIE. (*Helping to gather the flowers.*) Of course you wouldn't know what he'd be on either. Did you see the way he went for me? I had to leave the room for fear I'd say something unchristian about the man and he gone baserk.

JAY. (*Stunned, coldly.*) That's was good of you, Cissie.

CISSIE. So he's asked her to marry him. Of course it was what we suspected all along. Men are that bit weaker.

JAY. (*Disinterested.*) That a fact?

CISSIE. Oh, no doubt about it. Can't you see it in him, getting that bit older and worrying about himself and who's going to boil his eggs for him and put on his slippers and fill his hot water bottle when he's pushing up on the pension. And that man's supposed to be a servant of the public, God forgive me. Look what he's after doing to the flowers.

Mick has come in during the above. He is considerably cleaned up. He feels he is nearly the parish saint now. He comes in and stands behind Cissie.

CISSIE. (*Bumping back against Mick.*) Merciful hour.

MICK. God bless. God bless, Cissie.

JAY. (*Going back to the counter, rereading the letter, head down.*) How are you, Mick?

MICK. (*Brightly.*) Happy to be alive, Jay.

JAY. I don't suppose you'd like a drink?

MICK. I won't, thank you for your kindness in offering.

JAY. Nothing . . .

MICK. Now, Mrs Reidy, I haven't seen you all week . . .

JAY. Nothing at all . . .

MICK. And not for want of looking either.

CISSIE. I'm a busy woman Mr . . .

MICK. Michael . . .

CISSIE. Mr Michael . . .

MICK. Like the archangel.

CISSIE. And . . .

MICK. I owe you a debt of gratitude, mam . . .

CISSIE. What? Not at all. I hadn't . . .

MICK. You were instrumental in it, you were . . .

CISSIE. Well, I gave you the cigarette but . . .

MICK. You did, in your goodness and kindness, and for that I'd like to repay you. You helped me. D'you see if I hadn't died I wouldn't be alive now. If you follow. And God knows I feel as good now as a young boy and have a second go through the gap. I'm going to do it right this time, from now on in. (*He puts his hand on Cissie's shoulder.*)

CISSIE. Dear God. (*After a gasp, quick whisper.*) I don't think we should be talking, Mr Maguire, after the last time.

MICK. Sure wasn't it you gave me the kiss of life?

CISSIE. I did not!

MICK. You needn't fear but you'll be remembered in the hereafter for that.

CISSIE. But I did no such thing. (*To above.*) I didn't, honest to God. Ask Him yourself.

MICK. Amn't I right, Jay?

JAY. You'll excuse me now, please. (*Takes letter.*) I'll be inside. Not that any of you'll need me. (*Jay exits inside with the letter. Cissie sits with her back to Mick. There is a long pause.*)

MICK. Do you know what I was thinking, Cissie? (*Pause.*) Do you know the way it came to me afterwards and I up above at home thinking about it, and why I died here in the pub . . . with you there beside me?

CISSIE. (*Shaking her head, smoking furiously.*) Blessed mother of God.

MICK. Well do you know, couldn't it have been that maybe I was supposed to have a second chance? . . .

CISSIE. (*Not turning, hisses whisper.*) Mr Maguire . . .

MICK. Michael. A second chance, Cissie. And that maybe I'm a bit of a messenger, like the archangel . . .

CISSIE. Dear God . . .

MICK. Sent with the message of the second chance, d'you see. Like something dying and then living again, having a second chance. Like maybe a man and a woman who might . . .

CISSIE. Mr Michael, I think, if you'll excuse me in your presence I'd be happier if you didn't speak, thank you very much.

MICK. I know sure. There's things can happen too without speaking, don't the saints above in heaven know it. But that's just what I was thinking, the Messenger of the Second Chance . . .

CISSIE. Hail Mary full of grace . . .

MICK. (*Slow and loud to her speed.*) The Lord is with thee . . . (*Cissie and Mick duet the rosary. Kay comes along the beach from stage left. Sees Father collapsed on the sand, rushes to him.*)

KAY. Father Mac? Father? Francis? are you alright?

FATHER. (*Breathless, seems to be fading, very confused at first.*) What? Oh, I am, yes, just . . .

KAY. Sit up, can you?

FATHER. Where, you, you were swimming.

KAY. Deep breaths now, come on . . .

FATHER. Isn't it cold?

KAY. Are you cold?

FATHER. You were.

Des Nealon in *A Little Like Paradise,* by Niall Williams.
Courtesy Amelia Stein.

KAY. What?
FATHER. No. I thought.
KAY. Deep breaths now again, in and out.
FATHER. Oh, God . . .
KAY. Can you get up?
FATHER. No, I think, I'd better, I think, just sit here a min-
ute, I'll be . . .
KAY. That's it, just rest a minute . . .
FATHER. You were swimming.
KAY. What? No I . . .
FATHER. I saw you . . .

KAY. (*Shaking head.*) I wasn't . . .

FATHER. Well out there. I saw you. I, you were very far out . . .

KAY. I know just . . .

FATHER. Oh, dear, I'm very sorry, shouldn't be just . . .

KAY. Whist now and get your breath . . .

FATHER. I didn't think you were coming back in . . .

KAY. I know . . .

FATHER. For Marty, I . . . (*Pats his chest for pills.*) Would you ever open that. (*Hands over box of tablets, she opens it, he takes two.*) Thank you, Kay. You think the Lord would give me a clean death . . .

KAY. Stop that now, you'll be fine in a minute . . .

FATHER. If He was there at all. (*Finds cigarette.*) Dying has its privileges . . .

KAY. You're not dying . . .

FATHER. Do you love him, Kay?

KAY. Oh, God. Stop talking will you. Matron's orders.

FATHER. The person I loved most in the world was my father, you didn't know him . . .

KAY. No . . .

FATHER. He died after Martin was born . . .

KAY. Shush now . . .

FATHER. Of course I didn't love Martin or anyone much for a long time afterwards . . .

KAY. You were . . .

FATHER. Stupidist bloody thing. How we just get set on something. Nothing change us. I blamed him. The baby. He came, Dad went. D'you ever feel you'd like to start again? . . .

KAY. I'm too old to start again . . .

FATHER. It's only now you're old enough . . .

KAY. Stop talking now . . .

FATHER. Listen to your parish priest now, that's an order. Well humour me anyway. (*Laughs weakly.*) You love Marty, Kay?

KAY. I don't know what love is . . .

FATHER. (*Breathing with difficulty.*) 'It's what makes our souls grow wings', that's what Considine's young lady said at the confirmation year before last, 'isn't it Father?' And she looking up at me. And I thinking mine won't be flying so. Ha, I don't know if

Fionuala Murphy and John Olohan in *A Little Like Paradise,* by Niall
Williams.
Courtesy Amelia Stein.

there's any souls or wings, Kay, or anywhere to fly them in at
all . . .

KAY. I'm going to leave if you keep talking . . .

FATHER. I neglected Martin badly. Too busy with bloody
prayers . . .

KAY. I'm going now . . .

FATHER. You'd never be any good at confession. (*Moves his
side.*) Oh, that's better now. Wait a minute (*Pause, breathing deep*),
I'd like to do something for him . . .

KAY. For who?

FATHER. For Marty. I know, stupid bloody thing but I'd like to know he was . . .

KAY. Isn't he fine? . . .

FATHER. Let it through, Kay, let it through in the name of God, will you? You love him . . .

KAY. Well . . .

FATHER. Sure I know you do. . .

KAY. What if I do love him day after day and marry him and we live together in the bungalow beyond Crehan's there? And every day I'm getting older and I'm loving him but my eyes are getting dimmer and I'm starting to snore and cough at nights and all of a sudden he wakes up next to me in the bed and says to himself, is this it then? Is this the girl from Batty Melican's dance? Because it won't be. It won't be anymore. Then what? What if my hair falls out or I turn deaf and my legs seize up, will he still be loving me then? I don't know.

FATHER. I don't know either, Kay. I'd say he will, but . . .

KAY. I'm not a girl of eighteen now you know with bows and curls and red-and-yellow dresses, smiling and giggling at the wonder of things. I won't be throwing off my wrinkles all of a sudden and losing the swelling and pains in my ankles or growing white new teeth for the ones I put in a glass by the toilet when I go to bed. I won't be having babies and walking them through the village or playing with them on the sand. I won't be the girl he's been thinking of these past years. I've already been her, she picked a man she thought she loved and after eleven years feeding and washing for him found out she was wrong. That that man didn't really care about her anymore. That he had come and taken that girl with the tilt of his head and the boom of his voice in the classroom. Took her like you'd take a fly behind you on the breeze, or your shadow, without a though for her, without a look back for twenty-one years. That girl is gone, he took her, she died even before he did. I won't ever be her again. I won't be foolish and sweet and pretty and light, I'll be an old woman. That's all I'll be. (*Sits back.*)

FATHER. We're all old, Kay. It doesn't mean he can't love you.

KAY. Will he? Will he love me when he sees me at eighty like Bernie Crowley or Philomena Crowe, wetting their beds, drinking gripewater and sucking bullseyes and telling the matron the nurses are stealing their fortunes when they puff up their pillows, or that there's men hiding in the curtains? What's he going to be thinking then? Of a kitchen dance a lifetime ago and a dream of a girl he's kept carrying around with him all his life? Is that what he's going to be thinking? He'd want to be deaf, dumb, and blind, because she'll be gone, I'll drive her away without wanting to on the first morning he wakes up beside me. (*Pause.*)

FATHER. Do you believe in souls, Kay?

KAY. I don't know . . .

FATHER. I don't know myself.

KAY. Maybe.

FATHER. I'll tell you something young Mary said to me yesterday.

KAY. Poor Mary . . .

FATHER. 'We're all souls, Father', she says. 'That's all we are. Trapped like a bit of wind in a shirt on the line. You have to believe that', she says, 'don't you Father? I mean', says she, 'sometimes the wind escapes the shirt and goes, God knows where, everywhere I suppose, and tangling in another shirt and sort of touching it in a kind of way. Souls touching like wind, that's love', she says. (*Pause.*) It won't matter a damn to him whether your eyes fall out or your ears drop off in the night, Kay. He loves you that way. He's caught up inside you. Like wind in a shirt. (*Pause.*)

KAY. (*Softly.*) Oh, Christ.

FATHER. You know Maguire's becoming a bit of a saint? 'I'm really living since I died Father', says he. 'The new life of the Holy Spirit'. 'Well', I said to him, 'that's great, Mick, you're walking proof of life after death'. (*Pause.*) Don't be sure that girl is dead, Kay. If there's any miracles, they're ordinary things. Maybe she'd have a wonderful life again if you let her. (*Pause, seasounds.*) Well, if the good Lord's not going to kill me at the minute I'd say I'm late for the meeting. (*Getting up.*) It's getting very dark looking.

KAY. (*Getting up.*) You should go home.

FATHER. I will directly after. I promise, Matron.

KAY. All you need is a good rest.

FATHER. That's it sure. (*They walk to the bar, Kay stops.*)

KAY. Thank you.

FATHER. What in the world for?

KAY. I'm not sure. Something. I feel lighter somehow. Do you know, but you're a wonderful man.

FATHER. Of course I am, amn't I one of the McInerneys of Caherconn? Come on, Matron. (*They enter the pub to Cissie and Mick's prayers.*) God bless.

MICK. Father . . .

CISSIE. (*Finishes out her prayer, blesses herself, whispers.*) Afternoon, Father.

KAY. How are you, Cissie?

CISSIE. Oh, God bless me I think I'm after having an intercession.

MICK. What do you mean?

CISSIE. Just while we were saying the prayers, Father. Oh, I think I'm feeling a bit of a weakness coming.

JAY. (*Entering from shop.*) God Almighty!

MICK. (*Helping Cissie sit back.*) Here now, easy.

KAY. Are you alright, Cissie?

FATHER. Settle back there . . .

CISSIE. Oh, now. Now. Now. That's better now.

JAY. What happened to you?

KAY. (*Behind counter pours a drink.*) Here.

CISSIE. (*Drinks.*) Sorry Father. (*Lights cigarette.*) Only I'm after being a witness to the intercession of Our Lord and so I'm that bit peculiar, you know, you have to forgive me. (*Smokes.*) Up he went in a cloud of light.

KAY. Who? . . .

CISSIE. And the thing was you know how your mind can drift off on you, God forgive me, and you saying your prayers . . .

JAY. What did you see, Cissie?

CISSIE. I saw my Tommy, standing there, same as yourself, only my head was that bit dizzy and I could feel the bit of a weakness coming I'd have got up even saying the Hail Mary's and all as I was, Father, and here in the blessed site and gone over and joined him.

MICK. Almighty God. You never even turned your head . . .

CISSIE. What?

MICK. I was sitting behind you, you never once looked back there . . .

CISSIE. Are you questioning the Almighty? Didn't I see my Tommy there . . .

MICK. I'm not denying you . . .

CISSIE. And a lovely white suit on him . . .

KAY. Wings, Cissie?

CISSIE. What?

KAY. (*Turning away*.) No harp?

JAY. Kay . . .

CISSIE. A sharp tongue'll cut your throat, Matron. But I saw him. I saw him!

FATHER. Alright, Cissie, now . . .

CISSIE. I'm sorry, Father . . .

MICK. Easy now . . .

CISSIE. There's some kind of entrance, I'd say, right there and it's how you can maybe slide in or out the door a paradise, God in his mercy be good to us, Father, but it was as sure as when poor Tommy, God rest him, would be going to the county final in his grey suit . . .

KAY. Only is was bleached white?

CISSIE. Same as you'd picture on a blessed soul in heaven . . .

KAY. What're you having in the mug there, Cissie?

CISSIE. What?

MICK. Now be fair . . .

CISSIE. Father . . .

FATHER. I think perhaps it'd be for the best to leave it to one side for a minute and . . .

CISSIE. As God is my witness, Father . . .

FATHER. Yes, yes, well . . .

Mary hurries in. She is delighted with herself, bubbling with joy. During the following Marty will appear on the shore, shoeless, his jacket off, the hospital files in his hands as he begins to throw letters into the sea.

MARY. Hello. Hi everybody. Sorry I'm late . . .

JAY. Mary . . .

MARY. Sorry, sorry, sorry, but, I know. (*Her mother to herself*.) 'Now you're late again, you're always late, late every day of your life, Mary!' But (*Bursts out laughing*.) I'm late.

FATHER. That's alright Mary . . .

MARY. (*Laughter bubbling.*) I had the feeling I would be.

JAY. Is that a fact? . . .

MARY. Well, I always am . . .

JAY. It's no miracle so . . .

MARY. But no well now I don't like to say anything, but . . . I just had the feeling. I did and . . .

KAY. (*To Mary.*) And? . . .

MARY. Well, (*she does a mini bow*) Da-da . . .

CISSIE. Sacred Heart . . .

MARY. I am!

JAY. Jayz. Sorry, Father. What in the . . .

MARY. Aren't you going to congratulate me? (*They look at her.*) I'm late. I'm going to have a baby. (*A stunned silence.*)

FATHER. (*low whisper.*) A baby?

CISSIE. Merciful God . . .

MARY. Yes!

KAY. Oh, Mary . . .

MICK. Well congratulations to ye . . .

FATHER. A baby?

MARY. Yes . . .

FATHER. You're going to have a baby?

JAY. Jesus . . .

MARY. Yes . . .

FATHER. (*Breathless and stunned.*) Good God (*He has to sit down.*)

JAY. A baby. Well, you'll all have to have a drink now . . .

CISSIE. And your husband away in America?

MARY. Oh, he knows . . .

CISSIE. I'm sure . . .

MARY. I've told him . . .

KAY. He called?

MARY. I was sitting right over there when it happened . . .

JAY. Happened? . . . It happened in . . .

MARY. That corner there . . .

CISSIE. Holy God and his seven churches . . .

MARY. Is a high energy centre, according to my book, well, that's what you call it . . .

JAY. (*Getting a drink for Mick.*) Jesus, sorry Father . . .

MARY. And I could feel it happening . . .

KAY. Mary . . .

MARY. Well you do . . .

JAY. (*Feigned interest.*) Oh, yes . . .

MARY. That evening, Mr Maguire died, excuse me, and you're very well, you are, really but, well, that was a wonderful thing wasn't it and I had been reading all about it and thinking of Francie and well, you know, I knew. I came back in and breathing, that's the key, and I felt so funny doing it, well you do don't you? . . .

CISSIE. Lord save us . . . (*Cissie turns, Mick puts his hand on her arm.*)

MARY. You were out Jay . . .

JAY. (*A look to Cissie.*) Taking care of the . . .

MARY. And it happened.

KAY. When you said you were dancing with the child?

MARY. Oh, it was wonderful. I just, just floated out of myself and Francie was sort of all around me and there was this child, this baby, I could feel him and . . . I just knew I was pregnant.

CISSIE. Did you see Tommy Reidy?

MARY. No, I . . .

MICK. Isn't that something now?

FATHER. (*Shaken.*) When did you know—for sure, Mary? About the baby?

MARY. Well, I didn't want to say anything, Father. But I knew, that evening, and it's a boy. I knew it like it was my skin or something, just brand new. But I said I wouldn't say anything until I was really, really sure and took a test. So I took one today. And sure enough I failed it, or passed it, whatever, anyway I am, I'm, you know. Two months late.

FATHER. That's wonderful news. (*Begins to suffer pain he tries to disguise.*)

MICK. (*Raising his drink.*) Another vote for the McInerneys . . .

KAY. (*Hugs her.*) Congratulations.

MARY. Thank you. Francie said everything's nearly ready for . . .

KAY. (*Interrupting.*) He'll be here in no time so. (*Mary looks at Kay.*)

KAY. (*To Mary.*) I can't believe it. A baby in Caherconn . . .

MICK. God bless the child . . .

JAY. We haven't had a baby since . . . (*Pause of recognition.*)

FATHER. (*Quietly.*) Carthy's, God rest it . . .

KAY. Yes . . .

CISSIE. And may perpetual light shine upon it. (*A moment.*)

KAY. Yes, well, it's great, Mary, really, we're all delighted . . .

JAY. Of course we are . . .

MICK. (*Ordering for Cissie.*) Same again, Jay . . .

MARY. I'm as nervous . . .

KAY. Oh, don't be, Mary, you'll be fine . . .

MARY. I know, I know, well, they say the facilities out in . . .

KAY. We'll get everything for you . . .

MICK. Any chance of a Major? . . .

KAY. There isn't an attic in the parish that doesn't have a pram or playpen or cot or a highchair stored away. You wouldn't have to get anything at all, you could have it at home . . .

CISSIE. Oh, no, dear God you couldn't chance that, sacred saint Jude and his blessed protection but you could be one of the ones not to make it to Limerick, on the side of the road beyond Ennis there, and like Teresa, oh, a few years back and her waters burst and her little Hannah inside her deciding she's a bit carsick going all the way in from the west, wanted to be born there on the bend and Teresa with her legs up on the ceiling around the bull place in Clarecastle and fifteen farmers pulling and poking . . .

KAY. Cissie! (*To Mary.*) Here. Have it here in Caherconn, Mary.

MICK. Every man and woman'd be on standby . . .

CISSIE. Here? (*Smokes, looks at Mick.*) Are you mad? (*To Mary.*) No, no, I don't approve of that . . .

MICK. But . . .

KAY. It could be wonderful, Mary.

CISSIE. (*To Mick.*) You'll excuse me now, but you know nothing about the inner workings of a woman. (*To Mary.*) Complications . . .

FATHER. (*Standing.*) The best possible news I could ever hear, Mary.

MARY. Thank you, Father.

KAY. It's been a long time since I held a baby . . .

JAY. What about you, Cissie?

Brendan Conroy and Máire Hastings in *A Little Like Paradise,* by Niall Williams.
Courtesy Amelia Stein.

MICK. You'd drop it easy enough then . . .

CISSIE. I beg your pardon . . .

MICK. Wriggling and twisting in your arms, so you would . . .

CISSIE. I would not . . .

MICK. No, no, not you, Cissie . . .

CISSIE. Thank you . . .

MICK. Darling . . .

CISSIE. Mr . . .

MICK. Michael, but the likes of me, do you see, or Jay there, not that used to it, d'you know, but you now with your natural cuddle . . .

CISSIE. Well . . .

KAY. (*To Mary.*) We'll all want turns with it . . .

MARY. Oh, you can have them . . .

JAY. Well now, I'd fill bottles alright but . . .

KAY. (*Mock laugh at the though of him.*) You!

FATHER. Perhaps, Mary, you want to go home? Rest yourself?

MARY. Oh, no, no, no. I just wanted to tell Marty . . .

KAY. Let me. Let me tell him, Mary.

JAY. Best thing he could hear . . .

CISSIE. (*To Mick.*) Man's unchristian . . .

JAY. (*To Kay.*) He was in looking for you . . .

CISSIE. Went for me beserk . . .

KAY. Let me tell him, Mary. Let me tell him you're going to have a baby here in Caherconn . . .

MARY. Alright.

KAY. (*Quickly, moving away.*) Thank you. Thank you, Mary. I'll be back, Father. (*Kay exits.*)

FATHER. Well now.

JAY. Isn't that something now?

FATHER. Maybe, Mary, we shouldn't have the meeting now. I mean in your condition . . .

CISSIE. And what about my intercession, Father. (*To Mary.*) I'm after having a vision . . .

FATHER. Yes, well . . .

MARY. No no, I'm fine, Father . . .

FATHER. Alright then, maybe if we just started off with a few prayers and pray for, for God to, em, enlighten us and, well, Our Father . . .

ALL. Who art in heaven . . . (*At the end of the Our Father.*)

MARY. And deep breaths, Father. We can all start off with deep breaths.

FATHER. Yes. Righto.

MARY. Now. We all close our eyes.

MICK. That's right. (*A long pause.*)

MARY. And breathe.

CISSIE. (*Screwtight eyes.*) Breathe. In or out?

MARY. Em, in.

CISSIE. In, right, with your eyes shut?

MARY. (*Nods, deep breath.*) And in. (*Cissie can't hold hers as long, neither can Mick, both catch each other cheating, take second breaths.*)

MARY. And out.

CISSIE. Out.

MARY. In.

Jay gives himself a drink; overhearing, tries out instructions himself as he uncrates bottles, breathes in as if going underwater, then says quick In, etc. On the shore Kay finds Marty.

MARTY. (*Pulling pieces of notes and memoranda from inside files and tossing them into the sea.*) Nothing, nothing. Here, (*Throws a paper.*) Mrs Conway, here's nothing for you, Paudie Flynn, good man, nothing today, sit and wait for your wheelchair. Mickey Curtin, Ha! Jude Quinlavin you're joking me now, you, no, no, nothing for you, just die away there in your own time and what, you can't walk Maggie Flynn? Can't you dance to the Regional in Limerick because, let me see, no, no, nothing for you here, yes, and here's nothing for you Kathleen Maguane not a penny not a pound. Nothing. (*He falls down on hands and knees.*) Nothing.

KAY. Marty . . .

MARTY. (*Not looking up.*) Is it you?

KAY. What's the matter, Marty?

MARTY. (*Head in sand.*) Nothing. Nothing is the matter. Nothing's to be the matter with any of us. We're to thrive on nothing. Nothings, that we are until we fall into the sea. But no hospital, no clinic. Nothing. (*Raises his head.*) We got nothing, and more nothing.

KAY. From the Lottery?

MARTY. Excess of nothing.

KAY. Shite.

MARTY. I've failed.

KAY. Stop it . . .

MARTY. M McInerney has failed his . . .

KAY. Shut up . . . (*Kay sits down on the ground beside Marty.*) They gave us no money toward the hospital?

MARTY. No.

KAY. Well, feck them.

MARTY. What?

KAY. Feck them and God forgive them. They can all go and shite.

MARTY. We'll have nothing now.

KAY. Isn't it what we had before. Isn't it what we're used to?

MARTY. I said I would get a hospital. I said I would get it for you, for all of us and I didn't. I can't.

KAY. So.

MARTY. So? So that's it.

KAY. I see.

Kay takes on of the letters of the pile fallen on the sand between them and makes an aeroplane. Throughout the following she plays lightheartedly, throwing the balled papers and teasing Marty, letting off her shoes. She has a playfulness that at first seems out of place, until it spreads to Marty and they become children on the sand.

KAY. Well then. (*Firing a plane.*) There you go, Mrs Pender. (*Making another.*) What about John Joe here. (*Lies back and fires him.*) Now you're flying. Can you beat that?

MARTY. What?

KAY. Here, you take the Health Board. (*Gives him a letter.*) I'll have who, let me see, here, photocopy letter to Klaus Schlondorf outlining the benefits to his holiday house. Go on, make it. (*Marty makes one.*) Ready. Go! (*They fire off the planes.*) And good-bye to ye. Call again. Now, here letter from the Bishop for you, for me photocopy page one Caherconn petition.

MARTY. Kay, I failed . . .

KAY. Don't you fail to throw the Bishop now, come on. He's all set. Ready! (*They throw.*) Now here, A to C, Anglims to Cotters for you, oh, here, take Mickey Casey's medical history with them. (*She fires the papers at Marty.*) And you might as well take the wife or she'll be on the phone. (*Throws another one.*)

MARTY. Stop, will you, Kay, stop . . .

KAY. (*Throwing another sheet.*) Here's another bit of the parish, here's Downes to Hehir's . . .

MARTY. And what for you? Here's the bloody Chief Executive. (*He throws a letter back at her.*)

KAY. Oh, Christ don't give me him! Aaaah!

MARTY. (*Picking another and throwing it over at her.*) National Lottery Chairman, personal appeal! . . .

KAY. (*Rolling away from him in the sand.*) No! (*Kay throws the letter back at Marty and with it a handful of sand.*)

MARTY. Oh, Christmas! (*Kay gets to her feet and dodges about.*)

KAY. Now Marty . . .

MARTY. (*Getting up to chase her.*) Now, Kay. (*Waving letter.*) Here's Minister for Health himself . . .

KAY. Damn him to hell!

MARTY. To hell! (*Fires him exultantly, grabs another file.*) Minister for Tourism, private secretary, response to Caherconn appeal . . .

KAY. (*Grabbing it from him.*) Shite! To hell with you! (*Fires it.*)

MARTY. (*Pulling out several memos.*) Memos from useless bloody Taoiseach's office! For you!

KAY. No! Not him!

They dodge a moment on the beach. Kay falls down laughing. Marty stands over her with the letters. A moment, he throws all of them on top of her. He falls to his knees. They let their giddiness ebb. He reaches to touch her hair.

MARTY. You look like an angel. (*Kay turns her face to the sea.*)

KAY. Like a witch in the mornings . . .

MARTY. And radiant in your nightdress . . . (*Pause.*)

KAY. I like hot tea and cold toast . . .

MARTY. Every day . . .

KAY. I hate slippers . . .

MARTY. I have none . . .

KAY. Dirty bathrooms . . .

MARTY. Ajax and Omo . . .

KAY. Forget birthdays . . .

MARTY. April 12th, yours . . .

KAY. Can't get up in the mornings . . .

MARTY. We'll stay in bed . . .

KAY. Can't get to sleep at night . . .

MARTY. We'll stay awake . . . (*Pause. She turns to him.*)

KAY. I burn everything . . .

MARTY. We'll eat fruit . . .

KAY. I need glasses . . .

MARTY. (*points to himself.*) Two pairs . . .

KAY. Tablets for blood pressure . . .

MARTY. (*points to himself.*) Pink and blue . . .

KAY. I like bluntness . . .

MARTY. I love you . . .

KAY. Speak my mind . . .

MARTY. I'm listening . . .

KAY. (*Laughs.*) I sometimes snore . . .

MARTY. (*Points to himself.*) A chorus . . .

KAY. I lie in the middle . . .

MARTY. We'll meet there . . .

KAY. Leave the light on . . .

MARTY. So I can see you . . .

KAY. Talk in my sleep . . .

MARTY. And I'll answer. (*Pause.*)

KAY. Marty McInerney, you're a gorgeous man.

MARTY. If you say so.

KAY. (*Touches his face.*) The silliest bloody man I ever met, do you know that? You've the whole parish of us inside there, haven't you?

MARTY. And a great big wallpapered room for you.

KAY. I don't know what I'm doing. I feel. Oh, God, I feel light and (*deep exhale and breath*), ah. Think you can catch an old widow?

MARTY. I'll catch a young girl! (*A moment of false chase. They hold each other. Kay kisses him.*)

MARTY. (*Stunned as the kiss ends, silence, amazement, sighs away the twenty years then bursts, claps hands, leaps.*) Oh, Kay! *Kay!*

KAY. Okay.

MARTY. (*Jigs a tune, holds her in wild dance.*) Oh, Ha ha! Oh, bountiful heavens, Oh, Christmas! (*Dancing, shouting heavenward.*) Thank you! Thank you, thank you. Ahooo ya! Go raibh mile mhiath agat, if you're listening in Irish! (*Dances on.*) See the soul leaping sideways and backways and headoverheels in me little girl? Ahoooooya!

KAY. Well, try and keep it in your body anyway!

MARTY. (*He dances a moment wildly away from her.*) Ahhoooo!

KAY. Not bad for a grandfather-to-be.

MARTY. (*Stops.*) What?

KAY. You're going to be a grandfather.

MARTY. (*Pause.*) Oh, sweet God!

KAY. Mary said I could tell you.

MARTY. A baby.

KAY. A baby.

MARTY. God himself must be walking down Church Street today.

KAY. She might have it here.

MARTY. A baby.

KAY. Come on then. (*Kay takes Marty's hand and leads him away. They pause a moment before leaving the spilled papers.*)

KAY. Leave them for now. They won't be long gathering inside you again.

She leads him back to the pub where Mary, Cissie, and Mick are sitting silently. Father is sitting slightly behind them. During the following he dies very gently, unnoticed. As they enter Jay appears from the shop and the group, except Father, rouse.

MARY. (*Exhaling.*) Whewwww!

CISSIE. (*Waking.*) Dear God!

MICK. (*To Cissie.*) You were asleep were you, Cissie . . .

CISSIE. I was not. (*seeing Marty.*) Oh, my God . . .

MARTY. (*Coming forward to Mary and embracing her.*) We'll build you a fine house so we will, plenty of rooms and, there isn't any better place in the world than this, for a child Mary, no question, he'll have some life here . . .

KAY. (*Signals to Mary not to say anything.*) Be like a dream . . .

MARTY. Indeed it will, dream of paradise, be able to be walked out the cliff road on a fine day with the gulls like angels above him in the pram, I'll get new gravel for it, I will, and all the sea walks and the near strand and out by Carthy's and the dunes with the hares watching and darting over and back, the same I saw from my own pram sure, with Caherconn clouds in the sky and every class of peacefulness and beatitudinal beauty Mary as God in heaven made it, right there for him . . .

MARY. Oh, God!

Marty, silenced with emotion, hugs her. At this moment Father dies. He rises from his chair quietly and walks off toward the sea through the invisible wall. None of the characters pay this any attention but continue to react as if he were still in his chair.

MICK. In a way I suppose I'm responsible.

CISSIE. What are you talking about?

MICK. Amn't I the living miracle?

CISSIE. And don't some men get blisters from patting themselves on the back.

MICK. (*Indcating drink.*) Special dispensation for the circumstances I think, Jay.

JAY. (*Delighted to be serving drink.*) If your blessed self says so, Mick . . .

MARTY. And something for our new mother here . . . (*Marty turns to Father. He speaks to the empty chair as if the priest were plainly there and can be seen by all sleeping.*)

MARY. (*Aside to Kay.*) But we'll still be going back to San Francisco . . .

CISSIE. I don't drink by nature. (*As it is put before her.*) . . .

KAY. I know . . .

CISSIE. Only on the rarely occasional. (*Takes it.*)

MARTY. And Francis, you'll administer the wedding and the christening . . .

JAY. (*A look to Kay.*) Wedding?

MARTY. Happiest day in the parish, Donnellan's band there for the music . . .

CISSIE. Some nice traditional hymns . . .

MARTY. Every soul in every townland for miles around'll be there.

MARY. And the new soul . . .

MARTY. The . . .

KAY. The baby . . .

MARTY. The baby, Christmas yes, the baby. And what'll you . . . Francis? Are you alright? Francis? Did you doze off on us in the excitement? Come on, man. (*Reaches into the space to gently shake him. They all begin to move towards the priest-space.*) Francis?

JAY. Father?

MICK. Let him get air.

MARTY. Francis?
KAY. Father Mac?
MARY. Father?
JAY. Open his shirt and let him breathe.
MARTY. Francis, are you alright?
MICK. Air . . .
MARTY. Francis? God Almighty, are you with us?

*Stillness, lights slow fade, the seasounds and the cry of gulls, Father
stands stage right looking back. The light lingers on his face as it fades
from the others. Then freeze, and to black.)*

END OF PLAY